FROM ADAM SMITH TO
THE WEALTH OF AMERICA

FROM ADAM SMITH TO THE WEALTH OF AMERICA

Alvin Rabushka

Transaction Books
New Brunswick (U.S.A.) and Oxford (U.K.)

Library of Congress Catalog Number: 84-16170
ISBN: 0-88738-029-8 (cloth)
Printed in the United States of America

Library of Congress Cataloging in Publication Data

Rabushka, Alvin.
  From Adam Smith to the wealth of America.

  Includes index.
  1. Laissez-faire. 2. Supply-side economics. 3. Great Britain—
Economic conditions—19th century. 4. Asia—Economic conditions.
5. United States—Economic conditions. I. Title.
HB95.R32   1984   330.9   84-16170
ISBN 0-88738-029-8

Contents

Part I   Great Britain in the Nineteenth Century

Part II   The Miracle Economies of Asia

Part III   The Wealth of America

List of Tables

List of Figures

Preface

The single most impressive fact of the twentieth century is the dramatic growth in the scope and size of government. Since Franklin Delano Roosevelt's inauguration fifty years ago, federal revenues have expanded more than 160-fold. Federal spending on social programs has increased 270-fold, reflecting a decline in the importance of defense and the blossoming of the welfare state. From a historical laissez-faire approach to the economy, the federal government now regulates our activities in minute detail: the *Federal Register*, which lists government rules and regulations, has grown from 2,411 pages in its first annual edition in 1936 to 87,011 pages of much smaller print in its 1980 edition. But, above all, the federal government has so incredibly lived beyond its means that a national debt of $23 billion inherited by Roosevelt surpassed $1 trillion in October 1981. Topping this story is the even greater rate of growth in state and local government. In the last half-century, government spending at all levels rose from one-tenth to more than one-third of the gross national product.

On 20 January 1981, Ronald Reagan was inaugurated as President. He promised to cut federal spending, reduce taxes, deregulate the economy, and arrest inflation. By restoring economic incentives, these policies would stimulate growth, raise productivity and living standards, increase savings, create jobs, and stabilize the purchasing power of the dollar. Shrinking the size and scope of government would also promote individual liberty. The networks, press, political analysts, and scholars affectionately dubbed these new directions "Reaganomics."

Reaganomics became the catchword for a set of policies that, in truth, is a restatement of the free market economy. Adam Smith, one of history's greatest thinkers and the father of modern economics, set forth the intellectual foundations of the free market in *The Wealth of Nations*, published the same year as the Declaration of Independence. Smith strongly believed in a system of natural liberty which allowed the self-interest of the individual to be harnessed for the good of society. The creation of wealth, he argued, was properly the role of private individuals and firms, not of government. This principle is known by a number of names: free enterprise, economic liberalism, laissez-faire, economic nonintervention, and the competitive market economy. In Smith's view, the proper role of government was to provide defense against foreign enemies, internal law and order, public works (roads, bridges, canals, the post office), and education.

Reaganomics, too, emphasizes individual initiative and responsibility as the cornerstones of economic forces. Greater reliance on the free market means less reliance on government. Taxes must not discourage productive activity. Inflation must not erode savings or deter investment.

Reagan's revival of Adam Smith reverses a fifty-year trend toward bigger government, higher taxes, and more regulation of our affairs. Are Adam Smith's views on the free market relevant to a modern economy? Aren't Smith's ideas about economic organization outmoded? Is it politically feasible, or even desirable, to talk about shrinking government involvement in our lives? Since 1980, these questions increasingly are asked about economic policy. History may not literally repeat itself; it nonetheless affords a dispassionate look at old principles which have worked well in the past.

This book is divided into three parts. In Part I we cross the Atlantic and step back nearly two centuries to the England that exiled Napoleon to St. Helena. Taking mercantilism as our starting point, reinforced by twenty years of wartime controls that encumbered England with an oppressive tax system, a maze of protective tariffs, a ragtag collection of wage and price regulations, and a devalued currency, we can trace about fifty years of sustained liberal reform of economic policy. Low taxes, free trade, competition, and the elimination of government monopolies transformed England into the greatest and most prosperous economy the world had ever seen. Such brilliant political leaders as William Huskisson, Sir Robert Peel, and William E. Gladstone brought *The Wealth of Nations* to life in England. Not even Adam Smith envisioned repeal of the Corn Laws! An intellectual dream became an economic reality, although the passage from mercantilism to economic freedom was not smooth.

The application of liberal economic policies in nineteenth-century England was not a unique historical event. The principles on which England flourished brought Adam Smith into the twentieth century as well. In Part II we cross the Pacific to visit the most successful examples of post–World War II economic development in the world. From a virtual starting point of zero, Hong Kong, Singapore, Korea, and Taiwan have grown so rapidly that they are no longer part of the developing world. Low taxes, a minimum of governmental interference in private and business affairs, and responsible economic policies brought dramatic economic growth. As a result, millions of people escaped from poverty largely on the basis of their own efforts. These modern economic miracles vindicate Adam Smith more than two centuries after publication of *The Wealth of Nations*.

Adam Smith wrote in the late eighteenth century. England brought his dream to life in the nineteenth century. Modern Asia shows that these same principles are still in force in the twentieth century. Fully itemized, they constitute a coherent set of economic policies that foster economic growth and nurture individual freedom.

Of course, American social, economic, and political conditions differ from nineteenth-century England or postwar Asia. Even the language of economic policy has changed. "Supply-side economics" symbolizes improving individual incentives to work, save, and invest by reducing tax rates. A supply-side tax system means low tax rates. Talk about the need for economic deregulation supplants the historical phrase "nonintervention" or "laissez-faire." Monetarism, an economic theory that argues for a steady growth in the money supply to insure stable prices, is a descendant of the old gold standard.

Part III brings us back home. Reaganomics, a symbol for new economic policies, reflects the free-market ideas and practices embodied in nineteenth-century England and modern Asia. Its intellectual foundations owe much to Adam Smith, David Ricardo, John Stuart Mill, and other advocates of the free market. Milton Friedman brought new respectability to these concepts in 1962 in *Capitalism and Freedom*, and made them household notions in his television series and book *Free to Choose*. Social thinker George Gilder put supply-side economics on the best-seller list in *Wealth and Poverty*. Congressional staffer Bruce Bartlett documented the beneficial effects of prior tax cuts in America in the 1920s and 1960s in *Reaganomics*. Paul Craig Roberts and other economists have filled *Harper's*, *Fortune*, the *Wall Street Journal*, and other newspapers and magazines with a steady stream of analyses that defend or explain the new economic policies.

Part III traces the rise of the welfare state and big government in the last fifty years within the American social and political context. From the vantage point of recent history, we can evaluate the newly charted economic course to see how well the old principles have been understood and applied since 1981. What must be done for them to once again work their magic on a stagnant economy? The analysis suggests some successes and some failures. More important, it shows what should be done if growth and rising living standards are once again to benefit the American people.

The roots of this book date back to 1975 when Liberty Fund, Inc. of Indianapolis, through the Center for Studies in Law and Economics of the University of Miami Law School, now the Law and Economics Center of Emory University, funded a research project on the history of free-trade economies. I want to thank A. Neil McLeod, President of Liberty Fund, and Henry G. Manne, Director of the Law and Economics Center, for their assistance in getting this project off the ground. Richard N. Rosett, then Dean of the Graduate School of Business at the University of Chicago, subsequently invited me to deliver the 1976-77 William H. Abbott Lectures in International

Business and Economics, in which I set forth some preliminary findings from that research. Those lectures were published in 1979 by the University of Chicago under the title *Hong Kong: A Study in Economic Freedom.*

On June 6, 1978, California voters approved Proposition 13 by a two-to-one margin, slashing property taxes by half, and kicking off a nationwide tax revolt. In late 1979, Jeffrey Bell, then President of the International Center for Economic Policy Research in New York, since renamed the Manhattan Institute for Policy Research, suggested that the tax revolt which Proposition 13 spawned might induce a general trend towards government shrinkage, thus making a detailed case study of nineteenth-century Britain's experience with the reduction of government useful to academics and public officials. I then wrote a 100-page essay on the reduction of government in nineteenth-century Britain. Several of my colleagues at the Hoover Institution and other scholars outside Stanford read this draft and offered valuable suggestions and, in some instances, stinging criticism. My Hoover colleagues included Gerald Dorfman, Lewis Gann, Robert Hessen, Pauline Ryan, and then visiting scholar Michael Parkin. Readers outside Hoover included Richard Brady, Sir John Cowperthwaite (a retired Hong Kong government official), and Max Hartwell, an Oxford British economic historian of Australian descent, whose bibliographical assistance and reorganizational suggestions proved enormously helpful.

In 1980, George Gilder, who became program director at the Manhattan Institute, suggested that I broaden my treatment of nineteenth-century Britain by incorporating the Pacific Area Basin success stories and applying their lessons as well as those of Britain to the contemporary American economy. I took his advice, and a 100-page manuscript grew to 380 pages over the next few years. On that longer draft I received helpful comments from Ronald McKinnon of Stanford University and some stimulating questions from George Stigler of the University of Chicago. Others who read portions of the expanded manuscript included Bruce Bueno de Mesquita and Gerald Dorfman. Throughout the process of revision, Joan Kennedy Taylor of the Manhattan Institute provided encouragement and helpful suggestions on the organization and content of the manuscript.

My secretary, Ilse Dignam, did a superb job of typing multiple electronic drafts of the manuscript. Christina Peck executed the computer plots on which the figures are based. Don Bovee put the manuscript on magnetic tape for typesetting. I want to thank Gloria Watson, who found a print wheel with an English pound symbol, no small achievement.

I also want to thank the Hoover Institution for providing an exciting environment in which to tackle research questions of all shapes and sizes. The resources and intellectual latitude it allows facilitated the preparation of this book, and several others, during its long gestation. A key benefit for Hoover scholars is a set of interesting colleagues who can be counted on to provide constructive criticism.

If I were to dedicate this book, it would be to the memory of William E. Gladstone, to my mind the finest figure of public finance the world has ever known. It has been difficult to treat his management of British public finances in a wholly objective way, but I have tried to let the facts speak for themselves.

I gratefully acknowledge the help I received from all the above sources, who are, of course, not responsible for any errors, shortcomings, or conclusions in my book.

PART I

GREAT BRITAIN IN THE NINETEENTH CENTURY

1

Prelude to Liberal Reform

Nineteen eighty-one was a bad year for the U.S. economy. Interest rates hit 21 percent, inflation approached 17 percent, and unemployment threatened the horizon. Productivity and personal savings had declined for several decades. The national debt passed $1 trillion in October. Economic competition from Asia and Europe brought a chorus of cries for more protection. Every reputable economist warned of hard times ahead.

The federal government was blamed for these affairs. Since Franklin Delano Roosevelt's inauguration in 1933, federal revenues have expanded more than 160-fold. The federal tax system is now so complicated that over half of the American taxpayers have professional help in filing their returns. Federal spending on social programs has expanded more than 270-fold, providing benefits to nearly one-in-three Americans. From a historical laissez-faire approach to the economy, the federal government issued 87,011 pages of new rules and regulations in the 1980 edition of the *Federal Register*. When President Nixon closed the gold window in 1971, the money supply grew dramatically, leaving inflation in its wake.

Silicon Valley is famous for the "semiconductor chip" which promises to revolutionize economic life. Still, only a small fraction of the American population owns or regularly operates a computer. Indeed, there is widespread concern that the increasing encroachment of computers into daily life carries the threat of substantial unemployment as computers displace people on the job. Some prominent economists argue that increasing technology and automation will lower real incomes as workers attempt to forestall technological innovation by reducing their wages. But the technology tide will move relentlessly onward, they insist, and will leave a vast army of unemployed. Politicians have warned that growing dependence on machines instead of labor, and replacement of older, established craft or labor-intensive industries by high-technology, capital-intensive industries will create fewer new jobs per dollar invested, also fostering greater unemployment.

Academics, the media, and policymakers talk about the need for a new industrial policy, with a greater role for government planning in the economy.

Others advocate increased protection from foreign competition, subsidies to promote exports, the establishment of national financial corporations to allocate credit, and a growing partnership between big business, labor, and government.

To the student of economic history, what is happening in the United States in the mid-1980s is nothing new. In the aftermath of the Napoleonic Wars, Britain paralleled the contemporary United States. In the early 1800s, a group of British workers, concerned that machinery was eliminating jobs in the textile industry, destroyed such machines in the hope of saving jobs. They issued proclamations in the name of the mythical King Ludd of Sherwood Forest and became known as Luddites.

Britain in 1815 was the antithesis of a free economy. The list of regulations on His Majesty's Government statute book encompassed wages and conditions of work, a prohibitive tariff wall surrounding agriculture and manufacturing, a ban on the export of machinery and emigration of skilled artisans, an embargo on the export of precious metals, the Navigation Acts regulating colonial trade and overseas shipping, restrictions on limited joint-stock companies, maintenance of the monopolies of royally-chartered companies, and a system of thousands of separate taxes on all activities of economic life. An enormous national debt consumed half of all public spending. The government's heavy-handed approach to the economy reflected mercantilist thinking and practice, embellished by wartime controls and taxes imposed during the Napoleonic War. The British economy was a mixture of deliberate economic decisions of her rulers to achieve specific national goals and a collection of ad-hoc taxes and measures solely reflecting urgent wartime needs for more revenue or economic protectionism.

The industrial revolution, which fostered rapid economic change in the late eighteenth century, offered little prospect for renewed postwar growth in the early nineteenth century; the economy was firmly mired in a no growth quagmire of international recession. But, some influential statesmen were influenced by an alternative view published in 1776, in Adam Smith's *The Wealth of Nations*. Gradually, over a fifty-year period, a succession of statesmen implemented Smith's principles, replacing mercantilism with a policy of laissez-faire. These changes brought forth a torrent of economic growth, which from hindsight meant that early nineteenth-century Britain was at the beginning of its economic development. Policies of sound money, low taxes, minimal government regulation and spending, and free trade brought prosperity and a rising standard of living.

Great Britain arose from the Act of Union in 1707 that combined England, Scotland, and Wales into one common economic unit with a total population then of about 6.9 million. Population grew slowly and unevenly, with an initial upsurge about 1740 and a real up-turn from 1780. It passed 8.3 million in 1771, doubled to 16.4 million by 1831, and doubled again to 33.1 million by 1891.

Economic change accelerated throughout the eighteenth century. The agrarian revolution ran its course and the industrial revolution was in full swing. By mid-century a number of changes fostered higher yields in British farming. The Norfolk system consisted of a series of interrelated technical, economic, and legal processes, including the rotation of crops, the growing of turnips, clover, and new grasses, the production of grain and cattle rather than of sheep, and cultivation by tenants, under long leases, on large-scale holdings.[1] The enclosure movement, which encouraged more efficient agriculture, was well underway in the early 1700s; but, by the last third of the century, the number of Parliamentary acts surpassed a thousand and enclosed more than a half million acres.[2] Domestic grain output rose from 14.8 million quarters (one quarter equals 218 kilograms) in 1700 to 21.1 million in 1800, an increase of 43 percent.[3]

Historians date the industrial counterpart to agriculture from 1780. Invention of the jenny (1768), water frame (1769), boring mill (1775), seed drill (1782), improved steam engine (1776-1781), cotton-printing machinery (1783), iron puddling (1784), and improved lathe (1794) put manufacturing output on an upward trajectory.[4] Building on a sophisticated commercial and financial structure, a remarkable rise in foreign trade from the late 1740s, and the extension of the canal system from the 1760s, British entrepreneurs so successfully reduced production costs and increased output that historians call these changes "revolutionary."

Strange as it seems, Britain's agrarian and industrial transformation took place during a century of chronic war. Britain was at war for nearly half of the eighteenth century, which provoked a multitude of taxes, regulations, and an enormous public debt. Throughout this turbulence, the country enjoyed remarkable political stability considering that peasants were uprooted, workers displaced, and soldiers constantly sent abroad to fight. From the Glorious Revolution of 1688, Britain's public finances were firmly in the hands of Parliament, whose members were landed aristrocrats. Britain was truly an internal oasis of political stability.

The Mercantilist Legacy

Mercantilism is often defined as an economic system which increases power and monetary wealth through strict government regulation of the national economy. The goals of mercantilism are to accumulate bullion through a favorable balance of trade, to develop and protect domestic agriculture and industry, and to establish foreign trading monopolies. Features of this definition roughly characterize Britain in 1815, although many prior economic regulations were already fading or lacked enforcement. One historical interpretation sees in regulation not so much a reflection of economists' theories nor ministers' long-term commercial policies, but simply the urgent fiscal needs of a nation at war, especially the cumbersome tariff structure.[5] Still, Adam Smith wrote at great length on Britain's mercantilist practices in Book IV of *The Wealth of Nations*. To appreciate the extent of nineteenth-century liberal reform in Britain and its results requires a thorough description of the wartime and mercantilist regulations.

The Corn Laws

"Corn" in Great Britain connotes wheat, but the various schedules of the English Corn Laws embrace grain generally. The laws go back to 1436, when home producers were given legal monopoly protection.[6]

A succession of acts followed in later centuries. Although England exported more grain than it imported, the government often prohibited the export of wheat in periods of scarcity. In the reign of Philip and Mary, for example, wheat could not be exported if home prices rose above 6 shillings 8 pence (hereafter *s.* and *d.*) per quarter, and for cheaper grains in proportion. The home price for a quarter of wheat which limited exportation was raised from 20*s.* in 1593, to 26*s.* 8*d.* in 1604, to 32*s.* in 1623, to 40*s.* in 1660, and 48*s.* in 1663, largely reflecting the rising price of wheat over this period. A prohibition on wool and leather exports in 1647 prompted landowners to reduce sheep and cattle husbandry and expand domestic grain production. Other acts created sliding scales of duties on grain imports and authorized payment of treasury funds as bounties on grain exports when domestic prices fell below a specified level. Thus, producers were encouraged to export wheat when output was plentiful and domestic prices low. At the same time, consumers had access to duty-free overseas grain when domestic prices were high and home output did not meet demand. On balance, this system fostered exports through the middle of the eighteenth century. By 1765, grain exports dwindled to nothing in the face of rising domestic consumption and population; in the last third of the eighteenth century, Britain became a net importer of grain. The politics of corn switched from bounties to protection.

Late in the century, home producers feared that rising consumption of low-priced foreign grain would hold down domestic prices and agricultural incomes. Thus Parliamentary acts of 1791 and 1804 adjusted the points to 50*s.* and 63*s.*, respectively. Regulation of the wheat economy extended from heavy taxation of powder, in which grain was used, to a ban on the distillation of grain in areas of scarcity.

Various duties were abandoned in favor of an absolute prohibition of wheat imports up to 80*s.* in the Corn Act of 1815. Historian C.R. Fay observed that, "This law was defiantly protective, and differed both in principle and spirit from the legislation of the eighteenth century. It sought to fasten on a country at peace the protection furnished by a generation of war.''[7] The needs of greater domestic production during the Napoleonic War fostered expansion into marginal lands, and sharply increased agricultural rents. This expansion presumed high prices. Admission of low-priced grain imports on the return of peace threatened falling prices and widespread bankruptcy. Postwar fears of an agricultural depression prompted an aristocratic legislature to adopt the nation's most restrictive agricultural legislation.

The many statutes and effects of the Corn Laws on grain prices, consumers, and agricultural prosperity fill numerous books and articles. A discussion of the Corn Laws here demonstrates virtually complete government regulation of agriculture at the start of the nineteenth century. No sector of the economy was more heavily controlled than farming. These, then, were the obstacles that faced liberal reformers in the first half of the nineteenth century.

Regulation of Labor and Industry

Control of employment in the Middle Ages resided in the municipal guilds and manorial authorities. As economic life organized on a national basis, the central government assumed this regulatory power. In 1563, the government enacted the Statute of Artificers and Apprentices, an industrial regulation code that remained on the statute book for more than 200 years.[8] The act mandated apprenticeship in various crafts, set and revised maximum (not minimum) wages each year based on the prices of bread and ale, and required a minimum yearly term of employment to insure job security.

W. Cunningham published a marvelously detailed list of various wage assessments made under the Act.[9] Known as "The Middlesex Assessment of 166-," it appears as a form that might be periodically issued without substantial alteration. Its list of laborers and artificers ranges from free masons, carpenters, wheelwrights, and rope-makers through saddlers, coopers, and water-corn mills. Each category is divided into "the best sort" and "the second sort." Wages vary from an annual, to a six-month, to a daily basis. Cunningham's appendix of wage rates is accompanied by a list of forty-seven assessments made between 1560 and 1734.

The woolen industry exemplifies the extent of producer regulation. Wool was the staple trade of England until the end of the eighteenth century, enjoying considerable protection. Mantoux, a French historian of the industrial revolution, writes that, "The sole object of a whole series of laws and regulations was only to safeguard, to support and to guarantee the quality of its products and the high rate of its profits.''[10]

Commercial protection had its roots in the Middle Ages, but its full force was felt with the rise of foreign trade. The woolen industry, more than any other in England, was protected and regulated. Innumerable acts of Parliament contain prescriptions about the length, breadth, and weight of pieces, processes of stretching and dyeing, ingredients either prescribed or forbidden for the preparation of raw material, finishing of the cloth, and methods of folding and packing. It was forbidden to weave cloth unless it was of legal size and weight, to dry it in any manner which would stretch it, to dress it by dry pressing, or to dye the wool with substances considered detrimental to the fabric. In order to enforce these elaborate laws, England had a regular army of specially appointed officials, measurers, inspectors, and checkers, who weighed and measured the cloth and counted the threads. Each piece had to be stamped by them and bear the mark of the manufacturer. The justice of the peace guarded this army to insure the enforcement of industrial regulations and to prescribe penalties for offenders.

The system at times bordered on the absurd. Concern about industrial regulation and protection extended to a complete ban on the export of wool in any state but that of finished fabric, including the export of live sheep. It was an offense to shear sheep within five miles of the coast! The penalty was confiscation. The woolen industry found it unnecessary to innovate; rather, it kept asking for additions to the statute book.

Producer regulation was not uniform across industry. Contrast, for example, the cotton industry with the woolen industry. Manufacturing regulations, guild statutes, and even the Statute of Artificers and Apprentices of 1563 were measures with special and limited applications to specified trades. Newly created industries were often excluded. Unless a new industry became the subject of special regulations, it often could grow in economic freedom. From its birth the cotton industry was free of regulations prescribing length, breadth, or quality of its materials, and could use any method of manufacture. As a result, machinery quickly came into general use and many kinds of goods were produced. Similarly, neither the strict trade guild nor the apprenticeship system existed in the cotton industry.[11]

In the late eighteenth century, Parliament would not surrender its right to regulate industry. The Act of 1768 controlled the wages and hours of journeyman tailors and the Spitalfields Act of 1773 that of silk workers. Many skilled workers petitioned the government to enforce the apprentice system in their industry, together with a limitation on the numbers. By 1813 the movement encompassed the whole working class. Over 300,000 signatures and petitions were collected from every district and every trade seeking to maintain and save the apprentice system. However, Adam Smith's ideas took hold and the interests of manufacturers prevailed. Provisions for setting maximum wages were repealed by Parliament in 1813, and the apprentice clauses were largely repealed in 1814. Some still remained in force in the stronger crafts, which contrived to keep their labor scarce, and parish apprentices remained until 1844 when this relic of the Elizabethan poor law was abolished.

Chartered Trading Companies

During the late Middle Ages, England's import trade was in the hands of foreign merchants from the Hanseatic Leagues, France, Spain, Flanders, and the Netherlands. By the end of the sixteenth century, the steady development of domestic exporters and trading interests brought pressure to close the foreign trading concessions.

Abolition of the foreign trading concessions did not produce a free-for-all among English traders. Rather, from the late sixteenth century most overseas trade was restricted to members of English trading companies to which the Crown granted monopoly rights in specific regions.[12] Among the famous companies were the Merchant Adventurers (active in northern and eastern Europe), the Levant Company (founded in 1581), the East India Company (1600), which was not entirely abolished until 1858, the Royal African Company (rechartered in 1660), the several North American colonization companies—Virginia, Plymouth, Hudson Bay—and the South Sea Company.

Royally chartered trading companies epitomized mercantilist theory, which insured that economic policies were implemented that subordinated private commercial interest to the national interest. At the time it was widely believed that commercial investment would occur only if reasonable guarantees were given that those who took great risks would enjoy the profits. Some trading companies even became colonial powers when they established and governed settlements in North America, Africa and India. Several companies persisted well into the nineteenth century.

Navigation Acts

The Navigation Acts were the foundation of British commercial and naval power throughout the eighteenth century. Adam Smith thought them an appropriate instrument of national security; by encouraging seamanship, the nation would secure an adequate supply of seamen for the British navy. The Acts were a series of laws dating back to 1381. They were significantly expanded in scope from 1650 onward for the purpose of injuring Dutch commerce and merchant marine strength.[13] The Act of 1650 banned the carrying of goods from any English colony in foreign ships. The Act of 1651 limited the import of European goods to English ships or those of the country of origin; the same regulations applied for goods imported from Asia, Africa, and America. The Navigation Act of 1660 defined English ships as those built in England, Ireland (excluded after 1670), or the colonies, which were manned by an English captain and had a minimum of three-quarters English crew.

To encourage long-haul shipping, the Acts stipulated that goods from Asia, Africa, or America had to be brought directly to England from their place of growth or manufacture. Moreover, alien ships could not carry goods between any two English ports. Additionally, trade with the Russian and Turkish Empires was confined to English ships or those of the empire of origin.

In a move designed to weaken Dutch shipping, England prohibited the import of certain staples from the Netherlands or Germany on any vessel. To encourage shipbuilding and manufacturing, no foreign-built ship could become British by purchase. European goods destined for the colonies had to be shipped via England (to the benefit of the King's customs) and reshipped in English vessels (to the benefit of English shipping). This code was unaltered until after the American revolution, and was not fully abandoned until 1849.

J. R. McCulloch, in his essay on the commerce of Holland published in his *Treatise on Economic Policy*, disputes the alleged anti-Dutch effects of the laws.[14] He maintains that the decline of Dutch maritime power was not due to English navigation laws but to excessive taxation within Holland itself.

Regulation of the Colonies

His Majesty's Government controlled colonial and interimperial shipping through the Navigation Acts; it also controlled the objects of that trade through other measures. The Staple Act of 1663, for example, required that certain "enumerated commodities," notably sugar and tobacco, produced in the colonies be exported exclusively to England.[15] Iron, copper, naval stores, and hides were added to the list in the eighteenth century. At the same time, London restricted manufacturing in the colonies. Hardware, woolen cloth, and agricultural implements were thus exclusively imports from England. This colonial system thereby insured British access to raw materials and guaranteed a market for British manufactured goods.

The system worked well until the colonists and their descendents chafed under a succession of direct taxes imposed by the King's ministers, beginning with the ill-advised Stamp Act of 1765. American independence brought in its wake partial deregulation of the colonial trade. Since the bulk of the colonial West Indian commerce was with the new American nation, England broke with the Navigation Acts and allowed American vessels into West Indian ports, permitting return cargoes of any kind of goods. But English colonies were not granted control over their own economic policies and international trade until the reforms of the 1820s.

Tariffs and Taxes

Until the eighteenth century, tax receipts were limited to: (1) a 5 percent port duty on exports and imports; and, (2) excise taxes on alcoholic beverages, wine licenses, and other consumer articles (vinegar, coffee, tea, and chocolate). Other minor sources included a 2s. hearth tax, simple poll taxes, and others. Annual tax receipts in the late seventeenth century amounted to £3 to

£4 million, a modest 6 to 8 percent share of a total national income of £50 million.

For the next 125 years, unremitting pressures of war drove Chancellors of the Exchequer and English Parliaments into a relentless search for new sources of revenue. A relatively modest conflict with France in the 1690s was financed by a number of poll taxes that raised £2.5 million, a property tax that yielded £19 million, the extension of port duties and excise taxes to other consumer items, and the addition of £14.5 million in national debt (which implied future tax increases for repayment of debt).

The Treaty of Ryswick in 1698 brought peace to England for just four years when the War of Spanish Succession (or Queen Anne's War) broke out, which lasted eleven years, until 1713. When the Treaty of Utrecht was finally concluded in 1714, British taxpayers had incurred new taxes of £30 million and the national debt had been enlarged to £21.5 million. The land tax doubled from 2s. to 4s., customs duties rose, and import duties encumbered tea, coffee, and spices. Parliament levied excise duties on such essential manufactured goods as candles, leather, soap, paper, and printed goods and imposed stamp duties on deeds, legal instruments, and newspapers.

Britain remained at peace until 1739, except for a short, but inexpensive, military interlude with Spain from 1718 to 1721 that cost a modest £4.5 million. During this tranquil twenty-six-year interregnum, Sir Robert Walpole halved the land tax to 2s., repealed timber duties on American imports, refunded duties paid on imported raw silk used in the manufacture of exported finished silk products, repealed duties on imported chemicals used for dyeing of cloth, and lowered the high duties on spices.

The Peace of Aix-la-Chapelle in 1749 terminated ten years of war with Spain that had erupted on October 19, 1739. The war had halted tax reform and relief. New taxation raised £13 million, and new borrowing £30 million. The land tax again doubled to 4s., duties were imposed on the manufacture of spirits, the infamous window tax—a tax on light—was conceived and implemented, pleasure carriages were penalized, and the duties on imported goods rose to an overall level of 20 percent.

Glass-making was virtually ruined by a new tax on its manufacture, a story vividly narrated by Britain's foremost tax historian.[16]

> It is curious to observe, in the history of taxation in England in the last century, how frequently the rise to importance of a business or a manufacture is noted by an attempt on the part of the minister of finance to derive from its prosperity some additional revenue. As soon as it rises, in growth, to the level of his notice, so to put it, his fiscal hand is outstretched towards it with a grasp of welcome, from his point of view: "I rejoice to see you so prosperous, and— you shall be taxed." Perhaps no more signal case of the evil influence of taxation in crushing a prosperous manufacture is recorded in our fiscal annals

than that which occurs, at a future date, in regard to the useful and beautiful manufacture Pelham now thought fit to tax. Once before it had been taxed: the tax had been repealed as ruinous to the manufacture; and the repeal had been followed by an incredible improvement in glass-making. The new tax touched green, that is bottle glass, as well as flint, crown, that is, window, and plate glass, and a monopoly was secured to the native manufacturers by the imposition of high duties on imported articles of glass. The increase in the price of glass bottles consequent upon the tax was such as to cause Chesterfield, when writing to mr. Prior in Ireland, to suggest that he should start a manufacture of them in that country, to which the tax did not extend.[17]

Peace returned in 1749 for a short span of seven years and, with it, Parliament halved the land tax to 2s. But a burgeoning national debt increased debt servicing charges. Thus, most other taxes remained on the statute book.

Seven years of peace yielded to the Seven Years' War, officially concluded by the Treaty of Paris in 1764. It cost Britain £82 million of which £22 million was new taxes. The levies included the doubled land tax, cards, dice, wine licenses, deeds, newspapers, advertisements, homes and windows, and a new charge on official positions or titles with salaries exceeding £100. A 5 percent increase in import duties raised the general level to 25 percent. Beer consumers, too, felt the weight of heavier taxation.

Growing pressure in Britain to grant tax relief and find new revenue to service the public debt prompted Grenville to lay the historically infamous Stamp Act of 1765 on the American colonies. Although repealed the following year (with costs of collection outpacing receipts), Parliament approved Townshend's Act of 1766, which imposed port duties on manufactured articles imported from Britain. It, too, was repealed, but an intransigent British cabinet insisted on retaining a 3d. to the pound (a rate of 1.25 percent) duty on tea imports to establish the principle that Parliament could tax the colonies. The War of American Independence, which Britain lost, did not come cheap. A wartime expenditure of £97 million forced new luxury taxes on men servants, impositions on property sold by auction, and a general 5 percent increase in port excise duties. Once again wine and beer drinkers paid heavily for their indulgences.

A century of war showed its effects in the 1792-93 budget. Almost £17 million in total expenditure reflected £9.3 million in debt servicing, £5.5 million in military appropriations, and a mere £1.6 million in civil costs. The latter sum amounted to 0.5 percent of the national income. Government spending and taxes consisted almost solely of war-related costs.[18]

On 1 February 1793 war with France broke out which, along with the subsequent war with Napoleon, is termed the Great War. The four preceding wars had cost England £272 million and had enlarged the British national debt from approximately £12 million to £237 million.

The Great War by itself added £622 million to the national debt. In the peacetime years of the eighteenth century, annual public spending, including debt charges, averaged £15 million. During the 22 years of the Great War, it averaged £69 million. The Great War tripled the national debt; it also compelled the government to load an already harried British taxpayer with a steady succession of new and increased levies. The objects of new or increased taxation encompassed wines, spirits, materials for home building, licenses to practice law, paper, hair powder and wigs, ship insurance, the several stamp tax instruments, pleasure horses, tobacco, hats, inherited personal property, watches and clocks, general property, protection of shipping by naval convoy, and armorial ensigns, as well as a general rise of 5 to 10 percent in port duties. The first British income tax was imposed in 1798 at a rate of 10 percent on personal incomes above £200 and a sliding scale of lower rates assessed on incomes between £60 and £200. While the tax increased revenue during the war years, the great majority of British subjects, with per capita annual incomes averaging £20, were never subject to the income tax. It yielded an average of £6 million in 1799, 1800 and 1801. Abolished in 1802 during the brief Peace of Amiens, it was reimposed in 1803 at the rate of 5 percent (1s. to the £). This was half the former rate, but the revenue yield was nearly as great. The total exemption was lowered from £60 to £50, the deduction allowed on children was withdrawn, and the general rate was soon raised to 10 percent, yielding nearly £15 million a year in receipts. Concurrently, duties on such items as tea were increased to nearly 100 percent of value.

With the arrival of peace in 1815 came a budget of £68.3 million, of which £32 million was solely interest charges on the national debt accumulated by 125 years of war. The national debt increased about 70-fold from 1700 to 1815; annual government spending multiplied 30-fold.

John Noble, a historian of public finance, describes the state of British taxation in 1815:

> In order to meet this growing expenditure, fresh taxes were, year after year, imposed upon the people, until, at length, there was hardly an article that could be eaten, drank, worn, or used, that was not taxed. There was, it is true, no tax laid upon air or water, but the beneficent influence of the sun, as a sanitary agent, was made subject to tribute, and its rays were taxed by means of the window duty. To look through the list of articles on which duties were charged excites feelings nearly akin to horror. It seems like the work of some fiendish imp of the nether regions, some demon, alike the enemy of a beneficent God and of his creature man. Everything that was useful, or good, or beautiful in nature or in art; everything that was sweet to the palate, wholesome for the body, needful for raiment [clothing], grateful to the eye, or pleasant to the taste or smell, was taxed. All the fruits of the earth, everything that was necessary to eat or drink, with some exceptions, and they were prohibited; the rich man's sauce and the poor man's vinegar, the wines that inebriate and destroy, the

medicine that heals, and the poison that kills; everything that grew upon the face of the earth, or was produced from the waters under the earth, all were taxed, ruthlessly taxed—as if, by malignant and preconceived intention, it had been determined that nothing but things in the heavens above should be exempted, and, as if this were not sufficient to crush the people, a system of protection was maintained for the supposed benefit of landowners, manufacturers, shipowners, and Colonial proprietors, which effectually deprived the people of that liberty to use their own industry and their property for their own advantage, which, according to the principles of Political Economy, is essential to their well-being.[19]

Even more entertaining is an essay of Sydney Smith, published in the *Edinburgh Review* in 1820:

We can inform Brother Jonathan what are the inevitable consequences of being too fond of glory. Taxes upon every article which enters into the mouth or covers the back or is placed under the foot. Taxes upon everything which it is pleasant to see, hear, feel, smell, or taste. Taxes upon warmth, light, and locomotion. Taxes on everything on earth or under the earth, on everything that comes from abroad or is grown at home. Taxes on the raw material, taxes on every fresh value that is added to it by the industry of man. Taxes on the sauce which pampers man's appetite, and the drug which restores him to health; on the ermine which decorates the judge, and the rope which hangs the criminal; on the poor man's salt and the rich man's spice; on the brass nails of the coffin, and the ribbons of the bride; at bed or board, couchant or levant, we must pay. The schoolboy whips his taxed top; the beardless youth manages his taxed horse, with a taxed bridle, on a taxed road; and the dying Englishman, pouring his medicine, which has paid 7 per cent., into a spoon that has paid 15 per cent., flings himself back upon his chintz bed, which had paid 22 per cent., and expires in the arms of an apothecary who has paid a license of a hundred pounds for the privilege of putting him to death. His whole property is then immediately taxed from 2 to 10 per cent. Besides the probate, large fees are demanded for burying him in the chancel. His virtues are handed down to posterity on taxed marble, and he will then be gathered to his fathers to be taxed no more.[20]

Many of the more than 1,000 tariffs in place in 1815 had been strengthened or imposed during the Napoleonic War for purposes of granting complete protection, or obtaining higher revenue. Banned imports included silk, cottons, woolens, tobacco, and gold and silver wares. A punitive rate of 50 percent duty was levied on most manufactured goods. Raw materials of industry—hides, timber, wool, and silk—were burdened with high rates of import duty. Many consumer goods—tea, coffee, sugar, bacon, butter, and cheese—were also heavily taxed, thus they were denied to the majority of low-income Britons. Some scholars estimate that in 1793 as many as 40,000 smugglers were bringing banned or heavily taxed goods into Britain, since high duties made smuggling a lucrative industry.[21]

Augustus Mongredien described the postwar British tariff structure:

> In 1824 the fiscal regulations by which our commerce with the world was controlled and restricted stood as follows:—1. There was hardly an article obtainable from abroad that was admissible here without the payment of import duties, always heavy, sometimes excessive, and in certain cases all but prohibitory. . . . The tariff list of the United Kingdom formed a tolerably complete dictionary of all the products of human industry.
>
> To assess and collect these duties custom-houses were established in every part of the kingdom, down to the smallest fishing hamlet. At an expense which, in many cases, exceeded the sum collected, a multitudinous host was maintained of custom-house functionaries—commissioners, controllers, clerks, officers, examiners, collectors, &c. &c.[22]

Money and Currency

England adopted the gold standard as a practical consequence of a proclamation of 22 December 1717, which set the value of the golden guinea (because the gold from which the first issue of them was made came from the Guinea Coast) at twenty-one shillings of silver, although gold was not established as the sole legal monetary standard until Lord Liverpool's Act of 1816.[23] The value of the guinea held firm; from that moment, silver was tied to the value of gold in a guinea, rather than gold tied to the value of silver in twenty-one shillings, based on the market exchange of the two metals.

One troy pound of 22-carat gold was coined into 44 1/2 guineas. Anyone who had gold could demand that the government mint coin it for him at that rate. In practice, it was better to accept £46 10s. a pound or £3 17s. 6d. an ounce, given on the spot by the bullion office of the Bank of England. Gold was freely convertible into coin.

Silver coins were legal tender for amounts under £25; above that sum they were legal tender by weight, at the coinage rate of 5s. 2d. an ounce. However, anyone submitting silver at the official coinage rate lost heavily as against spending a similar quantity of coins in small amounts.

England had no legal tender paper. Bank of England notes in £10, £20, and a few larger denominations circulated freely in London. Outside London, notes in £5 and larger denominations, issued by over 200 banks with less than six partners known as "country banks," freely circulated. By law, country banks were not permitted to issue notes smaller than £5. Conservatism at the Bank of England kept its minimum notes at £10 until after the Great War began.

Money and currency in England revolves around the Bank of England, which received its charter in May 1694.[24] At that time, it agreed to lend the government £1.2 million at 8 percent interest. William III's predecessor,

Charles II, had clipped coins and confiscated £1.3 million from the gold-smiths, thus destroying the King's credit-worthiness and laying the foundation of England's national debt.[25] In exchange for this loan, the Bank of England was allowed to incorporate as a joint-stock company. The Bank became both a bank of deposit, accepting deposits, discounting bills, and granting loans, and a bank of currency issue. Its share capital offering of £1.2 million was quickly subscribed. Notes of that amount were printed with the Bank's seal, given to and paid out by the government throughout the country, and freely accepted at full face value. Cash notes without the Bank's seal were subsequently printed and these, too, circulated freely. In practice and policy, the Bank stood ready to exchange "cash" (gold coins or bullion) for its bank notes, assuring the holders and users of these notes confidence in their value.

The banking system of eighteenth-century England was rudimentary. Only the Bank of England enjoyed the limited liability of a joint-stock company; all other banks were compelled to operate as individuals or partnerships on the basis of unlimited liability. Between 1750 and 1800, 400 country banks sprang up, originating from the activities of small businessmen who managed to accumulate and loan surplus funds. Country banks in arrangement with London banks could channel surplus funds from agriculture into profitable lending opportunities to merchants and manufacturers who needed short-term credit. Even if the Bank of England tried to act as a central bank and lender of last resort, a legal prohibition of all interest above 5 percent often stood in the way of effective restriction on loans when speculative frenzy drove lending rates well beyond the legal maximum.

Events in the mid-1790s forced the government to suspend the cash convertibility of bank notes. At the end of 1794 the Bank directors complained of Prime Minister Pitt's excessive demands that the Bank accommodate rising government expenditure with the issue of new currency. Government spending of £17.5 million in 1792 rose to £29.5 million in 1794, but the revenue remained at £20 million. The £9 million the government borrowed in 1794 was a large sum in proportion to the annual savings of the people. Bank of England notes in circulation in 1793 stood at £12 million, with gold coins amounting to between £20 million and £30 million. By 1795 public spending shot up to £51.7 million. Revenue still held at £21.5 million. This situation threatened to inflate the currency.

The strain on the Bank of England was exacerbated by the French return to a metallic currency in 1796 from its worthless paper assignats of the early 1790s; gold was exported to France, despite the legal prohibition against export, where it was in strong demand. A number of small country banks folded under this drain of specie.

The Bank's position eroded quickly. In February 1794 it held £7 million of coin and bullion against £18.7 million of liabilities, of which £10.7 were notes in circulation. In early 1796, coins and bullion had shrunk to £2.5 million. By 31 August 1796, coin and bullion reserves barely exceeded £2 million against liabilities of £16 million. On Sunday morning, 26 February 1797, Pitt's government temporarily suspended cash payments, pending Parliamentary review and adoption of proper measures to deal with the financial and credit crisis. Opening Monday morning, the Bank exhibited the order of suspension.

Pitt's suspension was confirmed by Act 37 Geo. III. c. 45, called the "Bank Restriction Act," passed on 3 May 1797. Intended to continue only until 24 June 1797, the act was kept in force for nearly a quarter of a century. Three days earlier, another act authorized the Bank to issue bank notes for sums ranging between £1 and £5. However, the government did not make these bank notes legal tender. Gold coin was quickly hoarded or exported, and silver, too, became scarce.

The act of suspension gave the Bank the power to create money without limit. Prudence, coupled with the meteoric career of the French assignats, constrained the excessive overissue of bank notes. But self-restraint was less severe than the restraint convertibility imposed. Holders of notes demanded gold whenever £1 in notes became worth appreciably less than 123 1/4 grains of standard gold (or whenever gold rose above £3 17s. 10.5d. an ounce), since that redeemed note in gold could be sold for more than £1.

It was remarkable that the gold price of the pound held steady until 1808. This was partly because the Bank deterred excessive borrowing with a 5 percent interest charge, partly due to the Bank's innate conservatism, and partly because of a desire to prevent disaster to the "monied classes" and the country at large. But a wave of speculation in 1808, the opening of South America to British commerce, caused an excessive price rise in many articles. The 5 percent usury loan-ceiling prevented the Bank from raising its discount rate, thereby restricting the growth of credit. In early 1809 the price of gold went up to 90s., or to put it the other way, a £1 note only bought 107 grains of gold instead of 123¼. The value of the pound fell in its major foreign exchange markets. On August 29, 1809, the first of three letters from the distinguished economist David Ricardo appeared in the *Morning Chronicle* attributing depreciation in the pound to overissue of notes.

On 1 February 1810, Francis Horner moved in the House of Commons for a committee to consider the subject of bullion and currency. The committee was appointed on 19 February 1810. The Report from the Select Committee on the High Price of Bullion was printed on 8 June 1810. During 1909, the market price of gold ranged from 15 to 20 percent above the mint price. During the committee's deliberations, the price of gold sustained a premium of 15 to 20 percent, with a one-time fall to just over 10 percent in early April. The committee concluded that the premium price of gold and the fall in the pound's main exchanges of Paris, Hamburg, and Amsterdam was not due to the state of foreign trade but the overissue of domestic currency.

Statistics published in the Bullion Report trace the increase in the Bank of England notes in circulation from an average of between £10 million and £11 million in the several years prior to 1796, rising to £17 million in 1804 and reaching £19 million in 1809, when depreciation set in. A disproportionate share of the currency issue was in notes under £5. The report concluded

> That there is at present an excess in the paper circulation of this Country, of which the most unequivocal symptom is the very high price of Bullion, and next to that, the low state of the Continental Exchanges; that this excess is to be ascribed to the want of a sufficient check and control in the issues of paper from the Bank of England; and originally, to the suspension of cash payments, which remove the natural and true control. For upon a general view of the subject, Your Committee are of opinion, that no safe, certain, and constantly adequate provision against an excess of paper currency, either occasional or permanent, can be found, except in the convertibility of all such paper into specie.[26]

The committee naturally advocated restoration of convertibility—cash payments in exchange for Bank paper on demand. During the transition to full convertibility, the committee proposed that the Bank retain its low denomination note issue until gold coinage sufficed for the conduct of business.

A storm of criticism broke loose, especially from bankers and merchants. Horner, who had moved formation of the committee, on 6 May 1910, moved sixteen resolutions in support of the report. Following a four-day debate, the House overwhelmingly rejected terminating suspension in two years. In its place, Chancellor of the Exchequer Nicholas Vansittart brought forward seventeen counter-resolutions claiming that the divergence of value between notes and coin was not due to an overissue of notes but to the shortage of bullion, and was therefore quite proper. His seventeenth resolution declared it highly inexpedient and dangerous to fix a definite period for resuming cash payment until six months after the conclusion of peace. All his resolutions passed on 15 May. The result of Parliament's rejection of the committee's recommendations was to forbid all differences between payments in paper and in coin, which effectively made bank notes legal tender.

The price of gold fluctuated wildly from mid-1810 until 1816, when the Bank voluntarily resumed payment of gold for notes. In November 1810 the price of gold stood at £4 4s. 6d. an ounce, but by August 1813 it had risen to £5 10s., a premium of more than 30 percent. It fell, by October 1814, to £4 5s. During February 1815, just before the escape of Napoleon from Elba, the gold price stood at £4 9s. an ounce, rising sharply to £5 7s. at the time of the battle of Waterloo. Thereafter it fell rapidly to £4 3s. in October 1815 and to £3 18s. 6d. twelve months later, within a percentage point of the presuspension standard mint price.

In November 1816, with gold at £3 18s. 6d., only 7½d. above the coinage price, the Bank offered to pay gold on demand to all holders of £1 and £2 notes dated earlier than 1812. The Bank directors decided this on their own, not at the request of the government. Few notes were offered for gold by a confident public. Accordingly, in April 1817, the Bank offered repayment to all holders of £1 and £2 notes. Again, few takers materialized. Meanwhile, the Bank's gold reserve of £2 million in February 1815 had risen to £12 million by September 1817, when it offered to redeem all notes of every denomination in gold. In the interim, 300 country banks failed in 1815-16, and about £12 million of worthless country bank paper had been destroyed. In 1819, Parliament officially resumed cash payments, to take effect on 1 May 1823, restoring the standard at £3 17s. 10.5d. for an ounce of gold— a value that remained unaltered until suspension of convertibility during World War I. (Chapter 5 discusses the workings of the gold standard during the nineteenth century.)

The Changing Intellectual Climate

Mercantilism was a ragtag collection of trade, industrial, labor, and economic regulations, resting on a tariff structure that reflected revenue needs more than protectionist sentiment, save in agriculture. Mercantilist thinking showed up in the 1720s and 1730s when Sir Robert Walpole reduced import duties on raw materials and abolished duties on the export of English manufacturers to foster trade expansion. But the eruption of war in the 1740s halted further reform.

Adam Smith challenged mercantilist doctrine in *The Wealth of Nations*, arguing, in its place, for individual freedom and the market economy.[27] Smith's economic views grew from the broader philosophical claims put forth a century earlier by John Locke, who argued a theory of natural rights—a conception of society that consisted of independent, self-interested individuals, without any absolute duties toward the state.[28] Following the Glorious Revolution of 1688, Parliament asserted its dominance over the King. Justification lay on the intrinsic rights of the individual. The state, the instrument for general regulation and defense, became, conceptually, a means of protecting the rights of individuals. In turn, the individual's duty consisted of paying his share of the cost of this protection.

Smith pushed this line of reasoning in order to delineate the proper roles of government. According to him, the state had three functions. First, it must defend the society from external attack. Second, it must maintain law and order. Third, it must erect and maintain certain public works that individuals or small groups would never find profitable to provide on a commercial basis—roads, bridges, canals, the post office, and education. Smith's anti-mercantilist views did not encompass the Navigation Acts, which he believed were included under the national defense function of the state.

Classical economists envisioned the economy as a system of spontaneous cooperation. Consumers bought as they freely chose. Producers, workers, and owners were equally free to apply their labor and property in ways that brought the maximum reward. The market harmonized the interests of individuals. To use Smith's famous phrase, the individual seeking to direct industry that its produce may be of the greatest value "intends only his own gain," but "he is in this, as in many other cases, led by an invisible hand to promote an end which was no part of his intention."[29] This system was free from coercion or state control, and yet operated through the attempt of each to promote his own self-interest. In the process, the market economy allocated the total output of society toward more profitable lines through the price mechanism. In turn, rising profits attracted more investment. Gains from greater productivity, in turn, were passed on to consumers in the form of lower prices and by competing with each other for labor, businessmen drove up wages.

Obstacles to free trade and industry thus should be swept away: the privileges of regulated companies and corporations, the law of apprenticeship, restrictions on free movement of labor and capital, and restraints on importation.

Historian S.G. Checkland summarized the pervasive and convincing hold of Adam Smith on nineteenth-century Britain.

> Our starting point for the understanding of the economic facet of the nineteenth-century mind in Britain must be the system of Adam Smith. Its hold in the nineteenth century was real, but subtle. It was the outcome of an attempt by a moral philosopher to see economic behaviour as part of behaviour generally and to assimilate it to a unifying system. It was an extraordinary achievement. It seemed to synthesize philosophy and science, so rudely sundered by the speculations of the seventeenth century, when man was first dazzled by the fruits of the new empirical science. Secondly, it provided a philosophic apology for individual initiative. Yet, thirdly it implied that society, for all the disruptive activities of individuals within it, was nevertheless stable and free from any tendency to embark on cumulative accelerating change.[30]

Smith's system was in the Lockean tradition of resistance to authority, whether made by church or state. Men, living in a system of natural liberty, could make their own economic history. So long as competition was maintained, monopoly positions in business and industry would not occur. Indeed, minimizing the economic role of the state was the most effective means of depriving business cliques of their traditional sources of influence over potential competitors and consumers.

Smith advocated dismantling traditional economic controls and replacing them by a policy of governmental noninterference. Public spending and debt should be kept as small as possible to keep the tax burdens as small as possible.

Historian W. Cunningham documents the complete hold of the new classical economics on state action in the early nineteenth century. He writes:

> An impression began to be disseminated that the propertied classes were wholly indifferent to the sufferings of the poor. But this was not the case; the inaction of the House of Commons [in the 1820s] was due to the opinion, which had become more and more prevalent among educated men, that any interference on the part of the Government was injurious to the material prosperity of the community, and that no legislative remedy could be devised which would really mitigate the miseries of the poor.
>
> The paralysis which affected State action during this period, was chiefly due to the influence of the economic experts of the day. Ricardo, Malthus, the elder Mill and other writers of the school of Adam Smith, . . .[31]

Finally, Smith's views on taxation strongly influenced his first political pupil in the 1780s, William Pitt, and British taxation for much of the nineteenth century. Smith strongly opposed direct assessment of income, and hence an income tax, because it entailed an inquisition of each taxpayer. This he viewed as especially harmful to the commercial classes, adversely affecting capital formation. Second, he opposed taxes on necessary articles of consumption or on wages because they would raise the price of labor. Therefore, he favored taxes on non-necessary items of consumption or expenditure. Third, public works should be financed directly by users, that is, the government should run its public works by charging tolls or fees, and not place any burden on the general tax revenue. Fourth, taxes should be kept low. High taxes, especially in the case of customs duties, encouraged smuggling and often resulted in a smaller revenue than what might be collected from more moderate taxes.

Moreover, Smith set forth maxims of tax collection. Taxes—time of payment, manner of payment, amount of payment—ought to be certain and not arbitrary. Every tax ought to be levied in the manner in which it is most convenient for the taxpayer to pay it. "Every tax ought to be so contrived as both to take out and to keep out of the pockets of the people as little as possible over and above what it brings into the public treasury of the state."[32] It does little good to spend £1 1s. in salaries and overhead to collect £1 in taxes.

Notes

1. T.S. Ashton, *The Industrial Revolution 1760-1830* (London: Oxford University Press, 1967), p. 27.
2. E.L. Jones, "Editor's Introduction," in E.L. Jones (ed.), *Agriculture and Economic Growth in England 1650-1815* (London: Methuen, 1967), p. 13.
3. Phyllis Deane and W.A. Cole, *British Economic Growth 1688-1959*, 2nd ed. (Cambridge: Cambridge University Press, 1969), p. 65.
4. Ronald Max Hartwell, *The Industrial Revolution and Economic Growth* (London: Methuen, 1971), p. 147.
5. Ralph Davis, "The Rise of Protection in England, 1689-1786," *Economic History Review*, 2nd series, XIX, no. 2 (August 1966), p. 306.
6. See C.R. Fay, *The Corn Laws and Social England* (Cambridge: Cambridge University Press, 1932); Alexander Brady, *William Huskisson and Liberal Reform* (London: Oxford University Press, 1928), pp. 41-44; and J. Walker, *British Economic and Social History* (London: Macdonald & Evans, 1968), p. 123.
7. C.R. Fay, *The Corn Laws*, p. 35.
8. J. Walker, *British Economic and Social History*, pp. 108-10.
9. W. Cunningham, *The Growth of English Industry and Commerce in Modern Times* (Cambridge: Cambridge University Press, 1903), pp. 887-97.
10. Paul Mantoux, *The Industrial Revolution in the Eighteenth Century*, rev. ed., trans. Marjorie Vernon (London: Jonathan Cape, 1948), p. 48.
11. Ibid., p. 266.
12. J. Walker, *British Economic and Social History*, pp. 88-92.
13. Ibid., p. 112; and Alexander Brady, *William Huskisson*, pp. 74-76.
14. Cited in Sydney Buxton, *Finance and Politics: An Historical Study*, 1783-1885, vol. I (London: Murray, 1888), p. 97.
15. J. Walker, *British Economic and Social History*, p. 113.
16. The most comprehensive history of British taxation is that of Stephen Dowell, contained in four volumes. This section draws heavily from his *A History of Taxation and Taxes in England*, vol. 2, 2nd ed. (London: Longmans, Green, 1888). Other valuable sources include William Kennedy, *English Taxation 1640-1799: An Essay on Policy and Opinion* (New York: Kelley, Reprints of Economics Classics, 1964); Sydney Buxton, *Finance and Politics*, vols. 1, 2; John Noble, *National Finance: A Review of the Policy of the Last Two Parliaments, and of the Results of Modern Fiscal Legislation* (London: Longmans, Green, 1875); and Ronald Max Hartwell, "Taxation in England during the Industrial Revolution," *The Cato Journal*, 1, (Spring 1981), pp. 129-53.
17. Stephen Dowell, *A History of Taxation*, p. 116.
18. B.R. Mitchell with the collaboration of Phyllis Deane, *Abstract of British Historical Statistics* (Cambridge: Cambridge Press, 1962), pp. 366, 391.
19. John Noble, *National Finance*, pp. 3-5.
20. Reproduced in Stephen Dowell, *A History of Taxation*, pp. 259-60.
21. See William Kennedy, *English Taxation*, p. 32; and C.R. Fay, *Great Britain from Adam Smith to the Present Day: An Economic and Social Survey* (New York: Longmans, Green, 1928), pp. 29, 36, 57, 135-36.
22. Augustus Mongredien, *History of the Free-Trade Movement in England* (New York: Putnam's Sons, 1881), pp. 3-4.
23. A historical analysis of the workings of the gold standard in England is found in Roy W. Jastram, *The Golden Constant: The English and American Experience*

1560-1976 (New York: Wiley, 1977). Details of the wartime suspension of convertibility are found in Edwin Cannan, *The Paper Pound of 1797-1821*, with a reprint of the *Report from The Select Committee on the High Price of Bullion, House of Commons, 8th June 1810* (London: King & Son, 1919).

24. John Clapham, *The Bank of England: A History*, vol. I (1694-1797) and vol. II (1797-1914) (Cambridge: Cambridge University Press, 1945).

25. Alexander Johnstone Wilson, *The National Budget: The National Debt, Taxes and Rates* (London: Macmillan, 1882), p. 12. See also Walter Bagehot, *Lombard Street: A Decription of the Money Market* (Westport: Hyperion Press, 1979), pp. 45-46.

26. Edwin Cannan, *The Paper Pound*, p. 66.

27. Adam Smith, *An Inquiry Into the Nature and Causes of the Wealth of Nations*, ed. with an intro. by Edwin Cannan (New York: Modern Library, 1937), pp. 397-626.

28. John Locke, ''An Essay Concerning the True Original, Extent and End of Civil Government,'' in Sir Ernest Barker, *Social Contract* (New York: Oxford University Press, 1962), pp. 3-146.

29. *The Wealth of Nations*, p. 423.

30. S.G. Checkland, *The Rise of Industrial Society in England, 1815-1885* (New York: St. Martin's Press, 1964), p. 382.

31. W. Cunningham, *The Growth of English Industry*, p. 737.

32. *The Wealth of Nations*, p. 778.

2

The Reduction of Government Spending

The most remarkable achievement in the economic transformation of nine-teenth-century Britain was a steady reduction in government spending from 1815 to 1890. Britain's public spending historically comprised a small share of national income. While mercantilist doctrine supported state direction and regulation of trade, it never entailed direct government spending for any function other than national defense. Historian Asa Briggs described Britain's eighteenth-century government as "managed by an oligarchy, lacked an in-dependent civil service, [and] was abandoning older means of regulation and 'welfare' objectives inherited from Tudor and Stuart England."[1] For example, at the close of the seventeenth century, annual government spending ranged between £4 million and £8 million, or between 8 to 15 percent of the gross national product.

Government spending first passed the £10 million mark in 1747. Thereafter a succession of wars propelled spending to higher and higher levels. From 1775 until the Great War with France in 1794, annual spending fluctuated between £15 million and £25 million. Spending rose sharply in wartime, reaching its peak of £113 million in 1815. Despite a more than fivefold growth in the economy in the nineteenth century, public spending did not reach its 1815 level again until 1898. The period from 1815 to 1890 was the longest sustained reduction in government spending.

Table 2.1 vividly documents this steady reduction. Total central government spending fell from 27.1 percent of gross national income in 1811 to 7.3 percent by 1891 (see Figure 2.1). (Local government spending is discussed at the end of this chapter.) Excluding debt charges, the fall is even more dramatic, to about 5 percent of the gross national income, where it remained from 1840 to 1890. Nominal spending fell by half from 1811 to 1851. Indeed, as late as 1881, total nominal spending reached 1811 levels, but the economy grew fourfold in the interim.

At the end of the Napoleonic Era the three largest items of expenditure were central government spending on debt interest, military spending, and

Table 2.1
Government Expenditure as a Declining Share of National Income in
Nineteenth-Century Britain, 1770-1901

Year	Total Gross National Income (£ million)	Gross Public Expenditures Excluding Debt Charges		Gross Public Expenditures Including Debt Charges	
		(£ million)	(percent of national income)	(£ million)	(percent of national income)
1770	130.1	5.7	4.0	10.5	8.1
1801	232.0	34.2	14.7	50.9	22.0
1811	301.1	57.2	19.0	81.6	27.1
1821	291.0	26.4	9.1	58.4	20.0
1831	340.0	22.7	6.7	51.9	15.3
1841	452.3	23.7	5.2	53.2	11.7
1851	523.3	26.4	5.0	54.7	10.5
1861	668.0	46.6	7.0	72.9	10.9
1871	916.6	41.0	4.5	67.8	7.4
1881	1,051.2	51.4	4.9	80.6	7.7
1891	1,288.2	69.5	5.4	93.4	7.3
1901	1,642.1	173.5	10.6	193.3	11.8

Sources: Computed from B.R. Mitchell and Phyllis Deane, *Abstract of British Historical Statistics* (Cambridge: Cambridge University Press, 1962): national income, p. 366; public expenditure, pp. 389-91, 396-99.

local government spending on poor relief. Debt interest was gradually reduced from £32 million in 1822, to £26 million in 1860, to £20 million by 1900; it fell from half of all government spending in mid-century to a fifth in 1890. Military spending fell sharply from 1815 until the Crimean War, after which it typically exceeded debt charges. Nonmilitary spending remained at a very low level until later in the century, when public sentiment interplayed with universal male suffrage and party politics to support growing government spending in public health, housing, sanitation, and education.

The Intellectual Atmosphere

Laissez-faire was the intellectual atmosphere of the age. The creation of wealth, Adam Smith argued, was properly the role of private individuals and firms, not of the government. The proper role of government was limited to a handful of important tasks: external defense, internal order, public works, and education. Historian C.R. Fay gives us a strong feeling for the attitude that prevailed during this century of public retrenchment.

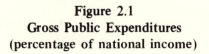

Figure 2.1
Gross Public Expenditures
(percentage of national income)

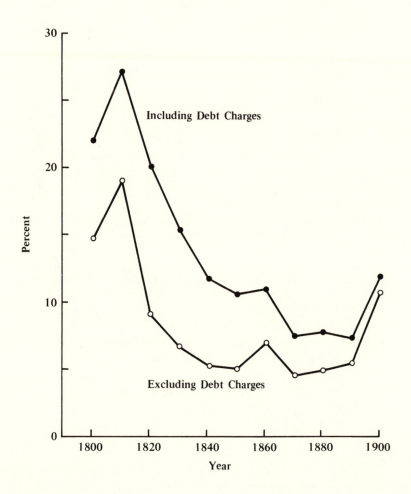

Source: See Table 2.1

The individualism of the 18th and 19th centuries was at once a state of mind and an expression of fact. The fact which it expressed was that nearly the whole of the economic services of the country were supplied by individuals pursuing, alone or in association, a profit-yielding occupation. By confining itself to a few simple tasks the State made itself efficient. In public finance it reduced economy to a science and built up a civil service free of corruption. It left foreign trade altogether to its subjects. It supplied the country with a sound currency, but did not embark on banking outside the reception of savings through the Post Office and it surrounded the banks of the country with a minimum of legal restrictions. The one effort of the State as a carrier, the Post Office Steam Packets, was a financial failure.[2]

Prefacing their account of the twentieth-century growth in British public spending, Alan Peacock and Jack Wiseman contrast the workings of nineteenth-century public finance. There was, they write, widespread agreement "that the level of government expenditure was to be kept at the minimum consistent with the provision of adequate protection against the Crown's enemies and the maintenance of law and order."[3] To the extent that members of different factions or parties quarreled over government spending, the disputes centered on how best to contain or reduce expenditure, rather than on the aims of public policy. It was, they conclude, taken for granted that government spending would be minimized.

Other historians of the nineteenth century render similar interpretations. Asa Briggs, for example, wrote that

in government there existed a strong sense of responsibility about the use and management of public money. In part this sense of responsibility derived from the accepted orthodoxies of mid-Victorian public finance, that individuals should be taxed no more than was absolutely necessary to cover certain essential national costs, and that government spending should be as small as possible.[4]

Arthur J. Taylor echoed in chorus:

In the nineteenth century British governments strove purposefully for the minimum: they abjured any right to direct the national economy. Their sole concern, expressed most cogently in the legislation repealing the Corn Laws and the Navigation Acts, was to make every element in the economy free to carve out its own path to prosperity. Gladstone's pleas that money should be allowed "to fructify in the pockets of the people" is well remembered because it expressed so clearly not only his own economic philosophy but that of all Victorian governments. Economy in public expenditure, long sought in the interests of the taxpayer, was now pursued as a policy virtuous in its own right.[5]

The obsession with economy in public expenditure is laid at the feet of William E. Gladstone, whose career spanned more than half of the nineteenth century. Shortly after completing his degree at Oxford, during which he gained distinction for his speeches in the Oxford Union, Gladstone won a seat in the House of Commons. At the age of twenty-five, in 1834, he was appointed a junior lord of the Treasury. Thereafter he enjoyed an illustrious career in public finance, first in the 1840s as vice-president of the Board of Trade (later president), from which he fashioned a major revision of the tariff, then as Chancellor of the Exchequer from 1853 to 1855 and again from 1859 to 1866, and, finally, as Prime Minister on two occasions between 1868 and 1885. He is best known to historians for his financial prowess and for his view that money should be allowed ''to fructify in the pockets of the people.''

Gladstone firmly believed that no Chancellor of the Exchequer ought to raise taxes until he made every effort to cut wasteful and unnecessary expenditure. He was convinced that the growth in private income should outpace that of public revenue. Individuals could look after their own well-being; government must wisely spend its limited funds on the few proper functions of government.

Gladstone's tenure as Chancellor of the Exchequer from 1859 to 1866 reveals his obsession with, and success in, cutting government spending. During debate on the proposed budget for 1860, Gladstone reviewed the development of national expenditure during the prior seventeen years. Apart from the increased debt charges due to the Crimean War, he pointed out that the annual total government spending rose by £14.7 million. In the decade 1843 to 1853, spending had grown at an annual rate of 5.5 percent, compared with 22.5 percent since 1853. Holding aside debt-servicing payments, optional expenditure under Parliamentary control rose only 9 percent from 1843 to 1853, as against 58 percent between 1853 and 1860. Gladstone used this comparison to emphasize his overriding principle of public finance: public spending must be steadily reduced. He meant what he said. He cut central government spending by 10 percent in a period of almost completely stable prices.

Year	Public Spending (£)
1861	73 million
1862	71 million
1863	69 million
1864	67 million
1865	66 million

In retrospect, it is incredible that Gladstone and the British government refused to be tempted by rising tax receipts into higher expenditures. No one could fault Gladstone for budgets that kept revenue and expenditures at a constant proportion of gross national product. Instead, he translated the spending cuts into a steady stream of tax cuts (see Chapter 3). Sydney Buxton, Gladstone's financial biographer, cited the beneficial effects of spending cuts on the long-run growth of revenue. By cutting government spending, Gladstone enjoyed the luxury of cutting taxes. Tax cuts stimulated economic growth which, in turn, brought greater receipts into the Treasury. From Buxton:

> The heavy load of expenditure with which the country had been burdened, and the consequent impossibility of remitting taxation, had done much to discourage the growth of revenue. It is always so; increased expenditure and deficiency of revenue naturally go together. The necessity of maintaining heavy taxation to meet the former, depresses the latter, and prevents its expansion—a vicious circle that can only be broken by economy. On economy follows reduction of burden, and elasticity of revenue; taxation can then be lightened, and the revenue further expands.[6]

The Composition of Government Spending

Reflecting the laissez-faire views of the age, early nineteenth-century budgets contained virtually nothing for education, maintenance of roads and bridges, administration of justice, and the police. Even the legitimate tasks of Adam Smith's limited government were resentfully funded at impecunious levels. Spending on law and justice, for example, did not reach the £1 million mark until 1850.[7]

Table 2.2 lists expenditures on social programs (which excludes the military and debt service) from 1801 to 1885. As a share of the overall budget, social programs comprised 10 percent in 1801, fell to 7 percent in 1821, recovered to 10 percent in 1831, and remained at that level through 1851. From mid-century social spending rose gradually, except during the Gladstone years, 1860-1865, until 1885 when its share of total spending reached 20 percent. But even 20 percent of a budget that comprised only 7 percent of gross national product puts government social spending between 1 and 2 percent of GNP.

The most dramatic growth in social spending occurred in public education and in the provision for law and justice; together they accounted for about £6.2 million of the £10 million increase in the twenty years spanning 1865 and 1885.

Nonmilitary spending escalated sharply between 1867 and 1873 due to government purchase and operation of the telegraphs and an expansion in public education. Between 1874 and 1880, spending grew rapidly. During this period, Disraeli's government actively adopted new social legislation (see Chapter 4). But the fiscal impact of these programs, as Buxton writes, strained

Table 2.2

Expenditures on Administration in Great Britain, 1801–1885

(in thousands of pounds)

Year	Works and Buildings	Salaries and Expenses	Law and Justice	Education	Foreign and Colonial Services	Non-Effective and Charitable	Miscellaneous	Consolidated Fund and Other Administrative Expenditures	Total
1801-02	85.6	70.4	57.8	62.1	165.7	322.2	40.1	4,756.4	5,560.3
1820-21	262.7	520.8	376.5	83.4	300.3	452.2	318.1	3,103.3	5,417.3
1830-31	398.9	504.3	266.5	75.7	308.3	224.6	160.8	2,982.9	4,922.0
1840-41	246.5	744.9	576.7	265.2	302.4	161.0	226.9	2,732.6	5,256.2
1850-51	504.3	1,007.0	1,168.7	445.3	399.6	195.6	136.4	2,901.3	6,768.2
1855-56	768.2	1,323.0	2,550.7	827.9	343.8	222.1	889.2	1,748.6	8,679.4
1860-61	639.7	1,425.0	2,484.1	1,233.3	451.6	237.4	940.7	2,296.4	9,708.2
1865-66	651.6	1,540.8	2,994.6	1,279.3	544.6	353.7	156.4	1,883.7	9,404.7
1867-68	724.4	1,731.4	3,021.2	1,597.4	544.7	400.2	294.1	1,893.9	10,385.0
1872-73	1,077.7	1,818.3	3,853.0	2,223.2	628.4	518.6	56.0	1,575.0	11,760.0
1875-76	1,326.8	2,107.4	4,622.3	2,603.8	663.9	520.6	129.3	1,583.6	13,557.7
1877-78	1,365.6	2,590.3	5,025.8	3,581.8	654.6	699.1	65.4	1,641.6	15,624.2
1880-81	1,446.4	2,581.9	5,922.4	4,288.2	607.0	1,211.2	51.6	1,669.8	17,418.5
1883-84	1,808.9	2,418.7	6,314.8	4,766.1	658.1	1,176.4	39.0	1,589.6	18,771.6
1885-86	1,766.7	2,442.9	6,236.0	5,268.4	673.1	1,212.4	126.3	1,638.4	19,364.2

Source: Sydney Buxton, Finance and Politics: An Historical Study, 1783-1885, vol. II (London: John Murray, 1888), p. 369.

the total budget: "The expenditure rose, the revenue lost its elasticity; the surpluses became small by degrees, and beautifully less; deficits supervened and all chance of fiscal reform came to an end."[8] By late twentieth-century norms, the increases in social spending between 1865 and 1885 were small in absolute terms and as a share of national income. But seen from the contemporary perspective of a century ago, Buxton exclaims, "The most striking and most disheartening feature of the last few years has been the disastrous expansion of the national expenditure."[9]

He bitterly complained that by 1880, too many Members of Parliament equated greater expenditures in social programs such as health, justice, and education with more efficiency in government. Objecting to the trend of rising expenditures and what he saw as growing inefficiency, Buxton charged that "if we cannot get economy, we ought at least to have efficiency; of late we do not seem to have secured either the one or the other."[10]

Public-sector employment remained modest throughout the century. The percentage of employed males in government service (excluding the military) ranged from 0.8 in 1841 (the first year for which figures are available) to 1.2 by 1881. Including women, those in government comprised 0.6 percent of the labor force in 1841, was 0.7 percent for 1851 and 1861, reached 1 percent in 1871, and fell back to 0.9 percent in 1881. Government employment did not pass 2 percent until the twentieth century.[11] (Today, one Briton in three works for the government.)

Peace and Internal Stability

Laissez-faire indeed restrained the growth of social spending throughout the nineteenth century. But even during the heyday of mercantilist regulation, government spending rarely surpassed a tenth of the national income. The dominant factor in the rise and fall of total government spending over the eighteenth and nineteenth centuries was the presence or absence of war.

Figures 2.2 and 2.3 show the relationship between military spending and overall government spending between 1688 and 1900. The plots move together with remarkable regularity. Military spending in this 212-year interval is the overriding cause of rising expenditures in the eighteenth and declining expenditures in the nineteenth centuries.

Recall the importance of debt payments since 1815. In 1691, the British national debt stood at £3.1 million; by 1818 it totalled £844.3 million, a level it did not again reach until World War I. From 1818 to the Crimean War, debt service equalled half of all public spending. By late century, it fell to one-fifth. Apart from the Crimean War costs of 1855-1857, Britain luxuriated in peace for nearly eighty-five years. Military requirements imposed relatively

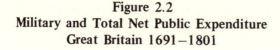

Figure 2.2
Military and Total Net Public Expenditure
Great Britain 1691–1801

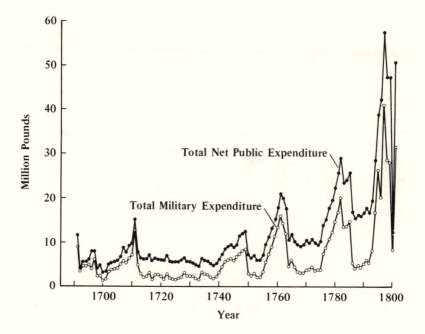

Source: B.R. Mitchell and Phyllis Deane, *Abstract of British Historical Statistics* (Cambridge: Cambridge University Press, 1962), pp. 396–99.

modest demands on public spending. And the rising trend in social expenditure previously noted did not begin until the latter third of the century.

Local Government Spending

Public spending at the local level of government in Britain— parish, county, town—was largely confined to the Poor Law and county expenditures on

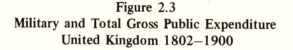

Figure 2.3
Military and Total Gross Public Expenditure
United Kingdom 1802–1900

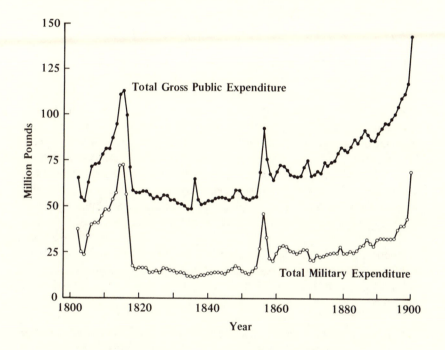

Source: B.R. Mitchell and Phyllis Deane, *Abstract of British Historical Statistics* (Cambridge: Cambridge University Press, 1962), pp. 389–91.

jails, prisoners, and bridges.[12] In all, local spending generally ranged from 10 to 15 percent of central government spending during the first half of the nineteenth century. During the second half, it rose due to municipal provision of utilities, housing, transport, education, libraries and museums, public baths, parks, and fire services. Supported with grants-in-aid from the central government, the largest increase in local government spending took place during the last quarter of the century. By 1890, poor relief fell to about 12 percent of local spending. This change in the pattern of local government spending reflected an improved economy with greater employment prospects, on the one hand, and the public health acts of the 1860s, county construction and maintenance of roads, general improvements in housing and sanitation, and rising participation in technical education and manual instruction by local governments, on the other.[13] Since the greatest reduction in spending occurred in the first part of the century, it is important to understand poor relief.

The Poor Law

Seventeenth-century Britain was largely a rural society with a large class of poor farm laborers. When conditions were favorable, this class survived on a combination of wages and charity. When conditions were unfavorable, rural unemployment depended on the generosity of others or public charity in the form of the Poor Law.[14] The Poor Act of 1601 authorized parish overseers of the poor, appointed by local justices of the peace, to levy a poor-rate on parish residents for the relief of the sick and aged, and to find work for able-bodied unemployed adults. In practice, the application of the Poor Law varied, reflecting differences in local wage rates and standards of living. In some parishes, the overseers genuinely assisted pauper children and orphans. In others, contractors were put in charge of dismal workhouses. Finding work for the able-bodied unemployed was never a high priority in the parish.

A series of settlement laws enacted in 1662, 1685, and 1693 made birth or residence in a parish a necessary qualification for relief. As a result, families and workers were discouraged from leaving the parish in search of work elsewhere.

> If a man left the parish in which he was domiciled, and remained in another for a full year, he lost his right to relief in the first and established a claim to it in the second. For this reason parish authorities were reluctant to receive outsiders, and employers who were large ratepayers would sometimes offer work only for a period short of a full year. If before a laborer had gained a settlement in a new parish he fell on evil days he could be moved back summarily to the parish from which he had come, and this made him think twice before leaving his native village to seek work far away.[15]

Structural changes in eighteenth-century English agriculture—the growth of large farms and the enclosure movement—increased rural unemployment.[16] The situation sharply worsened in the 1790s when the French War brought rising prices and greater dependence on the Poor Law. In response to rising prices, on 6 May 1795, the justices of the peace in the Parish of Speenhamland issued an historic ruling that dramatically altered the workings of the Poor Law. They declared that poor relief should include a subsidy to supplement wages that reflected the cost of living as measured by the price of a loaf of bread. The subsidy also included an allowance for a worker's wife, and his children, legitimate or otherwise. Poor relief instantly became a guaranteed minimum income independent of the amount of a worker's earnings. Although the scale was never formally enacted into law, it shortly became effective throughout the land.

If applied only to single men, poor relief might have been successfully confined to cases of acute distress. But ordinary agricultural wages, which were fixed, could not support a large family in contrast with allowances, which rose with the number of dependents. Thus the Poor Law actually encouraged large families on relief. The parish allowance system was transformed into a national welfare system.

By the early 1830s, the municipal workhouses generally were in a very bad state. Within them were dissolute, depraved, and promiscuous paupers— as described in the literature of the day.

Reform was inevitable. The 1834 Act was developed against the mounting pressure of poor rates, which after a period of falling prices were almost as large in 1832 as they had been in the grim post-war year of 1817. A royal commission recommended changes that resulted in the Poor Law of 1834. It rested on the two guiding principles of the workhouse test and reduced eligibility. First, an able-bodied man received poor relief only inside a workhouse. Outdoor relief and the per-capita allowance system were abolished. Given the deplorable state of most workhouses, these changes encouraged paupers to find work in a free, more mobile labor market. Second, was the principle of "less eligibility." Since relief was only given in the workhouse, that environment was made as unpleasant as possible: bad food, a minimum of social amenities and strict discipline. No one maintained by the parish was as well off as the poorest paid laborer. This policy made fewer people eligible.

The reform also took authority from the parish vestries and local justices of the peace, and placed it in the hands of an elected board of guardians, which in turn was supervised by a central board which laid down minimum standards. Rates imposed on the population per head of spending on relief fell sharply on adoption of the 1834 Act from 9s. 9d. in 1831 to 7s. 7d. in 1835, to 5s. 6½d. by 1851.[17] As seen in Table 2.3, overall spending fell from £6.8 million in 1831 to £4.9 million in 1851.

Buxton summarized the benefits of reform: "The old Poor Law system was a vicious one—a system of outdoor relief to able-bodied men, doles from rates in aid of wages, children, legitimate or otherwise, forming the standard of income. Self-respect and self-denial were at a discount. Corruption and maladministration pervaded the social system. The new Poor Law abolished outdoor relief for able-bodied men, mitigated the law of 'settlement,' consolidated parishes, reorganized the system of rating, and created a government

Table 2.3
Poor Rates Receipts and Expenditure on Relief of the Poor in Great Britain,
1748-1881

	Receipts (£m)	Expenditure (£m)
1748-50	.730	.690
1783-85	2.168	2.004
1803	5.348	4.268
1813	8.647	6.656
1821	8.412	6.959
1831	8.111	6.829
1841	6.352	4.761
1851	6.779	4.963
1861	7.922	5.779
1871	10.962	7.887
1881	12.410	8.102

Source: B.R. Mitchell and Phyllis Deane, *Abstract of British Historical Statistics* (Cambridge: Cambridge Univerity Press, 1962), p. 40.

Note: Other local taxation, about which information is patchy before 1825, indicates total receipts per annum from 1792 to 1830 of between £218,000 and £755,000. On the expenditure side, the largest item was "Goals and Prisoners" with increasing expenditure on "Bridges."

department armed with a general authority of rearrangement, supervision and correction. The poor rate, which in 1750 was but £730,000 a year (in England and Wales), had risen to over £6 million in 1814, and to £7 million in 1832; and was now within ten years reduced to £5 million, in spite of a population increase of two millions."[18]

Notes

1. Asa Briggs, *The Age of Improvement 1783-1867* (New York: David McKay, 1962), p. 30.
2. C.R. Fay, *Great Britain from Adam Smith to the Present Day: An Economic and Social Survey* (New York: Longmans, Green, 1928), pp. 321-22.
3. Alan T. Peacock and Jack Wiseman, *The Growth of Public Expenditure in the United Kingdom* (Princeton: Princeton University Press, 1961), p. 35.
4. Asa Briggs, *The Age of Improvement*, p. 444.
5. Arthur J. Taylor, *Laissez-faire and State Intervention in Nineteenth-Century Britain* (London: Macmillan, 1972), p. 59.
6. Sydney Buxton, *Finance and Politics: An Historical Study. 1783-1885*, vol. 1 (London: John Murray, 1888), p. 297.

7. In addition to central government spending on public services, county governments imposed rates on property, which financed a modest amount of spending on bridges, jails and prisoners, police constables, and the costs of prosecution. Total spending grew slowly, from £223,000 in 1792 to £348,000 in 1801. In successive ten-year intervals county spending grew to £474,000, £653,000, £773,000, £999,000, and finally broke the £1 million mark in 1842. The £2 million mark was reached in 1865. County government spending on public services and public works was always a small fraction of central government spending on social purposes. (Note also that county spending remained small compared with poor relief as shown in Table 2.3.)
8. Sydney Buxton, *Finance and Politics*, vol. 2, p. 191.
9. Ibid., p. 319.
10. Ibid., p. 322.
11. B.R. Mitchell with the collaboration of Phyllis Deane, *Abstract of British Historical Statistics* (Cambridge: Cambridge University Press, 1962), p. 60.
12. Ibid., pp. 410-13.
13. Alan Peacock and Jack Wiseman, *The Growth of Public Expenditure*, p. 39.
14. Asa Briggs, *The Age of Improvement*, pp. 57-8, 278-89; and C.R. Fay, *Great Britain from Adam Smith*, pp. 340-42.
15. T.S. Ashton, *The Industrial Revolution 1760-1830* (London: Oxford University Press, 1967), p. 110.
16. S.G. Checkland, *The Rise of Industrial Society in England 1815-1885* (New York: St. Martin's Press, 1964), pp. 273-74.
17. C.R. Fay, *Great Britain from Adam Smith*, p. 341.
18. Sydney Buxton, *Finance and Politics*, vol. 1, p. 31.

3

Fifty Years of Tax Reform

Britain entered the nineteenth century as a heavily taxed nation. She exited as a lightly taxed one. This transformation is almost as remarkable as the reduction of government spending that occurred in the same period. When the Napoleonic War ended, Britain endured a maze of tariffs and excises, a host of miscellaneous charges elegantly enumerated in the poetry of the day, and a burgeoning income tax that portended higher levels of government spending in the future. The British Parliament at once abolished the income tax, and then gradually simplified and reduced tariffs and excises.[1] By 1865 a half century of reform had been completed. Three great men provided the leadership: William Huskisson in the 1820s, Sir Robert Peel in the 1840s, and William E. Gladstone in the 1850s and 1860s. When Gladstone finished the last of his budgets as Chancellor of the Exchequer in 1866, Britain enjoyed virtual free trade including grain, an income tax rate under 2 percent, and the startling discovery that low tax rates could often generate more revenue than high tax rates.

Glimmerings of reform first appeared in the ministry of William Pitt, an early convert to Adam Smith, before the French War. Pitt became Prime Minister in December 1783, inheriting the fiscal chaos that resulted from resisting the movement of American Independence.

A first step was to curtail smuggling. An extensive system of smuggling had grown up around tea, an article of general consumption. Earlier, in 1745, First Lord of the Treasury Henry Pelham virtually abolished the contraband trade in tea through reductions on its duty. His successors reversed this policy, raising the duty to such high levels that smuggling once again became universal. High duties, or the costs of smuggling, were passed on to consumers, and converted tea into a luxury drink for the better-off classes of British society. Consonant with its luxury status, tea was often drunk in thimbleful amounts rather than by the cup. Reverting to the policy of Pelham, in 1784 Pitt reduced the heavy duties on tea from the existing rate of 119 percent to a single *ad valorem* (based on the value of) rate of 12.5 percent. This tax-rate reduction cut the ground out from under the smugglers' feet.[2]

Economic historian Francis Hirst attributes Pitt's reform of the tea duty to his study of *The Wealth of Nations*, in which Adam Smith contended that the extraordinary development of smuggling of any article proved that the duty on that article was excessive. In those circumstances, a reduction in duty lowers consumer prices and curtails smuggling. As to the revenue, at a level about one-tenth lower, the new duty yielded almost as much for Pitt as the old one—£650,000 against £700,000.[3]

Pitt did not swing his Mephistophelian axe helter-skelter through Britain's revenue system. Where possible, he strove to lower duties, but only if he could also preserve the revenue. A balanced budget was an overriding norm of public finance.

> Industries do not exist merely for purposes of taxation, and that judicious reductions, combined with simplification of levy, will, in the end, by stimulating consumption and by diminishing smuggling, increase the revenue. Pitt improved the system of warehousing, simplified the method and reduced the cost of collection, and—when he could find the means, for he would not risk a deficiency—lowered excessive duties.[4]

Pitt's reduction of the tea tax generated instant popularity. By this move he showed himself to be both a shrewd politician and a practitioner of public finance.

Pitt's second major success was the commercial treaty of 1786 (the Eden treaty) with France. Halting a century-long tariff war, the agreement reduced duties on a variety of goods on both sides of the English Channel. Trade expanded and consumer prices fell on many items.

Pitt's third major achievement was to consolidate the customs and excise taxes into one fund; in the old system, separate accounts were kept for each item. "So intricate, so chaotic, was the existing system, that nearly three thousand resolutions were needed to carry these reforms into effect."[5] Prosperity and rising tax yields before 1792 enabled Pitt to repeal the unpopular window tax imposed on small homes of seven or fewer windows and to reduce the tax on candles. From 1793 on, the story turns into an unending array of new and additional taxes to help finance the French War.

Phase One: The Income Tax Repealed in 1816

Of all the war-related levies imposed, British taxpayers most bitterly resented the personal income tax. Opponents of the tax regarded it as iniquitous, inquisitorial, and an interference with man's ideal state of natural liberty,[6] the same reasons that Adam Smith also opposed direct assessment of income.

It was widely felt that the income tax was too heinous a yoke to be imposed on any man because it would expose his finances to the scrutiny of the treasurer, who might then drag him through public disgrace.

Over the opposition of the Chancellor of the Exchequer Nicholas Vansittart and the Prime Minister Lord Liverpool, who regarded the income tax as essential to overall fiscal stability, on 13 May 1816, Parliament repealed the 2s. to the pound (10 percent) income tax by a vote of 238 to 201.[7] Moreover, the House of Commons ordered that all returns and documents in the hands of the tax commissioners be destroyed.[8] However, destruction was incomplete. Documents were discovered in the 1930s, along with various returns published in Parliamentary Papers, from which tax assessments have been estimated.[9]

Repeal of the income tax placed Vansittart in a most difficult quandary. It reduced revenue by £14 million from a budget of £72 million, thus compelling his unpopular government to maintain all war taxes, to impose new indirect taxation of £5 million, and to borrow the difference.[10] Given the pressing needs of debt service and other expenditures, further tax reform stalled in the postwar commercial and agricultural depression of 1816-1819.

Phase Two: Huskisson and Liberal Reform in the 1820s

Political action invariably lags behind changing intellectual winds. Adam Smith's manifesto on behalf of free trade appeared in 1776; yet, Britain of 1816 was not a free-trading country. In March 1817, Lord Brougham delivered one of the early speeches in Parliament on behalf of free trade, suggesting that a wholesale revision of the commercial code afforded a prosperous exit from the current commercial malaise.[11] The government's reply to his speech was to say, simply, that the exchequer could not afford the loss associated with tax reduction. Yet the failure to spell out any avenue of relief surrendered to the growing chorus of free-traders in Parliament the initiative in formulating fiscal and economic policy. In 1820, Alexander Baring presented the famous petition of the merchants of London in Parliament. As the basis of national trade, Baring proposed the guiding principle that nations should buy at the cheapest cost and sell at the highest price—the same principle that compels individual merchants in their own business affairs. Baring proposed that relief be granted from duties on Scandinavian timber, and that prohibitive duties be removed from imported goods and raw materials.[12] In response to the continuing commercial depression, Parliament set up a committee on foreign trade, which recommended simplification and liberalization of commercial policy.

In 1821, a select parliamentary committee dealt specifically with Baring's question of timber duties.[13] Since 1809, timber imported from British North

America entered British ports free of duty, while European timber was charged a duty of £3 5s. per load (a load is 50 cubic feet). It was generally acknowledged that American timber was inferior in quality. The select committee proposed a £1 reduction in the duty on the grounds that the customs schedule forced into consumption an article of inferior quality. Despite vigorous opposition from the shipping interests, the measure was enacted. The first victory for free trade, it signalled a series of reforms to come in the next few years.

A transformation in the 1822 administration of Lord Liverpool brought into power a group of liberal reformers known as the Canningites, named after their leader, George Canning. Their views built upon the pre-war reform tradition of William Pitt. The most important of these liberal figures was William Huskisson, appointed President of the Board of Trade in April 1823. His accession marked "a new era in fiscal history."[14] He was the dominant personality in fiscal and economic policy of his day, commencing important reforms in commercial taxation. The single most dramatic measure of his tenure was the repeal of the Spitalfield Acts, which had smothered the silk industry under a protective blanket. The tax-cutting experiment on silk has been well documented and forcefully demonstrates the beneficial effects of tax relief to that industry.

Silk manufacture in England enjoyed healthy development in the seventeenth century, when immigrant Huguenot weavers gave it a powerful boost in Elizabeth's reign.[15] Although French and other imported silks were prohibited, these protective measures were weakly enforced until 1697, when Parliament actively discouraged all European silk imports. Silks of China and India fell into this restrictive net in 1701.

The internal structure of England's silk industry also reflected changes in commercial tax policy. Throughout the early part of the eighteenth century, English silk weavers relied on foreign-thrown silk (to throw silk is to twist two or more filaments into a thread for weaving), much of it Italian. In 1765, only about one-ninth of the organzine (a raw silk yarn used for warp threads in fine fabrics) used in England was thrown in English mills. Having to import foreign-thrown silk made competition with continental manufactured silk fabrics difficult. A mid-century change in policy increased the duties per pound for thrown silk to 4s. between 1747 and 1765 and to 5s. 2d. by 1779; it sharply reduced the duty on raw silk from a high of 3s. 2d. per pound to only 11d. English silk throwers reacted by investing in filatures (a factory where silk is reeled from cocoons) in Bengal to take advantage of lower-cost raw material supplies.

Now that English manufacturers had developed their own sources of raw silk, they pressed for higher tariffs to shut out continental competition. During the Seven Years' War (1756 to 1763), English silk exporters captured much of the French silk trade. But peace brought a slump, and Parliament granted protection. In 1766, it granted a prohibition on all imports of foreign silk for five years; this prohibition remained in place for sixty years. However, the fiscal demands of war forced the government to raise import duties on all silks between 1779 and 1823: raw silk duties increased four to sixfold, and thrown silks nearly tripled. Overall, the silk industry expanded from the 1750s through the 1780s, but fell into a wartime slump until after 1810. These broad trends masked important changes in the structure, location, equipment, and products of the industry. New investment in water-powered mills contributed to the decline of traditional hand-throwers located in Spitalfields, the site of the seventeenth-century silk industry.

French immigrant weavers converted Spitalfields into the center for English silk manufacture, and it became the scene of wage riots between the manufacturers and weavers. In response, Parliament enacted the Spitalfields Acts of 1773, 1792, and 1811 which empowered local justices of the peace to regulate the wages of Spitalfields silk weavers by fixing weaving prices, limiting the number of apprentices, and forbidding union activity, thus stabilizing local conditions. The Spitalfields weavers thus enjoyed a protected status among British workers. But the acts could not prevent a depression which gradually drove the silk industry out of Spitalfields. Available labor at lower, uncontrolled wages was increasingly found outside London. Big London silk manufacturers, trying to reduce costs and improve their competitive position, invested in water-powered throwing mills in rural areas and country towns and gave work to weavers in these same districts.

In May 1823 Huskisson proposed repeal of the Spitalfields Acts, since the protected status of silk weavers in Spitalfields was not enjoyed by weavers elsewhere in the country. He substituted, in place of the prohibitions and high duties, a tariff of 15s. a pound on plain manufactured silks, 20s. a pound on figured silk, and an across the board maximum rate of 30 percent on the value of all other silk products. As Table 3.1 shows, he reduced sharply the duties on raw and thrown silk. In one gesture, Huskisson lowered the cost of raw silk imports and exposed British silk producers to overseas competition. From a comparison of rapid growth in the cotton industry, largely free, with dilatory growth in woolens, highly protected, Huskisson concluded that the British cotton industry flourished largely because it was forced to compete.[16]

Not only would native industry do better competing, in Huskisson's view, but lower duties would mitigate the harmful effects of smuggling, estimated at a £100,000 loss in uncollected customs each year for French goods alone. It did no good to levy high duties if imported goods were smuggled past the customs net.

A parliamentary committee was convened in 1832 and again in 1840 to evaluate the impact of Huskisson's measures on the silk industry. Nearly 1,000 pages of evidence was recorded in 1832 and a mass of statistics was

Table 3.1
Silk Import Duties in Great Britain, 1817-1829
(per lb. of 16 oz.)

Raw				Thrown (undyed)		
China	Bengal	Italy				
(British India)					*s.*	*d.*
1817-23 5s. 6d.	3s. 6d.	5s. 6d.		1814-23	14	8
March 1824	3d.			March 1824	7	6
				November 1825	5	0
July 1826	1d.			July 1826		
				organzine and crape	5	0
				tram and singles	3	0
July 1829	1s. per cwt.			July 1829		
				organzine and crape	3	6
				tram	2	0
				singles	1	6

Source: D.C. Coleman, *Courtaulds: An Economic and Social History*, vol. 1. *The Nineteenth Century: Silk and Crape* (Oxford: Clarendon Press, 1969), p. 66.

assembled in the 1840 hearings. Some witnesses claimed in the first hearings that exposure to French competition rapidly improved the quality of English silks. John Bowring, the commercial commissioner at Paris, testified that British exports to France rose sharply at the same time that silk exports to France from other countries fell. He told the committee that English silk exports to France rose from 1,087 kilograms in 1828 to 5,852 in 1830, with a corresponding fivefold increase in value; for all other suppliers of silk goods to France, the corresponding figures fell from 5,189 to 4,502 kilograms.[17] Other witnesses testified to a dramatic increase in the silk industry in Manchester.

The 1840 committee enjoyed an additional eight years of observation against which to judge Huskisson's silk reforms, and accorded them an even more ringing endorsement. G.R. Porter, head of the statistical department of the Board of Trade, testified to the vitality of the silk industry. In the ten years preceding the 1824 tax reductions, imports of raw and processed silk totalled 18.8 million pounds. In the ten years after 1824, these imports rose 95 percent, to 36.8 million pounds.[18] Exports of British manufactured silks rose even more sharply:

Year	Value of Exports (£)
1820	371,755
1825	296,736
1830	321,010
1835	972,031
1840	792,648
1845	766,405
1849	998,334

Presuming that home consumption of silk increased proportionally with exports, it is estimated that the total value of output in the silk industry rose from £6.5 million in 1820 to between £11 and £12 million by 1840.

J. R. McCulloch submitted a set of estimates that he published in 1839:[19]

Year	Index of raw material imports (1801–05 = 100)	Value (£ millions)
1770	87	2
1800	100	3
1812	110	3
1819	186	6.5
1836	449	10.5

Scholarly estimates extended McCulloch's figures through 1860:[20]

Year	Volume	Value
1847	521	11
1860	1,068	17

Both parliamentary committees contended that removal of the excessive tax on imported raw silk, coupled with the abolition of a protective shield of prohibitions and high duties, greatly improved the efficiency and output of the silk industry. In all, output doubled, exports tripled, and total employment rose.

An historian of the silk industry, D.C. Coleman, shows that the number of water- and steam-operated throwing mills, especially in the north, increased as firms took advantage of possibilities opened up by the removal of the duties on raw silk. In the Manchester area, for example, the number of silk mills rose as follows:

1820	1822	1824	1826	1828	1830	1832
3	5	6	10	12	14	16

Imports of thrown silk declined, those of raw and waste silk increased. Prices of raw silk fell sharply. Falling prices and sharpened competition put a premium on resourceful throwers with large units, up-to-date throwing machinery, and efficient sources of power; it put at a disadvantage small, remote, old-fashioned mills. Marginal producers were gradually driven out of business. On balance, the British silk industry grew for forty years after the first draught of free trade.[21] In 1824 the budget granted tax relief on imports and exports of wool. Rates on foreign wool imports were chopped from 6d. to 1d. per pound, thus being virtually eliminated, and export restrictions on British wool (which had been forbidden before 1824) were lifted, save for a token 1d. per pound export duty.

Rum duties were also reduced by 1s. 1.5d. a gallon, with an estimated loss in revenue for 1825 of £150,000.[22] But the revenue figures of 1825 showed a remarkable outcome: customs collections for rum did not fall. The volume of imported rum rose to such an extent that the lower tax rate applied to a larger volume of rum yielded the same revenue as had the 1824 higher rate.

This should have come as no great surprise. The experience of the two preceding decades demonstrated that, at some point, higher rates of duty on imported wines and liquor actually lowered revenue collections.[23] A duty of 12s. 6d. a gallon on foreign liquor in 1806 generated receipts of £1,463,000. In 1810, the rate rose to 15s. 1.5d. Imports fell, but the total tax receipts remained steady at about £1,500,000. Encouraged, the Chancellor of the Exchequer increased the duty to 19s. 1.5d., but total receipts fell. Taxation at this rate was counterproductive; similarly, when duties on French wines were raised between 1810 and 1815, the tax take fell almost 20 percent.

It is worth stressing the relationship between tax rates and tax receipts. A tax rate of zero yields no tax receipts. Private business may prosper in the absence of taxation, but the public treasury will be empty. As the tax rate increases, government tax receipts also rise. A modest tax rate may accomplish the twin objectives of private prosperity and ample public receipts, so long as public spending remains moderate. At some point in the tax-rate schedule, additional increases in tax rates harm business activity and cause receipts to fall. Tax evasion may become widespread. High taxes may also deter work, savings, and investment, leading to economic stagnation or contraction. To reverse the process, a reduction in tax rates may stimulate economic expansion, reduce tax evasion, and yield greater tax receipts. Simply put, low tax rates levied on a rapidly growing economy may yield more revenue than a system of high tax rates.

Huskisson's experiments on silks and alcoholic beverages confirmed that cuts in tax rates stimulated economic expansion and increased revenue. Both industries had been previously taxed at excessive levels. The flush of success in these two areas brought a more extensive sweep of the tax schedule in 1825.

Tariff Reform in the 1825 Budget

Huskisson had confronted a tariff wall surpassing one thousand separate customs charges. A duty had been imposed on virtually every imported item. To collect these duties, the government located customs officers and houses in every remote region of the country. For small volume imports the costs of revenue collection often exceeded receipts.

1825 was a boom year. Despite significant tariff reductions in 1824, revenue exceeded budgetary estimates by £1 million. Moreover, the government projected a succession of surpluses in the immediate years ahead. Taking advantage of these projected surpluses, and living within the balanced budget norm, Huskisson proposed further cuts in duties to stimulate trade, reduce smuggling, and lower consumer prices.

On 25 March 1825, Huskisson announced his proposed measures, which, taken together, constituted the first truly sweeping tariff reform of the century.[24] Duties on cotton goods ranging from 50 to 75 percent gave way to a much smaller uniform rate of 10 percent *ad valorem*. He retained a 10 percent rate in order to offset the small duty imposed on imported raw cotton. Duties on woolens that ranged between 50 and 67.5 percent were lowered to 15 percent. Linen rates fell from a range of 40 to 180 percent to a uniform rate of 25 percent. Duty rates on bound and unbound books declined by nearly half, rates on foreign glass were reduced from 80 to 20 percent, the duty on earthenware fell from 75 to 15 percent, and the prohibition on foreign gloves was lifted, and replaced with a 30 percent duty.

Minerals were an important component in the tariff reforms. Huskisson proposed to reduce the import tax on iron from £6 10s. a ton to £1 10s.; on raw copper, from £54 to £27 a ton; on zinc, from £28 to £14 a ton; on tin, from £5 9s. 3d. to £2 10s. per hundredweight; and on lead, from 20 percent *ad valorem* to about 15 percent.

Beyond tax reductions on imported fabrics and metals, which ranged from 50 to 75 percent, he also offered an omnibus reduction on all non-enumerated articles. Existing rates of 50 percent on the value of manufactured goods and 20 percent on unmanufactured commodities were cut to 20 and 10 percent respectively. With few modifications, these proposed reforms were all adopted.

What consequences flowed from these reforms? On 13 March 1826, F.J. Robinson, Chancellor of the Exchequer, opened the budget debate with a review of Britain's fiscal condition. He compared the quantities of goods that paid import duties in 1825 with those brought in during 1816 and showed a large increase across a whole range of items: tobacco, 13 percent; sugar, 19 percent; tea, 20 percent; leather, 29 percent; candles, 36 percent; coffee and cocoa, 43 percent; paper, 51 percent; hemp, 74 percent; wine, 88 percent; crown glass, 95 percent; flint glass, 104 percent; plate glass, 108 percent; hard soap, 113 percent; raw cotton, 119 percent; soft soap, 121 percent; thrown silk, 180 percent; deals, 182 percent; bricks, 188 percent; timber, 196 percent; tallow, 201 percent; raw silk, 274 percent; butter, 317 percent; sheep's wool, 443 percent. Receipts exceeded the estimated revenue over this period by £1.4 million, despite the repeal of more than £8 million in taxes. Furthermore, the expense of collecting the revenue fell by £500,000 compared with that of 1818.[25]

With hindsight, we might be tempted to fault Huskisson for his failure to have reduced or eliminated other duties. Customs receipts of 1827 show that 18 articles alone returned £17.7 million of a total customs take of £19.8 million; by contrast, 510 other items yielded only £585,072.[26] With trivial loss to the public revenue, Huskisson could have abolished all but the duties on the 60 most productive articles of import. Yet the tax cuts he achieved were proposed and enacted over the opposition of conservative opinion within his party and vested interests in the economy.[27]

One last episode, an accident in Huskisson's tax-cutting efforts. The 1826 budget was formulated in the midst of a commercial downturn which throttled major fiscal reforms. But the 4s. duty on tobacco was mistakenly reduced to 3s. for half of 1825. This change sharply curtailed smuggling, thus leading to its permanently lowered rate of 3s.[28]

Looking back over the Huskisson reforms during the debate on the 1830 budget, the year of Huskisson's unfortunate accidental death, commentators of the time concurred that tax cuts not only fostered economic growth but also maintained, and in some instances actually increased, government revenue. Poulett Thomson exemplified this position. There was a point in taxation, he said, where, by increasing the amount (rate) of duties, the revenue fell; conversely, by lowering duties, revenue actually increased and consumer prices fell.[29]

Whig Rule During the 1830s

The Electoral Reform of 1832 (see Chapter 6) ensconced Whig rule from 1832 to 1841, except for a short interlude of Tory government from late 1834 through early 1835. During this period, a number of social and political reforms held center stage—Catholic emancipation, abolition of slavery, the first factory acts, public education, and Poor Law reform (see Chapter 4). Tax reform received low priority during the decade.

During the seven years 1833 to 1839, Whig governments reduced total taxation by £4.6 million. This was a considerably smaller sum than the total of remissions during the prior decade, and smaller still as a share of national income. The breakdown and timing of these remissions revealed no particular pattern or underlying theory of trade or taxation.

1833. Repealed: duties on tiles, upon some taxed carts, upon shopmen, warehousemen, porters, commercial travellers, stewards, bailiffs, and others employed in trades. Reduced: the duty on advertisements, marine insurances, houses partly occupied as shops, raw cotton, and soap.

1834. Repealed: the house tax, duties on starch, stone bottles and sweets, some small assessed taxes, the stamp on almanacs. Reduced: Irish spirits from 3s. 4d. to 2s. 4d. per gallon, and some customs duties amounting to £200,000.

1835. New scale adopted for spirit licenses, in favor of small traders, reduction of duty on flint glass from 6d. to 2d. per lb., and of the stamp duty on awards in Ireland.

1836. Reduced: the excise on first class paper from 3d. to 1½d. per lb., further reduction of duties on taxed carts, South Sea duties remitted, stamp duties on newspaper reduced, excise on stained paper repealed.

1837 and 1838. No remission of taxation.

1839. The penny postage adopted, to come into effect on 5th December.[30]

In matters of fiscal reform, the 1830s are best remembered for the abolition of the beer tax in 1830 (to the delight of a gratefully drunken nation), a reduction in the duty on soap in 1833 (in the hope of a cleaner nation), and lower paper duties in 1839 (in search of a more literate nation).[31]

Lord Althorp, Whig Chancellor of the Exchequer in the late 1830s, was unable to resolve successfully a string of budget deficits. Indeed, after four successive deficits—it must be remembered that a balanced budget was considered an absolute hallmark of sound public finance— Althorp levied a 5 percent general increase in customs and excise and 10 percent on the assessed taxes (a form of personal property taxes). He forecast that the additional taxation would bring in nearly £2 million in revenue, but only a tenth of that sum materialized.[32] By 1841, Britain had reached the limits of indirect taxation on articles of consumption: higher tax rates only threatened lower revenue. Lord Althorp and his Whigs were left in fiscal disrepute. Moreover, real income per head fell between 1831 and 1841.[33] It is not surprising that fiscal reform again became politically paramount. The need for economic growth transcended social reform on the political agenda. In response, the Queen commanded Sir Robert Peel to form a new Tory ministry, which he assembled in September 1841. Peel appointed a very promising and brilliant William Ewart Gladstone as Vice-President of the Board of Trade, and he played a major role in the tax reforms of the 1840s. Peel and his followers enjoyed a majority of eighty in Parliament as he commenced his government.

Phase Three: Peel and Free Trade in the 1840s

Sir Robert Peel followed two key maxims of economic and fiscal policy. He believed in free trade. With equal conviction he opposed budgetary deficits. His predecessors in 1840 increased both the customs and excise duties by 5 percent which, in his view, exacerbated flagging trade and declining revenue yields. Thus Peel fashioned his economic and tax reforms on the twin pillars of free trade and fiscal balance. Progress in one area was not sanctioned at the expense of the other.

First Revision of the Tariff: 1842

Peel opened the budget in 1842 under adverse economic circumstances: high prices for food, stagnating industrial activity, rising unemployment, and a growing Chartist movement that advocated universal suffrage and annual elections (to the obvious dismay of the landed Tory interests).[34] Since 1834 military expenditures had risen, the Opium War had been fought with China, the costs of civil government had increased (with the formation of an education department in 1839), and servicing of the national debt consumed 60 percent of annual expenditures, the price of past wars.

Peel's chief mission was to revive commerce and manufacturing. British tariffs were still high in the early 1840s despite Huskisson's reforms, at an average rate of about one-third the value of net imports, with some articles much higher.[35] This situation entailed wholesale tariff reform—the abolition of import taxes, especially on raw materials, and export duties. In 1840 Parliament had convened an "Import Duties Committee." This select committee disclosed that eighty-two articles yielded ten/elevenths of all customs receipts, and that nine articles produced about six/sevenths of all customs revenue. The implication of this finding was obvious: virtually the whole customs net could be stripped away without jeopardizing the bulk of customs revenue. Buxton claims that Peel did not originate, but adopted, the recommendations of this committee.[36]

Peel was not prepared to surrender the customs revenue unless he could find some other means to maintain a balanced budget. He therefore proposed, for a limited period of four years, an income tax of 7*d.* to the pound, a rate of 3 percent. Unlike Pitt's earlier income tax, which had a graduated scale for annual incomes between £50 and £150, Peel exempted all incomes below £150. (Per capita income in 1842 was £24, thus the tax incidence fell only on a small minority of middle- and upper-income households.)[37] The estimated yield from this income tax was £3.77 million. With this new source of revenue in hand, Peel moved forcefully to stimulate commerce and manufacturing.

Historians of the mid-nineteenth century looked favorably on the substitution of a modest income tax for a very heavy customs charge. Checkland believed that a 3 percent income tax lessened the damaging and distorting effect of taxing trade at high rates, which discouraged economic growth.[38] Fay admitted that Britons detested the income tax and only swallowed Pitt's to defeat France in war. In 1842 "it submitted to fresh doses of the same medicine only because they were sweetened by remissions of taxes which it detested even more."[39]

In the first swath, Peel reduced, in some cases abolished, the duties on 750 of the 1,200 articles encompassed in the tariff. The principles underpinning his first tariff revision tariff were as follows:

(1) Removal of prohibitions and prohibitively high duties.
(2) Reduction of duties on most raw materials to a maximum rate of 5 percent.
(3) Reduction of duties on manufactured goods to a maximum rate of 10 to 20 percent, depending on the stage of manufacture.
(4) Abolition of export duties on manufactured products.

Peel's reforms met objections from those who stood to lose their protected status. These objections were forcefully treated by his accomplice in tariff reform, William Gladstone, who published an article in 1843 assessing the general merits of free trade and the specific effects of the 1842 tariff revision.[40] Gladstone's fundamental thesis was that tariff reductions stimulated trade and that increased consumption of imports sustained and, in some instances, increased public revenue. High duties discouraged imports, and in severe cases held down customs yields.

To prove his point, Gladstone set forth the effects of remission in 1842 of duties on hide, bark, turpentine, and oils. He estimated the loss of annual revenue from reduced duties as follows:

Hides and skins	£ 60,000
Bark for tanning	12,000
Turpentine	80,000
Oils	40,000
Total	£192,000

But just one year later, trade in the four commodities had dramatically increased in value in the following amounts:

Hides	£100,000
Oak bark	40,000
Turpentine	70,000
Olive oil	200,000
Total	£410,000

These figures showed that reduced taxes encouraged trade and consumption, thus improving national prosperity and individual well-being. Gladstone also noted in his article that reductions in coffee and copper ore duties stimulated considerable increases in consumption, which, in turn, offset the revenue loss from lower rates of duty. Convincing proof of these claims followed the second revision of the tariff two years later.

Second Revision of the Tariff: 1844 to 1845

Although the income tax proved unpopular, it enabled Peel to emancipate trade from the indirect tax burden imposed upon it. One observer, Stafford Northcote, Gladstone's private secretary and later Chancellor of the Exchequer (1874), assessed the impact of reduced rates of indirect taxation on public revenues:

> The seeming paradox, that a larger revenue might be obtained from smaller duties, had turned out to be the simple expression of an economical law, which appeared capable of more extensive application that it had yet received. Duties had been largely reduced, and even in some cases repealed; yet the [overall] revenue was as large as before and was evidently growing.[41]

Flushed with success from the 1842 revision, Peel pressed forward with an even more expansive tariff reform, granting threefold the pound value of relief compared with 1842.[42] With Gladstone's able assistance, Peel slashed the duty on nonslave-grown sugar, abolished all remaining export duties (including that on coal), removed the import duty on raw cotton, eradicated the excise charges on glass, and discarded all customs duties on 430 additional articles in the tariff, including silk, hemp, flax, and woods for furniture manufacture. Estimated loss of revenue from these tax remissions would exceed £3 million annually if no expansion in trade followed.

Among the excise duties imposed on domestic manufactures, Peel specifically earmarked glass for relief. A commission of inquiry into the excise duties reported that the tax on glass manufacture was iniquitous and harmful. Twice before in history this tax had ruined domestic glass manufacture, once in the reign of William III and again during the "Great War" with France. Gladstone's defense of Peel's second tariff revision was contained in a 65-page statistical survey analyzing recent movements in trade and revenue in Britain, which was published in early 1845.[43] Gladstone again examined a number of specific cases to determine the direct impact of remissions in taxation on the expansion of trade in, and revenues derived from, those items.

Gladstone reviewed those items surveyed in his earlier defense of the 1842 reforms, showing both the actual loss of revenue and value added to trade on each article:

	Loss of Revenue	*Value Added*
Hides	£ 36,971	£453,706
Turpentine	79,819	53,510
Palm Oil	8,423	123,774
Olive Oil	21,957	97,860
Bark	8,891	94,210
Mahogany	41,148	720
Rosewood	7,264	11,980
Total	£204,473	£835,760

The figures showed dramatic expansion in some products, minimal stimulus in others, and an overall boost to economic activity. The private sector gained £4 for each £1 surrendered in public revenue.

For other articles, Gladstone demonstrated that lower duties could actually increase revenue. The duty on sperm oil was reduced from £26 12s. to £15, on train oil from £26 15s. to £6, and on whale fins from £4 15s. to £1; yet, the increase in revenue from lower rates on these three items one year later amounted to nearly £50,000.

In 1842 the duty on copper ore yielded no revenue. The duty was lowered that year. By 1843 the yield amounted to £47,000 and, in 1844, £70,000, with an overall increase in copper smelting throughout Britain. Lard, at a duty of 8s. per hundredweight, yielded £30 in receipts in 1840; but with the 1842 reduction to 2s., its yield rose to £4,496 and £7,980 for the next two years.

Tariff reform stimulated trade and business activity; it also had a salutary effect on smuggling. Under former laws, watches were charged at 25 percent of value, and duties collected in 1840 came to £1,387. In 1842, this rate was reduced to 10 percent and the duty receipts increased to £5,391. The declared value of imported watches increased tenfold, from £5,085 to £52,622. As the benefits to smugglers fell, watch imports entered the tax net through normal import channels.

For other consumer goods, such as gloves, boots, shoes, corks, toys, tanned leather, fish, lard, and potatoes, Gladstone claimed that increased imports more than offset the immediate surrender of revenue from the rate reductions (see Figure 3.1).

Gladstone's assessment of specific cases is reinforced by the improvements in the overall trade picture. Between 1842 and 1846 ordinary public expenditure increased by about £1 million. But the public debt was reduced by £14 million, and a fall in interest rates reduced annual debt charges by £1.5 million. Over this five-year sequence of reforms, Peel remitted, on average, about £2.5 million each year (including the proceeds of the new income tax), yet economic growth increased total tax revenues from £50 million in 1841 to £55 million in 1846.[44] Economic historian W. Cunningham concluded that Peel's two major tariff revisions increased the volume of trade; moreover, the government collected revenue from low tax rates which equalled the sums previously collected from high rates, "which had so injuriously affected our trade."[45]

Repeal of the Corn Laws: 1846

By 1845 Peel had simplified and reduced the tariff wall that had burdened Britain's trade and commerce. While he reduced the duties on a number of agricultural goods, the Corn Laws restricting grain imports remained intact. Peel was a Tory and had come into office in 1841 committed to the principle of agricultural protectionism. However, the potato famine in Ireland forced him to open Irish ports to food imports in 1845, and the opening of British ports was a logical extension of his movement towards free trade.

The story surrounding repeal of the Corn Laws involves the machinations of cliques, factions, party politics, the interplay between the House of Commons and the House of Lords, and the survival of Peel's own career and government. Indeed, lacking adequate support among his own colleagues in the Cabinet for a proposal to repeal the Corn Laws, Peel offered his resignation to the Queen in December 1845. Since no cluster of personalities was able to form an alternative government, the Queen sought and got his return as Prime Minister just two weeks after his resignation.

Accordingly, in his 1846 budget, Peel proposed repeal of all grain duties to take effect on 1 February 1849, except for a 1s. registration fee per quarter of wheat.[46] Imported cattle, sheep, pigs, beef, bacon, pork, and other meats were wholly exempted from duty. The Corn Law Bill passed the House of Lords on 25 June 1846, after considerable political maneuvering, and received Royal assent on 26 June 1846. On 15 May it had secured approval in the

Figure 3.1
Customs Revenues and Value of Imports

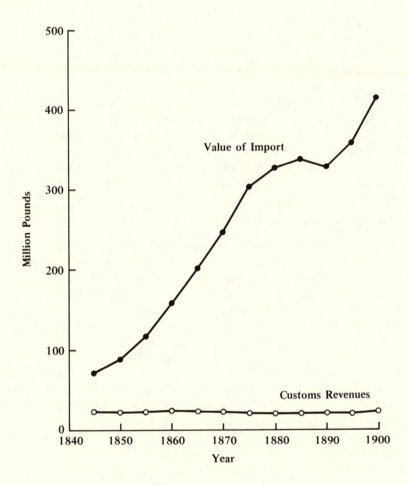

Source: B.R. Mitchell and Phyllis Deane, *Abstract of British Historical Statistics* (Cambridge: Cambridge University Press, 1962), pp. 282–84, 392–94.

House of Commons by a majority of nearly 100. However, Peel was not to escape the wrath of the landed Tory interests. Peel paid the penalty for repeal of the Corn Laws. In Ireland, famine was followed by disorder, which called for a Coercion Bill. On this he was defeated by a combination of Irish, Whigs, and Protectionist Tories—"some for the love of Ireland, more for hatred of Peel."[47] From 1846 to 1850 he was in opposition, supported by some of his former colleagues and lending a friendly support to the free-trade measures carried by his successor Lord John Russell. On 29 June 1850, he was killed by a fall from his horse on Constitution Hill.

Repeal of the Corn Laws owed much to the activities of the Anti–Corn Law League, whose chief spokesmen were John Bright and Richard Cobden.[48] The League's representatives held meetings around the country, lobbied Members of Parliament, and tried with every means at their disposal to get the Corn Laws repealed. During the debate in the Commons on Peel's motion to abolish, Cobden made only one speech. He said that if the motion were not passed, the free traders would make thousands into property owners, and at the next election would overwhelm both parties.[49]

Among the Tory aristocracy, the greatest resistance to repeal came from the Duke of Wellington. "Damned rotten potatoes put Peel in his fright," he said, but at length agreed. A report printed in the *Manchester Examiner and Times*, 4 April 1865, stated that Wellington was put in *his* fright on being told that Peel would have otherwise advised Queen Victoria to call on Cobden to form a government.[50] But even with the leadership of Peel and the support of the Manchester school of businessmen, Mother Nature carried the day. In Morley's biography of Cobden we find that, "It was the wettest autumn [1845] in the memory of man, and the rain came over the hills in a downpour that never ceased by night or by day. It was the rain that rained away the Corn Laws."[51]

It is useful to assess Peel's substitution of an income tax not quite exceeding 3 percent on annual incomes over £150 for many elements in a customs schedule that imposed a tax averaging one-third the value of net imports. It is hard to conceive that a 3 percent direct income tax would severely erode individual incentives to work, save or invest. But a tariff schedule imposing a tax rate on trade ten times as high could well hold down the volume of trade and manufacturing based on imported raw materials. A change in the structure of taxation in the 1840s, as studied by numerous economic historians, seems to have boosted British trade and industry, while the very modest low-rate income tax showed little adverse impact on the performance of the economy. These scholars claim that taxation on imports had entered the prohibitive range of the tax rate schedule, whereas taxation on income was in the very safe range of the low end of the rate schedule, at least in the mid-nineteenth century.

Phase Four: Gladstone and the Culmination of Fiscal Reform

The final major reductions in nineteenth-century British taxation owe much to the leadership of William E. Gladstone, who so aptly explained the rationale and results of Peel's two major revisions of the tariff.[52] Gladstone ascended to the post of Chancellor of the Exchequer at the end of 1852 in a coalition government of Whigs and Peelites under Lord Aberdeen; and, on 18 April 1853, he delivered what some economic historians regard as the nineteenth century's most elegant and carefully-reasoned statement of fiscal principles.[53] His discourse covered general principles of sources and equity of taxation, the harmful effects of tariffs on commerce and its burden on the living costs of the working classes, the use of a temporary income tax to diminish the general burdens of indirect taxation, and the principles on which any income tax should be constructed. Simplicity in the overall tax system was a feature of Gladstonian public finance.

Gladstone remained determined to extend the bounds of commercial freedom. But how was he to liberalize trade while maintaining a balanced budget? Gladstone proposed to renew the income tax for seven years, at a rate of 7*d*. on the pound for the first two years, at 6*d*. for the next two years, and 5*d*. for the remaining three years (a rate of 3 percent in 1853 gradually falling to 2 percent). Thus he borrowed from Peel the temporary imposition of an income tax to reduce the remaining indirect taxes collected from the customs net. The income tax took effect at £100 at the lower rate of 5*d*. and assumed its full rate of 7*d*. at annual incomes of £150. He also extended the tax to Ireland but, in exchange, cancelled an Irish debt of £4.5 million incurred during the famine on borrowings from the British Treasury.

The income tax fell disproportionately on middle-class professionals; to insure equity of taxation, Gladstone abolished the immunity previously accorded taxation of landed property. Real, as well as personal, property was now liable to duty on succession (death). With this inclusion of landed property in the succession duties, Gladstone publicly demonstrated that Parliament was no longer controlled by the landowning class and that all forms of property would contribute to the national revenue.

With these new sources of revenue in hand, Gladstone announced the third major tariff revison. Protective, discriminatory, and *ad valorem* duties were largely abandoned. Numerous articles (123) were removed from the tariff, and duties on 133 others were lowered. On the domestic tax front, Gladstone entirely repealed the excise charge on soap (to encourage habits of cleanliness), and revised a series of "assessed taxes" on servants, carriages, horses, dogs, hairpowder, and armorial ensigns, along with other simplifications in the tax code. The total annual value of these remissions in indirect taxation was estimated at £5.4 million. But the income tax, which made this possible, was a temporary seven-year imposition. Gladstone hoped that the stimulus afforded trade by these tariff reductions would increase public revenue and that he could permanently abolish the income tax by 1860.

Outbreak of war in the Crimea upset Gladstone's 1853 budget calculations. He firmly believed that wartime costs should be borne from taxation, not borrowing. This policy had the salutory effect of bringing home to the nation the costs of foreign military adventures, thus being a suitable damper upon them. Despite his prior commitment, he doubled the personal income tax from 7*d.* to 1*s.* 2*d.* on the pound (from a rate of 3 to 6 percent) until the end of the war and increased the duties on malt, spirits, and sugar.[54]

Disaster in the Crimea forced Lord Aberdeen's resignation. With him, Gladstone left office on 21 February 1855.

The Budget of 1860

In the 1840s, Gladstone had labored for four years on fiscal reform in Peel's administration. The Crimean War throttled his own reforms, begun in the "great budget of 1853." But his return as Chancellor of the Exchequer in 1859 gave him seven successive budgets with which to fashion his final financial reforms. His aim was to make commerce and manufacturing freer, virtually unencumbered by taxation or regulation.

He had little time to prepare the first of his budgets which he brought forward in July 1859. Higher expenses stemming from the Chinese wars had created an estimated deficit of £5 million, which he proposed to cover by raising the income tax rates from 5*d.* to 9*d.* on the pound. This increase in the rates of direct taxation would also leave him with a small surplus of £1.5 million on which to fashion the final tariff reforms. For Gladstone, as for Peel, the income tax proved a convenient vehicle for maintaining balanced budgets and eliminating impediments to foreign trade and manufacturing through reductions in customs charges.

The financial statement of 1860 was intricately bound up with the 1860 commercial treaty with France, successfully negotiated with the Emperor Napoleon III by Richard Cobden.

Gladstone opened the 1860 budget on 10 February.[55] Military adventures in China had increased war expenditure estimates by £1 million and the customs revenue stood to lose £640,000 from the treaty Cobden had negotiated with France. If the income tax, tea duties, and sugar duties lapsed on schedule, Gladstone would confront a deficit of £9.4 million. Recall that Gladstone had stated in the 1853 budget his intention to dispense with the income tax by 1860. Where had he gone astray?

In reviewing national expenditures in the intervening seven years, Gladstone noted that the fault was not his own. Apart from increased war-related debt charges, ordinary national spending had risen by £14.7 million. This money represented an annual charge equivalent to an income tax of 13 *d.* on the pound (or a rate of 5.5 percent). In the prior decade, 1843 to 1853, national and local expenditures grew annually by only 5.5 percent; by contrast, since 1853, the annual rate of growth of public spending stood at 22.5 percent. Debt-servicing payments aside, optional expenditures under Parliamentary control rose 58 percent between 1853 and 1860, compared with 9 percent in the decade preceding 1853. The excessive growth in public spending during his years in opposition now made it impossible to abandon the income tax as he had promised in 1853.

Still, Gladstone pressed forward with a final round of tariff reductions. As background to his new reforms, he examined the consequences of Peel's modifications. From 1832 to 1841, the revenue yield from customs and excise duties had grown £170,000 a year, while the export trade grew by £1.5 million a year. Then, from 1842 to 1853 (on Peel's two major tariff reductions), £12.2 million of taxation was remitted (an annual average of just over £1 million). But the aggregate return from customs and excise duties actually rose by more than £2.5 million (or £221,000 on an annual basis). Gladstone interpreted these numbers to imply that the customs and excise revenue grew more rapidly as a consequence of major tax remissions than they did when no remissions had been granted. Even more important, from 1832 to 1841, foreign trade grew by an annual rate of £1.5 million. Between 1842 and 1853, it expanded to the significantly larger annual rate of £4.3 million (see Figure 3.1).

Gladstone turned next to the new commercial treaty with France which would significantly reduce trade barriers in raw materials and manufactured goods between the two nations. But the immediate first year expected loss to the customs was £1.7 million under the headings of duties repealed on silk goods, gloves, artificial flowers, watches, oils, leather, China, glass woolens, and other miscellaneous articles. Duties on wine and brandy were cut by nearly half.

Apart from the tariff reductions embodied in the Cobden-Chevalier treaty of 1860, Gladstone also proposed a supplemental set of reductions, estimated to cost the public revenue £910,000 in receipts in the first year of implementation. These included abolition of the duties on butter, tallow, cheese, citrus products, eggs, nuts, nutmeg, paper, and other articles. Substantial reductions were proposed for timber, currants, raisins, figs, and hops, but Gladstone projected that increased consumption of these items would offset revenue losses. Finally, he proposed to abolish the excise duty on paper.

To safeguard the doctrine of balanced budgets, Gladstone raised the income tax rate from 9*d.* to 10*d.* on the pound, even as he harbored the wish to abolish the tax outright at the earliest possible moment.

Peel's initial reforms from 1842 to 1846 were fulfilled in Gladstone's 1860 budget. Numerous articles (1,052) were subject to customs duties on 1 January 1840. This number shrank to 466 with the 1853 reform, with further decline to 419 by 1 January 1859. After Parliament adopted the 1860 budget, only forty-eight items remained on the tariff.

This number itself overstated the true extent of the tariff wall. Of the 48 articles, only 15 were retained for the express purpose of raising revenue. None protected British producers. These 15 fell into 3 classes:

1. Five articles yielding from £1 million to £6 million a year—sugar, spirits, tobacco, tea, and wine.
2. Four articles yielding from £200,000 to £1 million a year—coffee, grain, currants, and timber.
3. Six articles yielding from £20,000 to £200,000 a year— chicory, figs and fig-cakes, hops, pepper, raisins, and rice.

Besides these fifteen items, twenty-nine other articles were retained on special grounds. Five were kept because of coutervailing duties on domestic articles, and twenty-four because of their resemblance to one of the other fifteen leading revenue duties. All protective and differentiated duties disappeared in the 1860 budget.

In some areas, the impact of these tax cuts was immediate. The export trade of 1860 was the largest on record, having risen in value to £136 million from the 1859 figure of £130 million. Although timber imports rose only modestly, imports of butter, cheese, eggs, and rice rose from £4.7 million to £7.4 million in the first full year following implementation of the tax cuts.

For those items untouched in the 1860 reforms, the import value fell slightly, from £138 million to £137 million. Those on which duty rates had been reduced rose from £11.3 million to £13.3 million, an increase of 17.5 percent. Those on which duties had been completely repealed skyrocketed 40 percent in one year, from £15.7 million to £22.0 million. Gladstone estimated that the French treaty alone added £9 million in value to the nation's trade.

The statistical abstract shows that British imports and exports in 1859 were valued at £179 million and £155 million, respectively. Ten years later they stood at £295 million and £237 million, which represents a per capita increase in one decade of from £11 14s. 2d. to £17 4s. 6d.

The 1860 budget brought complete victory to the free traders. Even though Adam Smith made the case eighty-four years earlier, and William Huskisson had marked out sharp new directions in commercial policy thirty-seven years earlier, and Peel had repealed the Corn Law fourteen years earlier, entrenched opposition still rose to fight each new round of reform. As late as 1859, for example, there were still twenty-one duties in the tariff for leather and forty-two duties for silks. Special interests resisted complete repeal of all these protective duties until the end. As Buxton writes, "Those who desired the maintenance of the existing state of things were all thorough free traders in every article, except the particular one in which they were personally interested, and which invariably seemed to deserve special treatment."[56] On the eighty-fourth anniversary of *The Wealth of Nations*, free trade triumphed.

Predictions of contemporary free traders were justified by the surge in British exports on signing of the Cobden-Chevalier Treaty. Before the treaty, total trade between the two countries was under £20 million a year. Trade increased to £43.5 million in 1862 and £63.5 million in 1866. Thereafter trade fluctuated with general business conditions and the Franco-Prussian War of 1873, but rose again until the treaty lapsed in 1880.[57]

The Budgets of 1861 to 1866

Gladstone used the income tax in 1853 and 1860 (as Peel did in 1842) to complete the tariff reforms that emancipated international trade from the import and export duties. The robust expansion in trade that followed these tax remissions justified Gladstone's faith in the free trade policy.

Gladstone remained troubled by the potential misuse of the income tax and was determined to take whatever steps necessary to reduce the rates and ultimately abolish it. He had been greatly troubled by the increase in public spending that occurred between 1853 and 1860. He worried that much of this growth derived from the availability of easily-generated income tax revenue and the propensity of an electorate-oriented House of Commons to spend it. To curtail this propensity, he planned to reduce and ultimately abolish the income tax. Along with substantial reductions in the duties on cheese, tobacco, sugar, and stamps, and complete repeal on hops, Gladstone systematically cut the income tax from a rate of 4 percent to 1.7 percent by 1866.

Fiscal Year	Change in Income Tax Rate
1861-62	Reduced from 10*d*. to 9*d*.
1862-63	No change
1863-64	Reduced from 9*d*. to 7*d*.
1864-65	Reduced from 7*d*. to 6*d*.
1865-66	Reduced from 6*d*. to 4*d*.

It is important to restate Gladstone's objections to the income tax. He never claimed that a tax rate of 4 percent would discourage productive economic activity. Rather, his chief concern was that the revenue such a tax could "painlessly" generate would encourage rising public expenditure and reduce efficiency in government. He could not have possibly contemplated the high rates of 50 percent that prevail in most Western countries today.

Despite significant cuts in direct and indirect taxes in 1861 and 1862, overall revenue increased; and, Gladstone opened his 1863 budget with a prospective surplus that he applied to further cuts in the income tax (as we have seen) and the tea duty. Revenue remained high despite military expenditures in Asia, the American Civil War and the blockade of cotton that severely damaged Lancashire, and the export trade to America. During this period Britain also suffered three consecutive bad farm seasons. Still, the economy grew so rapidly that a surplus of £3.7 million permitted additional tax reductions in 1864.

Surpluses accrued at the start of each of the next several budgets and Gladstone availed himself of the opportunity to lower the income tax and other select duties. By 1865 the tea duty was cut to 6d. per pound (it had stood at 1s. 5d.—triple the new rate—just three years earlier in 1862), and the income tax was lowered to only 4d. on the pound. The value of these two tax cuts alone was put at £4.9 million; yet the total national revenue still rose by £1 million. A growing economy continued to generate rising tax receipts from all sources despite systematic reductions in the rates on several main sources of income and indirect taxes.

Gladstone's last year as Chancellor of the Exchequer, 1866, began with a £2 million surplus which he applied to abolish the timber duties, repeal the duty on pepper, and reduce the national debt. His remarks on the nation's experience with timber duties, presented in Parliament in May 1866, merit reproduction as a vivid illustration of the disincentive effects of high taxes.

> The consumption of timber in this country is remarkable. In 1811 the consumption of timber amounted to 417,000 loads [a load is 50 cubic feet]. At that time the duties were augmented, and in 1814 the consumption fell so low as 218,000 loads. However, the growing wealth of the country brought about a gradual increase; and I will pass over the long period of years to 1841, from which time the House will observe that every reduction of duty has been answered by more than a corresponding increase in the use of this essential material. In 1841 the total consumption was 829,000 loads. In 1842 the duty on foreign timber was reduced from 56s. 6d. to 31s. 6d; and on Colonial timber from 11s. 6d. to 1s. The reduction only took effect in October 1842. In 1843 the consumption was 1,298,000 loads. In 1850 the consumption was 1,723,000 loads. In that year the duty on foreign timber was further reduced from 15s. to 7s. 6d., and on deals from 20s. to 10s. [A deal is a board of fir or pine.] The consequence was that, from a consumption of 1,723,000 loads in 1850, the consumption rose until, in 1859, it reached 2,408,000 loads. In 1860 we went to work again, and further reduced the duty from 10s. to 2s., and from 7s. 6d. to 1s. At that time a highly respectable gentleman from the Colonies, who represented Launceston (Mr. Haliburton), predicted that ruin would sweep

down upon the timber industry of New Brunswick; but the consumption of all kinds, which in 1859 was 2,408,000 loads, actually had increased in 1865 to 3,700,000 loads, or to sixteen times the consumption of 1814.[58]

From 1866, when Gladstone completely abolished all timber duties, to 1874, timber imports rose more than 60 percent, further vindicating Gladstone's conviction that taxes, protectionist or otherwise, impeded rapid growth of the private economy.

Just two months after his exposition on the timber duties, Gladstone resigned his position at the Exchequer with the defeat of the Russell government in which he served.

Gladstone as Prime Minister

From 1868 to 1874 Gladstone took the final step up in his political career and served Queen Victoria, much to her distaste, as Prime Minister and, again, in a second administration from 1880 to 1885.[59] Near the end of his first administration he even became his own Chancellor of the Exchequer and devised a scheme to abolish the income tax. But the defeat of his Liberal Party and the installation of a Conservative government between 1874 and 1880 were accompanied by a rise both in national expenditure and the income tax rates.

Robert Lowe, Gladstone's Chancellor of the Exchequer from 1868 through 1872, maintained the Gladstonian tradition of reducing taxes and public spending on a regular, systematic basis. He managed, in his first budget, to repeal the residual 1s. registration fee on grain imports (worth £900,000) and the tax on insured property. He also abolished the old "assessed tax" system, which included such antiquated taxes as that on hairpowder, armorial bearings, menservants, and horses. He lowered the income tax from 6d. to 5d. The increased rate had been set by Disraeli to pay for the military expedition into Abyssinia to rescue British prisoners.

In his second year, 1870, Lowe further reduced the income tax and repealed half the duties on sugar; and, despite the Franco-Prussian War of 1870, the British economy flourished and revenues still increased. But military and social expenditures grew even more rapidly, and the tax-cutting episode came to an end: he increased the income tax by 2d. in 1871.[60]

A return to a budgetary surplus in 1872 saw a reduction in income tax rates to 4d. and an increase in the exemption from £60 to £80, with the full charge taking effect only on incomes exceeding £300. In the next two years, the income tax was cut in steps to 3d. and 2d., the taxes on hops were repealed, and the sugar duty finally abolished.

Thus in his first administration, Gladstone's ministers reduced taxes where possible, but gradually rising public expenditures put complete abolition of the income tax at risk. Tax rates on income rose and fell with the need to maintain growing military and civilian expenditures.

In 1874 Gladstone campaigned to abolish the income tax altogether. With his defeat, and Disraeli's accession to power in a six-year Conservative government, Gladstone's third and final attempt to end the "temporary" income tax of 1842 failed.[61] Gladstone and Peel had invoked Pitt's wartime income tax for the purpose of commercial reform, using its yields to offset remissions in indirect taxation since 1842. With the completion of commercial reform, Gladstone feared increasingly that the income tax would only encourage unnecessary government spending.

Sydney Buxton, Gladstone's financial biographer, notes the irony in the financial wizard's fate. In 1858, out of office, the statesman vehemently opposed the maintenance of the tax at 7*d*. in support of Disraeli's proposed budget. But on returning to office in 1859, Gladstone himself pushed the rate to 9*d*. just to meet an ordinary deficit—the highest point the tax ever attained in peacetime.[62]

Since 1859 one government after another found the income tax a convenient vehicle for making up deficiencies on ordinary annual expenditures. It was commonplace for a government to adjust the income tax rate annually up or down a pence or two. In prior years, changes in taxation had been simultaneously made in direct and indirect levies, either to raise new revenue or remit excess receipts. From 1867 resort alone was made to the income tax. Despite his personal desire to abolish the income tax, Gladstone was a culprit "by accustoming the country to the use of the tax as an ordinary annual makeweight,"[63] thus making it a perpetual feature of the tax code.

Gladstone had refused to graduate the income tax according to the size of income since this constituted a penalty for hard work and enterprise. While he managed rate reductions during most of his years at the Exchequer or as Prime Minister, he had recourse to rate increases too often to stay beyond reproach. It is worthwhile to examine the Parliamentary record to appreciate the intensity of feeling surrounding just a one penny change in the tax (a rate of 0.4 percent). 12 April 1869 was given over to acrimonious, heated debate on just such a modest change.[64] By 1874, when Gladstone proposed abolition of the tax, each penny was generating more than £1.5 million; two years later, one penny yielded £1.8 million. As Table 3.2 shows, total receipts from the income tax quadrupled in the ten years between 1875 and 1885, confirming Gladstone's fears.

The Conservative government of 1874 to 1880 was a mixture of fiscal modifications. Increases in military and civilian expenditures and a commitment to maintain repayment of the national debt necessitated several tax

Table 3.2
Income Tax in Great Britain, 1799-1888

Total Receipts	Year	Rates (*d*. per £)
(£ million)		
6.0*	1799-1801	24*d*. on incomes above £60; between £60 and £200 there was a sliding scale of abatement
	1802	Repealed
5.3	1803	Reimposed at 12*d*. on incomes above £60; between £60 and £150 there was a sliding scale of abatement
4.1	1804	Same as 1803
6.4	1805	Raised to 15*d*.
12.8	1806	Raised to 24*d*., and levied on all incomes above £50, with abatement on certain incomes between £50 and £150
15.6 (in 1815)	1807-15	Same as 1806
	1816	Repealed
5.5*	1842-44	For three years at 7*d*. on incomes above £150
5.8*	1845-47	For three years at 7*d*. on incomes above £150
5.8*	1848-50	For three years at 7*d*. on incomes above £150
5.9	1851	For one year at 7*d*. on incomes above £150
5.9	1852	For one year at 7*d*. on incomes above £150
7.2	1853	Reimposed for seven years at 7*d*. above £150; at 5*d*. between £100 and £150; and extended to Ireland
14.4	1854	Raised to 14*d*. above and to 10*d*. below £150
16.6	1855	Raised to 16*d*. above and to 11½*d*. below £150
16.9	1856	Until a year after the end of the war
7.9	1857	Reduced to 7*d*. above incomes of £150 and 5*d*. between £100 and £150

Since 1857 the tax has been an annual tax.

5.8	1858	5*d*. for all
10.4	1859	Raised temporarily for one year at 9*d*. and 6½*d*.
11.6	1860	Raised to 10*d*. and 7*d*.
11.0	1861	Reduced to 9*d*. and 6*d*.
11.3	1862	9*d*. and 6*d*.

Table 3.2 (Continued)
Income Tax in Great Britain, 1799-1888

Total Receipts	Year	Rates (*d.* per £)

On all incomes above £100, with an abatement of £60 under £200.

9.0	1863	7*d.*
8.3	1864	6*d.*
5.8	1865	4*d.*
5.9	1866	4*d.*
7.6	1867	5*d.*
9.2	1868	6*d.*
7.9	1869	5*d.*
6.7	1870	4*d.*
10.4	1871	6*d.*

On all incomes above £100, with abatement of £80 up to £300.

7.2	1872	4*d.*
5.8	1873	3*d.*
4.0	1874	2*d.*
4.0	1875	2*d.*
5.9	1876	3*d.*

On incomes of £150 a year and upwards, with abatement of £120 on incomes below £400.

5.9	1877	3*d.*
9.8	1878	5*d.*
9.8	1879	5*d.*
11.8	1880	6*d.*
10.2	1881	5*d.*
13.5	1882	6½*d.*
10.7	1883	5*d.*
12.7	1884	6*d.*
16.7	1885	8*d.*
—	1886	8*d.*
—	1887	7*d.*
—	1888	6*d.*

Source: Sydney Buxton, *Finance and Politics: An Historical Study*, vol. 2 (London: John Murray, 1888), pp. 378-79.
*Average.

increases. On net, the Conservative administration accumulated deficits of £6 million and imposed over £5 million in additional taxation; by contrast, Gladstone's previous five years achieved surpluses totalling £17 million despite tax cuts of £12 million.[65]

Gladstone's second administration, 1880 to 1885, encountered trouble in Ireland, and wars in South Africa, Egypt, and the Sudan, all of which placed the revenue system under pressure. Public spending had increased from £81 million in 1881 to £89 million by 1885. His second period ended with the rate at 8d. Besides increasing the income tax, he imposed additional duties on beer and spirits, also reversals of his previous policies.

Summary

Huskisson, Peel, and Gladstone dismantled tax barriers to trade, commerce, and manufacturing. They succeeded beyond Adam Smith's visions of commercial freedom. Except for the very low income tax, the British revenue system in the late nineteenth century also showed Smith's visible influence. The following statistics demonstrate how fifty years of tax reform stimulated economic expansion and simultaneously lowered individual tax burdens.

	1825	*1850*	*1870*
Imports (value)	£37,500,000	£105,750,000	£303,250,000
Exports (value)	£59,000,000	£190,000,000	£244,000,000
Shipping (tons)	5,500,000	14,500,000	36,500,000
Population	22,000,000	27,000,000	31,000,000
Per capita taxation	£2 9s. 3d.	£1 19s. 3d.	£1 18s. 5.5d.
Yield of 1d. of income tax	—	£867,000	£1,500,000

As the economy grew, broadening the tax base meant that each 1d. in the income tax generated higher and higher revenues. Thus, throughout the nineteenth century total revenues grew even as the per capita overall rates of taxation fell: the decrease between 1825 and 1870 amounted to a 22 percent reduction in each Briton's average tax burden.

Postscript: The Income Tax in the Twentieth Century

One pound contains 20 shillings. One shilling, in turn, has 12 pence. Thus every 1d. increase in the tax rate is equivalent to a rise of 0.4 percent. Every

1*s*. increase is 5 percent. A standard rate of, say, 2*s*. on the pound is a tax rate of 10 percent.

Throughout the nineteenth century, the income tax rate only once reached a level of 10 percent, at the height of the Napoleonic War. Thereafter, from its restoration in 1842, the rate ranged from a low of almost 1 percent to a high of 6.7 percent (1855).

Pitt originally imposed the income tax to help finance the French Wars. Peel reimposed it to finance tariff reform. Thereafter, Chancellors of the Exchequer raised or lowered the rates a pence or two to balance the budget. But the rates moved both ways: they were reduced about as often as they were raised.

By 1890 circumstances changed. Rising expenditures on social programs propelled the rate upward. Too, the principle of graduation came into play. World War I pushed the standard rate up sharply, beyond 5*s*. (over 25 percent). However, with peace, the government did not cut the rates to the prewar 1*s*. level. Instead, it maintained a 4*s*. rate. In the course of the Great Depression and World War II, it further upped the standard rate to 10*s*. (50 percent). British income tax rates have remained at those levels or higher in the post-World War II era (see Figure 3.2).

All of which brings us back to William E. Gladstone. He used the income tax, at a low rate, to overhaul the customs, which stood at a high rate. In retrospect, he perhaps maintained this "temporary" imposition too long, for in the end he could not abolish it. His fears that the income tax would lead to more public spending did not materialize until World War I, and Gladstone himself advocated tax increases instead of borrowing as an appropriate means of war finance. But the failure of the postwar 1918 government to cut tax rates crystallized his nightmare.

At the time, it seemed to make economic and fiscal sense to substitute a low income tax for a high duty. How Gladstone would relive that period with the benefit of twentieth-century hindsight is an interesting question!

Notes

1. An import/export duty is both a fiscal and commercial device. I have chosen to discuss tariff reform in the context of this chapter on tax reduction rather than in the next chapter on the reduction of government regulation.
2. Stephen Dowell, *A History of Taxation and Taxes in England*, Vol. II (London: Longmans, Green, 1888), p. 184; and C.R. Fay, *Great Britain from Adam Smith to the Present Day: An Economic and Social Survey* (New York: Longmans, Green, 1928), p. 35.
3. Francis W. Hirst, *From Adam Smith to Philip Snowden: A History of Free Trade in Great Britain* (New York: Adelphi, 1925), p. 7.
4. Sydney Buxton, *Finance and Politics: An Historical Study. 1783-1885*, vol. 1 (London: John Murray, 1888), p. 3.

Figure 3.2
Summary of Income Tax Changes
1793–1960

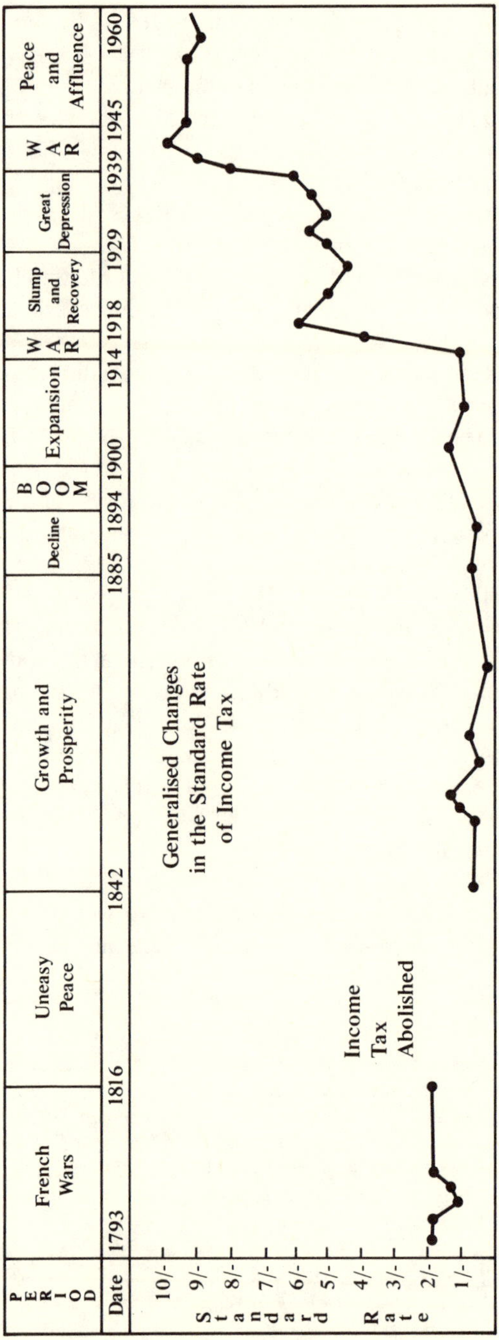
PERIOD
French Wars
Uneasy Peace
Growth and Prosperity
Decline
BOOM
Expansion
WAR
Slump and Recovery
Great Depression
WAR
Peace and Affluence
Date
1793
1816
1842
1885
1894
1900
1914
1918
1929
1939
1945
1960
Standard Rate
10/-
9/-
8/-
7/-
6/-
5/-
4/-
3/-
2/-
1/-
Income Tax Abolished
Generalised Changes in the Standard Rate of Income Tax

Source: James Clifford, *Aspects of Economic Development 1760–1960* (London: Longman, Green, 1967). p. 200

5. Francis W. Hirst, *From Adam Smith*, p. 10.
6. Asa Briggs, *The Age of Improvement 1783-1867* (New York: David McKay, 1962), p. 169; and Stephen Dowell, *A History*, p. 263.
7. Asa Briggs, *The Age*, p. 187.
8. Sydney Buxton, *Finance and Politics*, vol. 1, p. 12.
9. Phyllis Deane and W.A. Cole, *British Economic Growth 1688-1959*, 2nd ed. (Cambridge: Cambridge University Press, 1969), p. 323; Albert H. Imlah, *Economic Elements in the Pax Brittanica* (Cambridge: Harvard University Press, 1958), p. 14; and, Arthur Redford, *The Economic History of England 1760-1860* (Westport, Conn.: Greenwood, 1960), p. 185.
10. J.D. Chambers, *The Workshop of the World: British Economic History from 1820 to 1880* (London: Oxford University Press, 1961), p. 91.
11. Alexander Brady, *William Huskisson and Liberal Reform: An Essay on the Changes in Economic Policy in the Twenties of the Nineteenth Century* (London: Oxford University Press, 1928), p. 83.
12. Ibid., p. 86. For the text and an interpretation of the merchants' petition see Augustus Mongredien, *History of the Free-Trade Movement in England* (New York: Putnam's, 1881), pp. 39-44.
13. Alexander Brady, *William Huskisson*, pp. 87-88; and William Smart, *Economic Annals of the Nineteenth Century 1821-1830* (London: Macmillan, 1917), p. 33.
14. Stephen Dowell, *A History*, p. 273.
15. A marvelous history of the silk industry is found in D.C. Coleman, *Courtaulds: An Economic and Social History, vol. 1, The Nineteenth Century, Silk and Crape* (Oxford: Clarendon, 1969). See also Alexander Brady, *William Huskisson*, pp. 99-106; and William Smart, *Economic Annals*, pp. 197-98.
16. Statistics encompassing the period 1765-1825 appear in Alexander Brady, *William Huskisson*, p. 114.
17. Cited in ibid., pp. 103-4.
18. Cited in ibid., p. 105.
19. J. McCulloch, *Account of the British Empire*, vol. 1 (1839), pp. 682-90, cited in Phyllis Deane and W.A. Cole, *British Economic Growth*, p. 209.
20. Phyllis Deane and W.A. Cole, *British Economic Growth*, p. 210.
21. D.C. Coleman, *Courtaulds*, pp. 67-69.
22. William Smart, *Economic Annals*, p. 195.
23. Ibid., p. 219.
24. Ibid., pp. 264-68; and Alexander Brady, *William Huskisson*, p. 106.
25. William Smart, *Economic Annals*, pp. 358-59.
26. Alexander Brady, *William Huskisson*, p. 121.
27. Sydney Buxton, *Finance and Politics*, vol. 1, p. 17.
28. William Smart, *Economic Annals*, p. 359.
29. Ibid., p. 552.
30. John Noble, *National Finance: A Review of the Policy of the Last Two Parliaments, and of the Results of Modern Fiscal Legislation* (London: Longmans, Green, 1875), pp. 58-59.
31. Stephen Dowell, *A History*, pp. 288-315.
32. Sydney Buxton, *Finance and Politics*, vol. 1, pp. 53-54, and J.D. Chambers, *The Workshop*, p. 102.
33. S.G. Checkland, *The Rise of Industrial Society in England 1815-1885* (New York: St. Martin's, 1964), p. 20.

34. Francis W. Hirst, *Gladstone as Financier and Economist* (London: Ernest Benn, 1931), pp. 50-52.
35. S.G. Checkland, *The Rise*, p. 19.
36. Sydney Buxton, *Finance and Politics*, vol. 1, pp. 47-51.
37. Albert Imlah, *Economic Elements*, p. 150.
38. S.G. Checkland, *The Rise*, p. 22.
39. C.R. Fay, *Great Britain From*, pp. 64-65.
40. Gladstone's article was published anonymously early in 1843 in a new journal entitled *Foreign and Colonial Quarterly*, cited in Francis W. Hirst, *Gladstone*, pp. 58-72.
41. Francis W. Hirst, *Gladstone*, p. 73.
42. Ibid., pp. 73-75; and Stephen Dowell, *A History*, pp. 8-79.
43. Gladstone's essay was entitled "Remarks Upon Recent Commercial Legislation, suggested by the Expository Statement of the Revenue, from Customs, and other Papers, lately submitted to Parliament by the Right Hon. W.E. Gladstone, M.P. for Newark," London: John Murray, 1845, cited in Francis W. Hirst, *Gladstone*, pp. 76-81.
44. Arthur Redford, *The Economic History*, p. 198.
45. W. Cunningham, *The Growth of English Industry and Commerce in Modern Times*, 3rd ed., *Laissez-Faire* (Cambridge: Cambridge University Press, 1903), p. 837.
46. Stephen Dowell, *A History*, pp. 329-30; Francis W. Hirst, *Gladstone as*, p. 112; and C.R. Fay, *The Corn Laws and Social England* (Cambridge: Cambridge University Press, 1932), pp. 88-108.
47. C.R. Fay, *Great Britain*, pp. 67-68.
48. William D. Grampp, *The Manchester School of Economics* (Stanford: Stanford University Press, 1960), *passim*.
49. Ibid., p. 45.
50. Ibid., p. 93.
51. The citation of Morley's *Life of Cobden*, vol. 1, p. 334, is found in W. Cunningham, *The Rise and Decline of the Free Trade Movement*, 2nd ed. (Cambridge: Cambridge University Press, 1905), p. 62.
52. For a comprehensive exposition of Gladstone's financial principles and practices see Francis W. Hirst, *Gladstone, passim*.
53. Ibid., pp. 138-54. For the full text of the 1853 budget see Arthur Tilney Bassett, *Gladstone's Speeches, Descriptive Index and Bibliography* (London: Methuen, 1916), pp. 182-252.
54. Francis W. Hirst, *Gladstone*, pp. 159-61.
55. Ibid., pp. 176-99. For the full text of the 1860 budget see Arthur Tilney Bassett, *Gladstone's Speeches*, pp. 253-311.
56. Sydney Buxton, *Finance and Politics*, vol. 1, p. 204.
57. Ibid., p. 236; and R.A. Church, *The Great Victorian Boom 1850-1873* (London: Macmillan, 1975), p. 62.
58. Francis W. Hirst, *Gladstone*, pp. 239-40.
59. Stephen Dowell, *A History*, pp. 389-427.
60. To his later discomfiture, Lowe proposed a tax on matches in 1871 to help close the revenue gap on the ground that it would also prevent fires and improve the quality of matches. Of this John Noble says, "If that were so, it would accomplish what no such tax has ever yet done; in every other known instance, taxation has deteriorated the article taxed." *National Finance*, p. 108.

61. Sydney Buxton, *Finance and Politics*, vol. 2, pp. 165, 169.
62. Ibid., vol. 1, p. 187.
63. Ibid., vol. 1, p. 194.
64. John Noble, *National Finance*, p. 76.
65. Francis W. Hirst, *Gladstone*, p. 263.

4

The Flowering of Economic Freedom

Early nineteenth-century Britain was a heavily taxed, highly regulated nation. A contemporary of 1800 would observe a net of labor and industrial regulations, wage and price controls, commercial monopolies held by royally-chartered trading companies, a complex set of shipping regulations in the Navigation Acts, and rules that bound the colonies to Britain in trade, shipping, manufacturing, taxation, and administration. Some of these regulations became obsolete in the late eighteenth century and were repealed before the conclusion of the Napoleonic War. For example, the 1563 Statute of Artificers and Apprentices was largely repealed in 1813 and 1814. Industrial regulations became increasingly inapplicable or weakly enforced. The privileges of chartered trading monopolies were under growing challenge. An Act of Parliament in 1815 ended the domestic price control on an assize of bread, on the petition of 800 master bakers.[1] And American independence forced rethinking of both the Navigation Laws and colonial regulations.

But governments rarely overhaul regulations overnight. Huskisson's reform of the tariff, drastic in his day, paled against the wholesale reforms of Peel and Gladstone. Despite the merits of the free-traders' arguments in 1820, full free trade materialized only in the 1860s. Change was slow in other dimensions of economic policy too. Internal laissez-faire did not fully blossom until midway in the nineteenth century. And, when laissez-faire did describe the British economy, Parliament enacted a spate of social and economic regulations that went in the opposite direction. As the nineteenth century wound to a close, Britain was the foremost example in the world of a free-market economy. Nonetheless, late nineteenth-century measures prescribing social regulations foreshadowed a return to the heavily taxed, regulated eighteenth-century economy of mercantilism.

Huskisson and Liberal Reform in the 1820s

William Huskisson's fiscal and economic reforms between 1823 and 1825 make him the giant of his day. Yet he owes much to his two predecessors,

Frederick John Robinson and Thomas Wallace, President and Vice-President of the Board of Trade, who introduced sweeping reforms in the commercial and navigation regulations in 1822. The new measures repealed 300 obsolete statutes and clauses.[2] The Wallace-Robinson code also authorized foreign ships to bring goods from any European port, abolished the ban on Dutch shipping, allowed goods of Asian, African, or American origin to be brought from Europe (instead of directly from those areas) if scheduled for reexport, and permitted ships of newly independent South American countries to transport indigenous goods to Britain. British colonies in America were also accorded greater freedom of trade with the United States, South America, and Europe.

In April 1823, Robinson became Chancellor of the Exchequer, and Huskisson was appointed President of the Board of Trade.[3] Wallace was not shifted to the presidency; instead, he became Master of the Mint. Indeed, some of Huskisson's initial measures followed the plans laid out in the report issued by the Parliamentary Committee on Free Trade that he had chaired in 1820.[4]

Huskisson moved with haste. A first measure was a warehousing bill, which gave foreigners the right to import and warehouse goods in Britain, free of duty, if reexported.[5] With this stroke of the pen, Britain was now eligible to be an entrepôt for world trade.

Huskisson quickly followed with the reciprocity duties bill. Under the Navigation Acts, cargoes carried in foreign vessels bore higher rates of duty than those brought in British vessels. Similarly, the government allowed smaller drawbacks (refunds of import duties) on goods exported in foreign, rather than British, vessels. The retaliation of the United States against British vessels, to the detriment of overall British-American trade, induced Britain to equalize the duties and drawbacks for both American and British bottoms. Huskisson extended the principle of equalized duties and drawbacks to cargoes carried in ships of any nation that afforded reciprocal terms to Britain. Within a few years agreements were reached with Portugal, Holland, Prussia, Denmark, and most of Britain's other trading partners.

Huskisson capped his first year in office with two additional reforms.[6] His Scotch linen manufacture bill deregulated the manufacture of linen which had been governed by forty sections that prescribed precise details of length, width, and shape of manufactured linen cloth. The second was the already mentioned repeal of the Spitalfields Acts.

In 1824, Huskisson's second year at the Board of Trade, he proposed that Parliament remove or relax legislative restraints on the free movement of goods and people.[7] Parliament did, authorizing the free export of gold, lifting the ban on the emigration of skilled craftsmen to practice or teach their trade abroad, and permitting the export of machinery. It also repealed the Combination Laws of 1799 and 1800 that had disallowed lawful trade union activity. Labor disturbances led Parliament to modify its repeal of the Combination Laws in 1825 by limiting unions to peaceful bargaining, with severe penalties for violence or intimidation by strikes.[8]

A renewed attack on the Navigation Acts in 1825 tended to treat the colonies as economic supplements to Britain. In Huskisson's view, the American Revolution was partly a reaction against British restrictions on colonial trade. And, it was increasingly questionable if Britain could effectively monopolize the trade of her colonies, even if she wanted to. The newly independent South American countries sought trade with Europe and North America and would capture this trade if the colonies and Britain were shut off from this new outgrowth of commercial intercourse.

The Wallace-Robinson code reformed the Navigation Laws to allow trade between the colonies and other nations in the western hemisphere. Huskisson now proposed to open the colonial trade to all states that reciprocated. Trade within the empire was still the preserve of British and colonial shipping, but trade between the colonies and foreign countries was free, except for the restriction that cargoes be carried only in vessels of the reciprocating countries.

Other measures he suggested included removing prohibitions on goods entering colonial ports, though preferential duties remained for British goods, authorizing installation of the warehouse system of duty-free imports for subsequent reexport to colonial ports in the western hemisphere to foster entrepôt trade, and granting special import terms to Canadian grain shippers. He also persuaded Parliament to repeal quarantine duties, abolish shipping fees in the colonies, and repeal the stamp duty on transfer of shares in ship ownership. Paying British consular officials in foreign ports a government salary, instead of imposing costs directly on British ships, undermined the powerful position of the Levant Company, which had enjoyed a monopoly over British trade in the eastern Mediterranean. The company voluntarily surrendered its charter in 1821.[9]

Consolidation occurred in 1826. Overaggressive bank lending for purchase of goods by British merchants and speculation in joint-stock companies brought a financial crisis which produced vocal opposition and criticism of Huskisson's tariff and trade reforms. His critics alleged that interference with the navigation codes and protectionist tariff system directly caused the commercial crisis of 1826.

Huskisson never was a thorough-going freemarketeer. His reforms reflected the visions of an imperialist. "In the navigation laws he reserved inter-imperial trade; in his tariff revisions he created, or maintained, imperial preference over a wide range of commodities; and in the corn laws he not only secured and maintained the colonial preference in the corn-law schedules, but also secured an important modification for Canada in 1825."[10]

How did Huskisson's partial dismantling of the Navigation Laws affect British shipping? G.R. Porter, director of the statistical department of the Board of Trade, answered this question before a select committee of Parliament in 1847.[11] In 1824, he noted, 893,987 tons of goods from British possessions entered Britain's ports under the protection of the Navigation Laws, which meant a monopoly for British shipping. By 1846, this figure had risen 95 percent to 1.7 million tons. However, on the unprotected routes, the percentage increase in British shipping was even greater. In 1824, British vessels imported into Britain 904,223 tons of merchandise from noncolonial sources; by 1846, that figure rose 183 percent to 2.6 million tons. British shipping grew twice as fast on the unprotected routes as on the protected interimperial trade channels. Even the volume of goods carried by British ships to the United States grew by leaps and bounds, from an amount in 1821 which equalled 7 percent of the total volume of goods carried by American vessels in the foreign trade of the United States, rising to 39 percent in 1839, and reaching 56 percent by 1849.[12]

It is appropriate to bring the story of full repeal of the Navigation Acts to a conclusion here. In 1836 Parliament abolished the Tonnage Acts and in 1849 the remaining elements of the now greatly weakened Navigation Laws. British shippers now emulated American designs, and competition weeded out the less efficient managers. The discovery of gold in Australia (1848) simultaneously opened up a new, profitable long run. Still, by 1860, the American merchant fleet had all but achieved parity with that of Britain.

Steam came to the rescue. With its developed iron, coal, and engineering industries, Britain had a comparative cost advantage— British ships could carry more, faster and cheaper. Transatlantic trade became a British monopoly, while American shippers were confined to coastal waters. Between 1852 and 1864, British tonnage rose 50 percent. By the 1870s, iron ships comprised five-sixths of the fleet. By 1890 Great Britain, with nearly half of the world's tonnage, had twice as much as America, eight times as much as Germany and ten times as much as France.[13] Success had been achieved, in Checkland's words, "under competitive stimulus."[14]

The End of Monopoly Privilege

Prior to the nineteenth century, a number of firms were incorporated by Royal Charter and enjoyed a monopoly in the right to function as a joint-stock enterprise. This privilege accorded legal recognition, limited liability, and transferable stock. The majority of these enterprises consisted of the chartered commercial trading companies, the Bank of England, and two insurance companies—the Royal Exchange Assurance and the London Assurance.[15]

After 1800, in keeping with the free-trade movement, exclusive privileges were gradually withdrawn. The East India Company lost its monopoly in 1813. The Levant Company, with its monopoly of trade with Egypt and most of the Middle East, became moribund and gave up its charter in 1821. In 1822 Parliament refused to renew the monopoly of the original London Dock Companies. In 1825, it repealed the Bubble Act of 1720, which removed an obstacle to broadening the principle of joint-stock enterprise. In 1826, Parliament legalized joint-stock banks outside the London radius, but still protecting the Bank of England; by 1833 it permitted them to conduct business within the London radius. In that year it also opened the China trade to all firms. Two years later, Parliament abolished the ancient privileges of municipal corporations which authorized only the freemen of the City of London to keep a shop or trade there.[16]

In the absence of joint-stock incorporation, business was limited to a simple partnership which ended when a member died. In the 1830s, the government expedited the formation of new businesses. In 1837 it authorized incorporation by the mechanism of "letters patent," which meant that new corporations did not require an Act of Parliament. Incorporation by registration was permitted from 1844 onwards, although without the principle of limited liability. Passage of the Limited Liability Act of 1855 ended the exclusivity of joint-stock privileges and granted limited liability to any firm registered since 1844. In 1858 it extended limited liability to joint-stock banks. Finally, in 1862, every registered firm received the right to become a joint-stock enterprise with limited liability.

From the 1860s to the 1870s, this new method of industrial organization became widespread. New companies arose at a sharply accelerating rate.

The Factory Acts: The Rise of Economic Regulation

Writers on the subject of the heyday of laissez-faire also point to the simultaneous growth of social and economic regulations. They cite as examples of this trend the Factory Acts, public health legislation, the rise of public education, municipal provision of gas and water services, and a variety of other measures. Because the first Factory Act was passed as early as 1802—Sir Robert Peel (the Prime Minister's father) sought to impose equal conditions upon all spinners of cottons with his Health and Morals of Apprentice Act of 1802—many critics of laissez-faire see nineteenth-century Britain as the story of growing state regulation of business. However, Checkland claims that Peel's 1802 Act was intended to stop competitive deterioration in his industry.[17]

The state first entered the field of factory regulation to protect pitiful pauper children who were forbidden to work at night and limited to a twelve-hour day. But since "there was to be no prying into the concerns of free men," the legislation contained no provision for inspection or enforcement.[18] If prosecuted, penalties for infringement were negligible.

An Act of 1819, proposed by moralist-businessman Robert Owen, prohibited the employment of children under nine and limited maximum hours for all under sixteen years of age to twelve hours a day in cotton factories. It, too, contained no provision for enforcement. The measure was subsequently broadened in 1825 and 1831 to an age limit of eighteen and prohibited night work until age twenty-one.

The first effective Factory Act was adopted in 1833, providing for an inspectorate and powers of entry. However, since there were no age records available, inspectors could not readily establish violations of its child labor provisions. This fact led to a Parliamentary Act in 1837 providing for compulsory registration of births.[19]

Next came the Mines and Collieries Act of 1842 which limited labor in the mines to men. The Factory Act of 1844 extended state protection of children to women and strengthened the system of penalties. The Ten Hours Act for women and children was passed in 1847. The Coal Mines Inspection Act of 1850 provided for regular inspection in the mines to insure safety, proper lighting, and ventilation. An Act of 1860 kept boys under twelve out of the mines. These and later Acts culminated in the comprehensive Act of 1878 which extended state regulation to all factories employing fifty or more workers (with minor exceptions) and to workshops employing fewer than fifty.[20] By the 1880s the state had accepted the role of industrial policeman. Growing state control laid the foundations for a bureaucracy that increasingly controlled business.

Economic historian Walter Rostow finds in the passage of the Factory Acts motives of economic self-interest to accompany those of good intentions.[21] Many of the Factory Acts received parliamentary approval during years of depressed economic conditions, the low point of the business cycle. Acts adopted in 1819 and 1842 typify such business troughs. To some extent, children and women working in the factories and mines competed with men for scarce jobs. Rostow argues that it would only be natural for unemployed men to reduce or eliminate this form of labor competition. A driving force behind the movement leading to the Act in 1833 was the hope of absorbing idle men. In the case of the Ten Hour Bill of 1847, Rostow claims the role of economic depression was clearer. Once defeated in 1844, it passed quietly in 1847. "So great was the depression of trade that mill owners found it impossible to keep their mills working for so long as ten hours."[22] Labor unions viewed the limitation on hours as a means of restricting labor supply and maintaining wage rates during serious economic depression.

Similar forces worked to pass the Mines and Colliers Act of 1842, when indignation over children and women in the mines found full expression. Checkland concludes that "no doubt indignation was able to become effective without real resistance because women and children were rapidly becoming uneconomic in this employment."[23]

Nor was it purely coincidental that Parliament passed additional Factory Acts during the Corn Law controversy. Protectionists in Parliament wished to retaliate for the Corn Laws repeal campaign conducted by the Manchester businessmen. "Their major counterstroke was the introduction of additional factory regulation."[24]

Other worker legislation was adopted by Parliament early in the century, but enforcement measures lagged far behind. In 1831, for example, Parliament passed the Truck Act which was designed to reduce the exploitation of workers through their purchases ("truck" is paying workers in goods instead of cash). However, it provided no means of enforcement. Enforcement provisions were added in 1887, but workmen still bore the initiative and expense of prosecution.[25]

The Extension of Social Regulation

In addition to the factory and coal mine acts, social reform encompassed chimney acts, emancipation of slavery in the colonies, broader rights to picket and unionize, and a variety of measures dealing with sanitation, public health, foods and drugs, housing, and women's rights.

Even before Parliament approved the Public Health Act of 1848, Liverpool and Manchester had assumed responsibility for health and housing improvement.[26] By its Police Act of 1844, Manchester had started to control housing. The next year it adopted a sanitary improvement act. And, in 1848, it began to build the first large reservoir in the country to assure a safe, dependable water supply. Liverpool obtained a sanitary act and appointed the first borough engineer and first medical officer of health in the country during 1846 and 1847. By 1855 towns were responsible for providing water; by 1870, many had their own municipally-owned gas services. The effects of these health measures, coupled with a general rise in incomes and living standards, reduced filth-related diseases of fevers, smallpox, cholera, and diarrhea.[27]

State intervention in public education took a large step forward with the Education Acts of 1870 and 1876, resulting in sharp increases in public spending on education (see Table 2.2). Liberal reform expanded during Gladstone's last term as Prime Minister. Between 1880 and 1885 Parliament dealt with the issues of the Irish Church, Irish land, university admissions, the secret ballot, corrupt practices at municipal elections, partial abolition of imprisonment for debt, greater freedom for trade unions, and it enacted competitive entrance by examination into every branch of Civil Service except the Foreign Office. To show how the social regulations imposed in the latter half of the nineteenth century laid the groundwork for a manyfold expansion in government regulation and spending in the twentieth century would take us too far afield from this review. Yet despite the burgeoning social regulation of the state, Britain remained the world's foremost example of a free-market economy in which government's general economic policy would best be described as noninterference in the private sector.

The Philosophy and Practice of the Free Market Economy

Mercantilist principles held sway in the late eighteenth century. Laissez-faire took its place in the nineteenth century. Reduction of government spending, massive tax and tariff reform, and the steady removal of government interference from the economy resulted in the golden age of laissez-faire. Historian A.J. Taylor emphasized its intellectual convictions.

> Victorian governments, like the Classical economists, had no explicit theory of economic growth. But implicitly they believed that an economy thrives best when left to the free play of market forces. In this respect, therefore, the commitment to laissez-faire was positive, and the continuing expansion of the British economy throughout the nineteenth century seemed to validate this approach.[28]

The more doctrinaire wing of this school of thought was epitomized in the views of John Bright, a Manchester economist,

> who boasted that he had opposed every enactment for the regulation of labour in factory or mine, every measure for the promotion of public health or for the abatement of the smoke nuisance in large towns, and even the restriction of the licensing laws. He himself was a model employer, a virulent hater of landlords, and a radical democrat in favour of manhood suffrage, but he regarded State interference as unnecessary and as an intolerable invasion of the private domain of the citizen.[29]

> It is probably not far from the truth to say that the period from 1815 to 1885 in Britain represents that range of human experience in which individual economic initiative had its greatest opportunity to operate upon men and things, and in so doing to re-make an ancient society.[30]

Other features of laissez-faire showed in the lack of government statistics on the increasingly free movement of British subjects. Throughout the nineteenth century, Britain experienced massive inward and outward migrations of people, from Ireland, and to the colonies and dominions. "Consistent with the liberal outlook, the state kept no adequate record of its human exports and imports."[31] Another instance was the Cobden-Chevalier Treaty of 1860 with France which abolished the passport system for British subjects in France.[32] Historian A.J.P. Taylor provides a vivid summary of the full extent of economic freedom which nineteenth-century Briton's bequeathed their twentieth-century descendants.

> Until August 1914 a sensible, law-abiding Englishman could pass through life and hardly notice the existence of the state, beyond the post office and the policeman. He could live where he liked and as he liked. He had no official number or identity card. He could travel abroad or leave his country for ever without a passport or any sort of official permission. He could exchange his money for any other currency without restriction or limit. He could buy goods from any country in the world on the same terms as he bought goods at home. For that matter, a foreigner could spend his life in this country without permit and without informing the police. Unlike the countries of the European continent, the state did not require its citizens to perform military service. . . . The Englishman paid taxes on a modest scale: nearly £200 million in 1913-14, or rather less than 8 per cent. of the national income. The state intervened to prevent the citizen from eating adulterated food or contracting certain infectious diseases. It imposed safety rules in factories, and prevented women and adult males in some industries, from working excessive hours. The state saw to it that children received education up to the age of 13. Since 1 January 1909, it provided a meagre pension for the needy over the age of 70. Since 1912, it helped to insure certain classes of workers against sickness and unemployment. This tendency towards more state action was increasing. Expenditure on the social services had roughly doubled since the Liberals took office in 1905. *Still, broadly speaking, the state acted only to help those who could not help themselves. It left the adult citizen alone.* [emphasis added][33]

Notes

1. S.G. Checkland, *The Rise of Industrial Society in England 1815-1885* (New York: St. Martin's Press, 1964), p. 329.
2. Alexander Brady, *William Huskisson and Liberal Reform: An Essay on the Changes in Economic Policy in the Twenties of the Nineteenth Century* (London: Oxford University Press, 1928), pp. 89-91.
3. Sydney Buxton sees Huskisson as the prime mover of reform in the 1820s. He writes that "Huskisson—for Huskisson was the prime mover, the good-natured but feeble Robinson being little more than a cipher. . . . Everybody knows that Huskisson is the real author of the finance measures of Government, and there can be no greater anomaly than that of a Chancellor of the Exchequer who is obliged to propose and defend measures of which another minister is the real though not the apparent author," Charles Greville, *Memoirs*, 1st S., i, p. 81. Cited in Sydney Buxton, *Finance and Politics: An Historical Study 1783-1885*, vol. 1 (London: John Murray, 1888), p. 17.
4. William Smart, *Economic Annals of the Nineteenth Century 1821-1830* (London: Macmillan, 1917), pp. 157-58.
5. Alexander Brady, *William Huskisson*, pp. 92-94.

6. Ibid., p. 95.
7. Ibid., p. 106. In 1843, Peel removed all final impediments to the free export of machinery.
8. Ibid., pp. 107-108, and S.G. Checkland, *Rise of Industrial Society*, pp. 326, 330.
9. Alexander Brady, *William Huskisson*, pp. 124-29.
10. C.R. Fay, *The Corn Laws and Social England* (Cambridge: Cambridge University Press, 1932), p. 122; and C.R. Fay, *Great Britain from Adam Smith to the Present Day: An Economic and Social Survey* (New York: Longmans, Green, 1928), p. 56.
11. Porter's statistics appear on pages 391-92 of his book, *Progress of the Nation* (London: J. Murray, 1851), cited in Alexander Brady, *William Huskisson*, p. 141.
12. Albert H. Imlah, *Economic Elements in the Pax Britannica* (Cambridge: Harvard University Press, 1958), pp. 171-72.
13. Richard Tames, *Economy and Society in Nineteenth-Century Britain* (London: Allen & Unwin, 1972), pp. 79-81.
14. S.G. Checkland, *Rise of Industrial Society*, p. 157.
15. James Clifford, *Aspects of Economic Development* (London: Longmans, Green, 1967), pp. 101-106.
16. C.R. Fay, *Great Britain*, pp. 318-19, and S.G. Checkland, *Rise of Industrial Society*, pp. 343-44.
17. S.G. Checkland, *Rise of Industrial Society*, p. 245.
18. Ibid., p. 246.
19. Ibid., p. 247.
20. J.D. Chambers, *The Workshop of the World: British Economic History from 1820 to 1880* (London: Oxford University Press, 1961), p. 204.
21. W.W. Rostow, *British Economy of the Nineteenth Century* (Oxford: Clarendon, 1948), pp. 118-19.
22. Ibid., p. 119.
23. S.G. Checkland, *Rise of Industrial Society*, p. 248.
24. William D. Grampp, *The Manchester School of Economics* (Stanford: Stanford University Press, 1960), p. 85.
25. S.G. Checkland, *Rise of Industrial Society*, p. 231.
26. G. Kitson-Clark, *The Making of Victorian England* (Cambridge: Harvard University Press, 1962), p. 101.
27. S.G. Checkland, *Rise of Industrial Society*, pp. 254-57. It is easy to attribute improvements in public health to official public health measures. It may well be that improvements in real incomes over this period played a more important role than state-directed measures in eradicating disease. I will address this controversy in Chapter 7.
28. Arthur J. Taylor, *Laissez-Faire and State Intervention in Nineteenth-Century Britain* (London: Macmillan, 1972), p. 60.
29. J.D. Chambers, *The Workshop*, p. 203.
30. S.G. Checkland, *Rise of Industrial Society*, p. 103.
31. Ibid., p. 34.
32. Sydney Buxton, *Finance and Politics*, Vol. 1, p. 236 fn.
33. A.J.P. Taylor, *English History 1914-1945* (New York and Oxford: Oxford University Press, 1965). p. 1.

5

Monetary Stability: The Gold Standard at Work

Britain officially went on the gold standard with Lord Liverpool's Act of 1816. Unofficially, Britain had been on a gold standard since the 22 December 1717 proclamation which proscribed the value of a golden guinea at 21 shillings. Except for emergency periods of suspension, the Bank of England stood ready to exchange its bank notes for gold coins and bullion. The price of gold remained virtually unchanged until 1808, rising to a premium following a speculative binge in Latin America. With the return of peace, Britain restored a now official gold standard.

The Coinage Act of 1816 provided for the free coinage of gold at the mint price of £3 17s. 10.5d. per ounce of gold 11/12 fine. Silver coin became legal tender for amounts up to 40 shillings (£2), thus becoming mere change. The 1816 Act also put a new gold coin into circulation, the sovereign, which was worth 20s., or £1. The sovereign was more convenient for trade and business than the 21 shilling guinea.

Return for a moment to the 1810 Report of the Select Committee on the High Price of Gold Bullion. Its authors feared entrusting discretionary authority to individual bankers to determine how much money should circulate to insure both prosperity and stability of the currency. The Committee had determined that the suspension of cash payments, when notes could not be converted into bullion, had led the Bank of England to overissue paper currency. This had resulted in the pound's falling value on the European exchanges. They saw gold as an automatic mechanism of currency management, free from the potential mistakes of human misjudgment.

> The most detailed knowledge of the actual trade of the Country, combined with the profound science in all the principles of Money and Circulation, would not enable any man or set of men to adjust, and keep always adjusted, the right proportion of circulating medium in a country to the wants of trade.[1]

Currencies based on precious metals or convertible paper, through world exchanges, adjust internal circulating mediums to the actual operation of commerce; discretionary issue of paper money cannot be as effective. In their view, the overissue of currency fostered speculation and unsustainable business expansion. This could produce a crisis during the first loss of confidence in the value of paper money. In contrast, a gold-based system restrained excessive issue of paper money, yet supplied enough liquidity for the normal operation of business.

Money and the Bank of England

The Bank of England (Bank) always played an important part in Britain's monetary system. The first charter granted to the Bank was sealed on 27 July 1694. In return for its charter, the Bank subscribed the whole of its capital (£1.2 million) as a loan to the government at 8 percent interest. However, the Bank's loan was not made in cash. On 2 August the new bank paid into the Exchequer a first installment of £112,000 in the form of bank bills— Bank of England notes—with their corporation seal being Britannia sitting on a bank of money. In return, the Bank took government's promise to pay in the form of interest-bearing tallies. Early sealed bills, not to exceed £1.2 million in total value, bore interest at 2d. per £100 per day. During the twenty-two years that such bills were in regular use (1694-1716), they usually bore interest at 2d. or 3d., a rate of 3 to 4.5 percent, although from 1698 some non-interest-bearing bills were sealed. As an historical note, interest payments on the sealed bills in the first six months came to less than £3,000, as against a 6 percent dividend of £72,000 to the Bank's shareholders in the first half-year. On the greater part of the bills, interest claims were rarely made. The practice soon fell into abeyance, but Bank documents show that interest payments were unimportant even in its early days.[2]

Immediately the hard-pressed government transferred these notes to creditors and contractors, who, in turn, circulated them in the mercantile world. Due to the prestige that government backing gave to the new Bank, and partly because the first notes bore interest, they were readily accepted. The cash shareholders put up remained in the Bank's hands, and was used as a basis for normal banking operations. Each time the Bank's charter was renewed, the government took a fresh loan which the Bank raised by a new issue of capital, leading to an additional bank note issue. The Bank again used the newly subscribed capital to expand its normal banking operations.[3]

The Bank initially performed two functions: note issue and management of the government's account. The Bank granted advances to government in anticipation of taxes, and government loans provided opportunities for the Bank to circulate its notes. Until the mid-nineteenth century, the Bank made little effort to draw banking business from private bankers by offering interest on deposits.[4]

By the late eighteenth century, the Bank held the only important gold stock in the country. Country bankers held their reserves in Bank of England notes, keeping only as much gold as they needed for till money. When checks supplanted bank notes as commercial instruments, bankers held their balances in the form of a credit balance with the Bank rather than in bank note form. The Bank gradually became a bankers' bank in the course of the development of Britain's overall banking system.[5]

As the business activity of the Bank steadily grew—the purchase of government securities, commercial discounting, or increased deposit acceptances from the public—its note issue correspondingly increased. If the supply of money increased faster than the supply of goods and services, prices rose. Any failure of confidence in the soundness of a business expansion led people to return bank notes issued by country bankers to the country bankers in exchange for Bank of England notes, the reserves of country bankers. If the crisis became severe enough, they demanded gold in exchange for the Bank's notes. If the Bank's supply of gold was inadequate, it stopped payments (as in 1797), thus jeopardizing business activity. The crux of the system was the relationship between the gold holdings of the Bank and its outstanding obligations in the form of notes. The Bank's liquidity position served as a barometer for the soundness of the entire economy.[6]

The Act of 1819 (59 Geo. III, c. 49) ordered the return to cash payments, giving the Bank four years to make the transition. It also created a free market in bullion and gold coin. Gold was free to flow in and out of London. Thus Britain's gold stock was an intrinsic element in its overall balance of trade and payments. Fiscal reformers such as William Huskisson, a member of the Bullion Committee of 1810, and Sir Robert Peel, chairman of the Commons committee of 1819 on the resumption of cash payments, regarded free trade in gold and other commodities as complementary.

The mechanics of the gold standard were straightforward. The Bank of England paid out gold at the rate of £3 17s. 10.5 d. per ounce—the Bank's selling price for gold. It purchased gold at the rate of £3 17s. 9d. per ounce—the Bank's buying price for gold. The requirement to buy and sell gold within this range restrained the Bank in its issue of currency, since holders of bank notes could exchange them for gold if they lost confidence in paper money. Exchanging notes for gold reduced the stock of paper money in circulation, arresting its erosion. A rapid drain in the Bank's bullion and coin reserves signalled that credit growth in Britain was excessive. A run on the Bank's gold reserves thus stemmed overly rapid credit creation although the process did not always work overnight.

Through the balance of payments, the gold standard worked as an automatic correction mechanism to determine increases or decreases in Britain's domestic money supply and the resultant levels of income and employment. A favorable balance of payments resulted in an inflow of gold, an expansion of the domestic money supply, a fall in domestic interest rates (due to the greater availability of credit), and increased business activity. As incomes and employment rose, Britons purchased more imported goods and holders of capital would invest some of it overseas where it earned higher interest. This process would ultimately reduce the balance of payments surplus, stopping or reversing further inflow of gold.

Conversely, an adverse balance of payments induced an outflow of gold to pay for the excess value of imports over exports. An outflow of gold, in turn, contracted the domestic money supply, pushed up interest rates and reduced business activity. Incomes and employment fell. Reduced income and employment permitted fewer imports. At the same time, falling domestic costs and prices made British goods more competitive on overseas markets. As imports fell and exports rose, the outflow of gold was stopped or reversed.

This kind of monetary system is automatic in that it works without government interference or management. The economy, in turn, automatically adjusts to the money supply determined by the balance of payments. Throughout the nineteenth century gold was bought for the magic price of £3 17s. 10.5d. an ounce by all holders of British currency anywhere.

Government policy towards the Bank and its responsibility for the management of Britain's currency changed occasionally to accommodate imperfections in the original legislation or new economic circumstances. For example, the government always distrusted small-denomination bank notes. It authorized the Bank to issue £1 and £2 notes during the Napoleonic War when golden guineas disappeared from circulation. However, by 1826, it suppressed Bank issue of all notes under £5, believing that small-paper notes drove sovereigns from circulation. The 1826 Act thus made the gold sovereign the dominant piece of pound-level money in circulation for most Britons throughout the nineteenth century.[7]

Seven years later, the Act of 1833 addressed two problems. First, it restored legal-tender status to bank notes. When convertibility of the note issue was restored in 1819, bank notes had ceased to be legal tender. Thus the 1832 Act relieved the Bank from unexpected withdrawals of gold by provincial bankers who feared a run on their cash reserves; provincial bankers settled their obligations with bank notes. Second, usury laws limited the Bank from raising its discount rate above 5 percent. It could not constrain credit when speculative zeal pushed the effective market rate beyond 5 percent—resulting in a banking crisis in 1825 and commercial hardship in 1826. The 1833 Act abrogated the 5 percent limit. Finally, it contained the provision that the Bank should send its accounts to the Chancellor of the Exchequer for publication. Each month it had to report the amount of its bullion, the size of its note circulation, and the total of its deposits. This information was published in averaged form three months later in the *London Gazette*.[8]

In 1844 the Bank's Charter was renewed for the ninth time. The 1844 Act complemented the 1819 Act which called for the resumption of convertibility; it dealt solely with the question of currency issue. It was more of a "Bank Note Act" than a "Bank Act."

Underpinning the 1844 legislation was concern by Peel and others that no legal guarantee existed to prevent an overissue of notes in time of pressure, thus endangering the doctrine of absolute convertibility of notes and gold. The Act thus separated the issue department of the Bank from its commercial banking department: each had separate offices and maintained separate accounts. The issue department took custody of all the Bank's bullion. It confined its note issue to a fixed value of government securities—a fiduciary issue of £14 million—and the stock of bullion or gold coin in its possession. If the stock of bullion diminished, bank notes were called in; if the stock increased, the issue of notes might be enlarged. The Bank was to render a weekly statement.[9]

The government decided that the power of country banks to issue notes at their discretion threatened monetary stability. Thus the 1844 Act confined all future note issues to the Bank of England. Country banks could maintain existing note issues, but they could not establish a new private issue. If a bank voluntarily surrendered its note issue, the Bank of England could issue new notes up to two-thirds the amount of the lapsed issue after it had compensated the surrender of notes from other banks.[10] The significance of the Act of 1844 was that it ended any serious prospect of state interference in the monetary system.[11] Apart from the fiduciary issue and gold-backing rules, the state prescribed nothing about the Bank's manipulation of money and credit.

By 1870 the Bank became the pivot of the London money market, the money market of Great Britain. The London loan-fund was by far the world's dominant source of credit.

Money Markets	Loan Funds £ (in millions)
London (31st December 1872)	120.0
Paris (27th February, 1873)	13.0
New York (February, 1873)	40.0
German Empire (31st January, 1873)	8.0

Also, deposits in banks which did not publish their accounts were much greater in London than in other major financial centers.[12]

As the Bank learned how to control the credit policy of the London market by its discount rate, it regulated the interest rate on short-term commercial loans throughout the world. If the Bank raised its discount rate, i.e., the rate at which it lent on approved security, the Bourses of the Continent followed suit. A sufficient rise in the rate caused gold to flow in from all corners of the world. Gold flowed freely in because it could flow freely out.[13]

The purpose of a gold standard—the guaranteed exchange of notes and gold at a fixed price—is to prevent the overissue of currency, which could result in inflation and a depreciation of the currency's value in foreign exchanges. A sound currency was for Peel and other supporters of the currency school a "sine qua non" of economic policy. Bank of England notes had to be literally as "good as gold."

But a guarantee of the gold-value of paper money does not guarantee that prices will remain stable over time, or that holders of gold will be protected from the effects of inflation in commodity prices, or that the country will forever remain free of serious financial crises. Unless gold supplies increase, nations may lack sufficient liquidity to support growing world trade.

The Price of Gold

Jastram has thoroughly studied the price of gold and its relationship to the wholesale price of commodities between 1560 and 1980.[14] With postwar return to convertibility, the price of gold stabilized at its pre-Napoleonic figure of 1792. Between 1820 and 1900 (indeed, up to 1930), the price of gold remained virtually constant, and never fell more than 0.7 percent from the Bank's official buying price. Holders of English bank notes bought one ounce of gold at £3 17s. 10.5d.; holders of gold bought £3 17s. 9d. quantity of bank notes per ounce. For eight consecutive decades in the nineteenth century, Britons and other holders of English currency enjoyed the convenience of paper with the security of specie.

Gold and Commodity Prices

A constant paper money and silver coinage price for gold did not necessarily guarantee that commodity prices would be equally stable. Therefore, holders of gold enjoyed an increase, or suffered a decrease, in their real purchasing power depending on the swings in commodity prices.

Britain entered a long deflationary period between 1813 and 1851. From their historical peak in 1813, prices fell abruptly for three years and then moved generally downward for the next thirty-five years. Agricultural prices led the decline, followed by those in the manufacturing sector. For twenty-two of the thirty-five years beginning in 1817, Britain's economy languished in a recession or depression. Prosperity characterized only nine of those years. Commodity prices fell over 58 percent during this period, the most severe price deflation in British history.

However, the price of gold held firm. Holders of gold coin or bullion enjoyed a 70 percent increase in their purchasing power over the period. Those whose wealth consisted largely of gold did very well under the gold standard until mid-century.

Between 1851 and 1855, prices rose sharply and then remained on a stable plateau for nearly two decades. Prices recovered to levels that prevailed during the last third of the eighteenth century and the Huskisson "prosperity" budgets of the 1820s.

At the end of 1873, another deflationary period began which ended in 1896. Commodity prices fell 45 percent, reaching a low point in the summer of 1896. The purchasing power of gold rose 82 percent between 1873 and 1896. However, real wages and economic growth surged during this period (see Chapter 7).

To summarize, a gold standard gives holders of paper currency confidence in its value, but it does not insure what that currency will buy nor what producers will get for their products in the market.

Gold and Commercial Stability

A gold standard implies monetary stability and, as we have seen, Britain enjoyed totally stable gold prices throughout the nineteenth century. But a stable bank note-gold relationship is not an ironclad guarantee of economic prosperity. Nor does it preclude the occurrence of business cycles and financial crises.

The industrial revolution took hold in late eighteenth-century Britain. In its wake followed a series of business cycles that produced at least one general collapse of credit in every decade: 1763, 1773, 1783, 1793, 1797, 1810-11, 1825, 1836-1839, 1847, 1857, and 1866. Most commercial crises developed during wartime or as a result of an extremely rapid growth in some new aid or outlet of production, buttressed by a dramatic growth of credit. The direct cause in 1793 was war with France and the English canal boom; in 1797, war; in 1810-11, overtrading in the new markets of South America; and in 1825, speculation in Mexican mines and other overseas enterprises. The great American crash of 1837, coupled with the domestic promotion of joint-stock banks, brought about stringency between 1836 and 1839. The home-railway boom precipitated the crisis of 1847; the American railway boom spurred that of 1857. The crisis of 1866 resulted from the abuse of bank credit by limited companies established under the Companies Act of 1862.[15]

The Bank Act of 1844 was suspended by government decree during the three financial crises of 1847, 1857, and 1866. In each case, a collapse of business confidence led to the destruction of credit in the economy. By official letter, the government advised the Bank, if necessary, to extend its discounts and advances on approved securities by issuing notes in excess of the legal limits fixed by the Bank Act. Parliament granted the Bank directors immunity from violation of the banking law if the Bank carried out its critical function of acting as lender of last resort to prevent an excessive collapse of credit. The public fact that the government stood behind the Bank stemmed panics in 1847 and 1866 and quickly ended the crises in these two instances without the Bank having to issue notes beyond their legal backing.[16]

The Crisis of 1857

The commercial crisis in the autumn of 1857 was a worldwide crisis. Gold was plentiful in the summer, and the Bank lowered its discount rate from 6 to 5.5 percent in July. But bad financial news came from America in September.

During the prior year, 1856, between a quarter and a fifth of all British exports had been shipped to America. British investors also held some £80 million of United States stocks and bonds. A collapse of credit prompted 150 American banks to stop payments in four Eastern states between 25-29 September. Prices of American securities sagged. In October 1857, sixty-two of sixty-three New York banks suspended payments; across the entire country, 1,415 stopped. Business along the Eastern and Southeastern seaboards came to a standstill.

The shock spread to Liverpool. The first financial institution in Britain to fold was the Liverpool Borough Bank on 27 October. Its rediscounted bills were largely held by bill brokers in London, who passed on the shock. The discount rate shot up in Continental markets to 6.5 percent. Within two weeks the Bank of England raised its rate from 6 to 8 percent.

At the same time the Scots and Irish were losing faith in their own locally issued bank notes. By mid-November, the Bank of England sent £2 million in gold coins to relieve these pressures.

Within days the rate reached 9 percent. A powerful firm of American bankers and brokers next stopped payment for £2.1 million. On 11 November, Sandersons, the bill brokers, suspended payments on £5.3 million of liabilities. The Bank rate went to 10 percent.

The Bank's stock of bullion stood at £6.7 million on 11 November. On 12 November, two ships arrived with fresh gold supplies. On that same day, a collection of banks and bill brokers presented the Bank with requests to discount some £1.4 million in bills and notes. By now the Bank's banking reserve had collapsed to £1.5 million.

The government instructed the Bank not to let the bill brokers firm of Alexander's go down and to meet its request for £400,000 on doubtful security. The Bank gave Alexander's £355,000 for fourteen days. Between 13 and 17 November, the Bank averaged £440,000 a day in discounts. The Bank used the authority granted it by the government, and the Issue Department transferred to the Banking Department two million pounds worth of "illegal" notes in excess of the legal maximum in exchange for securities. By 14 November £554,354 of these were circulated.

On 16 November new failures were announced in Birmingham and Leeds, along with a continued run on gold in Ireland. On 19 November the Bank sold stock and restricted the circulation of new notes, which peaked at £928,000 on 20 November. The monetary phase of the crisis eased by the end of the month when all excess notes were removed from circulation. By Christmas Eve, the Bank rate was reduced from 10 to 8 percent, falling sharply to 3 percent by 11 February 1858. By that date there was £15.7 million of bullion in the Issue Department and £11.4 million in the banking reserve. Prompt action had allayed the panic.[17]

Peel had urged the 1844 Act to prevent an overissue of notes in time of pressure, and to minimize any serious prospect of state interference in the monetary system. The crisis of 1857 belied both objectives. However, the British government was obligated to protect the integrity of the nation's monetary system. It had given the Bank of England a virtual monopoly with respect to note issues and had also granted legal-tender status to Bank of England notes in 1833. It therefore was morally obligated to take whatever steps were necessary to enable the Bank to defend the currency. These steps might include urging the Bank to raise its discount rate, to advance funds on the basis of questionable securities, to circulate "illegal notes," or to help arrange for foreign loans or gold imports. These obvious interventions in times of crisis were responsible exceptions to the general policy by which the gold standard, working through the balance of payments, automatically adjusted the money supply and the level of economic activity.

Gold and the Growth of World Trade

Britain enjoyed a strong creditor position among world traders in the nineteenth century. However, it did not attract and hold an undue part of the world's stock of monetary gold. Britain's exports of goods and services closely matched imports and the loans British investors placed abroad. As a result, the British balance of payments was in remarkable equilibrium. There was only a modest net inflow of gold into Britain during the century, and at no time was there an excessive accumulation. As a vehicle of international money and exchange, the gold mechanism functioned effectively with almost no governmental intervention.[18]

The net gain of bullion to Britain was relatively small before the 1850s. No large reserve of gold built up in Britain in the first half of the nineteenth century. The annual flows of bullion in and out of Britain averaged over five-year periods between 1815 and 1850 ranged from a high inflow of £2.3 million to a net outflow of £0.98 million. By mid-century the inflows increased, often ranging between £3 million and £8 million a year until 1880.[19]

After 1849 new gold fields came into production which doubled the world's stock of monetary gold by 1885. Between 1851 and 1890, annual world gold production ranged from 5 to 7 million ounces, falling to just under 5 million ounces only during 1873 through 1875.

Thanks to the free-trade policies of chief-creditor states, gold flowed to areas where it was useful in meeting the currency needs of rapidly expanding business activity and financing world trade, which was quadrupling in value during this period. Concurrent with the development of banking and credit techniques in more advanced countries, the expanding gold supplies were generally sufficient for expanding business needs.[20]

Notes

1. Edwin Cannan, *The Paper Pound of 1797-1821*. Includes a reprint of the bullion report: *Report of the Select Committee on the High Price of Gold Bullion, 1810* (London: King & Son, 1919), p. 52.
2. Sir John Clapham, *The Bank of England, A History*, vol. 1, 1694-1797 (Cambridge: Cambridge University Press, 1945), pp. 8-24.
3. C.R. Fay, *Great Britain from Adam Smith to the Present Day: An Economic and Social Survey* (New York: Longmans, Green, 1928), pp. 99-100.
4. Ibid., p. 100.
5. Ibid., pp. 101-102.
6. S.G. Checkland, *The Rise of Industrial Society in England 1815-1885* (New York: St. Martin's Press, 1964), pp. 193-94.
7. C.R. Fay, *Great Britain*, p. 96.
8. Ibid., pp. 97, 104; and S.G. Checkland, *Rise of Industrial Society*, p. 197.
9. Sydney Buxton, *Finance and Politics: An Historical Study, 1783-1885*, vol. 2 (London: John Murray, 1888), p. 16.
10. C.R. Fay, *Great Britain*, p. 97.
11. S.G. Checkland, *Rise of Industrial Society*, p. 201.
12. Walter Bagehot, *Lombard Street, A Description of the Money Market* (Westport, Connecticut: Hyperion, 1979), p. 2.
13. C.R. Fay, *Great Britain*, p. 103.
14. Roy W. Jastram, *The Golden Constant. The English and American Experience 1560-1976* (New York: Wiley, 1977), pp. 26-37, 79-80, 113-17.

15. C.R. Fay, *Great Britain*, pp. 103-104.
16. Sydney Buxton, *Finance and Politics*, p. 18.
17. Sir John Clapham, *The Bank of England, A History*, vol. 2, *1797-1914*, pp. 226-34.
18. Albert H. Imlah, *Economic Elements in the Pax Britannica* (Cambridge: Harvard University Press, 1958), p. 11.
19. Ibid., pp. 70-73.
20. Ibid., pp. 158-59.

6

From Factions to Parties: The Transformation of British Politics

Huskisson, Peel, and Gladstone directed the liberal transformation of Britain's economy in three great spurts. During the same period, political reform also passed through three stages.[1] In 1800, cliques and factions, reflecting narrowly-focussed aristocratic, landed interests, dominated British politics. By 1900, mass-based political parties replaced the landed elements. Major political reforms in 1832, 1867, and 1884 extended a limited franchise, where one man in twelve could vote to a system of universal male suffrage. This political metamorphosis took place peacefully, although sometimes grudgingly.

Political and economic reform moved in tandem. Expansion of the franchise both reflected and furthered the political influence of manufacturing, trading, and middle-class interests. Further expansion acknowledged the reality of trade-union influence. Recall that Gladstone completed his reforms by 1866. Britain prospered as a free economy throughout the balance of the nineteenth century. But the extension of the franchise to all males in 1884 shifted political power away from men of property, money, or education to those who could marshall the support of sheer numbers in the electorate. Bidding for votes with promises of government programs fostered sharp increases in spending and taxes and led to a full-blown welfare state following World War II.

Agricultural protectionism was the hallmark of aristocratic politics throughout the eighteenth century. But the industrial revolution, which began in 1780, prompted a landed Parliament to reform itself in 1832 to accommodate the new commercial, manufacturing, and middle-class interests. A reformed Parliament, in turn, accelerated liberal economic reform. It approved free trade in grain, overhauled the tax and tariff code, and reduced government spending as a share of national income. This enlightened Parliament reformed itself a second time in 1867 and gave the vote to well-paid, skilled workmen. However, only a minority of British males could vote. Since the income tax granted a personal exemption of £100, voters and taxpayers were largely synonymous.

New government spending programs meant higher taxes for them. The 1884 reform, which granted universal male suffrage, thus became the watershed of British politics. The two-thirds of the electorate who paid no income taxes comprised the political majority. Successive Parliaments graduated the tax rates and steadily raised the top marginal rate. The transition from a predominantly landed franchise to a limited middle-class electorate facilitated free trade and tax relief, but its subsequent extension to the working classes reversed the liberalizing trends that had characterized the era of Huskisson through Gladstone.

Late eighteenth-century British politics is a story of shifting factions, cliques, and major personalities that is hard to keep straight. To explain the process of political change during the nineteenth century requires some background of prereform political life in Britain.

Prereform Politics

A good place to begin is with the unpopular American War of Independence which produced a challenge to Britain's eighteenth-century political constitution. King George III's Prime Minister, Lord North, supported the British war effort. When General Cornwallis surrendered to George Washington at Yorktown in October 1781, the House of Commons repudiated the King's war policy and Lord North's ministry. In March 1782, a new ministry assembled under Lord Rockingham, who had led the opposition to the King's American policy. This group, known as the Rockingham Whigs, wanted to impose constitutional restrictions on the King and curb royal patronage. The new ministry was short-lived, dissolving on Rockingham's death, and his successor was unable to hold his followers together.

King George III, who sought to retain the monarch's traditional influence in British politics, struggled with those antimonarch Whigs who had opposed the American war and wished to convert the King's humiliation in defeat into a permanently smaller role for him. The King regained the upper hand for a few short years with the accession of the young promonarch William Pitt to the post of Prime Minister. But rivalry between the pro- and antiroyal factions highlight the structure of the British constitution at the beginning of the nineteenth century.

The British Constitution

Unlike the American Constitution, the British Constitution has never been codified. Rather, it is a set of evolving relationships between the British government and its subjects, on the one hand, and the powers of, and interrelationships between, the several branches of the British government, on the other. Most educated or propertied Englishmen venerated the British Constitution as a bulwark of individual liberty. They saw it as a mixed monarchy which combined the benefits of absolute monarchy, aristocracy, and democracy, without the dangers of rule by just one of these. The English Constitution evolved from the Glorious Revolution of 1688 which stressed individual liberty, the rule of law, and the preeminence of Parliament as against absolute monarchy. Do not confuse the concepts of individual liberty and the rule of law with the idea of equality for all. The rights of Englishmen did not extend to the rabble, the illiterate, and the propertyless. However, contemporary political commentators stressed the importance of checks and balances as guarantees of liberty, in which the monarch had a proper role to play. In the words of the most brilliant jurist of his day, William Blackstone:

> Herein indeed consists the true excellence of the English government, that all the parts of it form a mutual check upon each other. In the legislature, the people are a check upon the nobility and the nobility a check upon the people . . . while the King is a check upon both, which preserves the executive power from encroachments. And this very executive power is again checked and kept within due bounds by the two Houses. Thus, every branch of our civil polity supports and is supported, regulates and is regulated, by the rest.[2]

Checks and balances in late eighteenth-century Britain reflected the trinity of King, the House of Lords, and the House of Commons. Educated thinking about authority abhorred both extremes of royal autocracy and single-chamber government. Parliamentary government in 1800 lacked organized political parties and an independent civil service. The King chose his ministers from inside Parliament and both Houses had to approve legislation.

Government ministers were not party leaders in any modern sense, nor did they concern themselves with public opinion. Their chief tasks were to garner a majority of support from Members of Parliament. To accomplish this, they had available a considerable amount of public patronage, rewards, places, honors, and pensions which they employed to buy influence among a very limited electorate.

No precise constitutional formula or convention determined the distribution of power among the three elements. In practice, influence ebbed and waned with different personalities and with the pressure of events. Seen in this light, the challenge to the King's authority by the Rockingham Whigs, if successful, would have converted the monarch into a figurehead and made Parliament absolutely supreme, leaving political power to be parcelled out between Lords and Commons. Nothing in this assault on royal power implied the extension of political privilege to the middle classes, much less to the working classes. It was simply a straightforward attempt to wrest all political influence from the King.

Although Lords and Commons were constitutionally divided, an aristocratic element prevailed in both. Heads of families sat in the Lords, with younger brothers, sons, and nephews sitting in the Commons. As leading representatives of the propertied, many of the Lords controlled elections to the Commons. It is estimated that about 150 Members of Parliament were elected through the influence of peers. Commons took the lead in questions of financial policy and assumed steadily greater political importance, but an adverse vote in the Lords often led to the fall of a ministry until the middle of the nineteenth century.

The eighteenth-century Constitution was admired and defended by men of rank, property, and education because, in part, it protected their interests. Their primary means of ensuring political dominance lay in a severely restricted franchise: only one in twelve men could vote. We can say with hindsight that nineteenth-century constitutional change facilitated the expression of the popular will.

Regardless of the substantive disputes on domestic or foreign policies, Kings, Lords, and Commons all agreed about the imperatives of property—only the landed interest enjoyed the right of representation. Property holders never converted their constitutional conflicts with the Crown into fundamental debates about natural rights or popular sovereignty. Nor was the King, who may have been irritated by the pretension of an aristocratic opposition, ever tempted to side with the multitude against the aristocrats. All respectable people feared the "mob" and suspected "the people." Governmental power reinforced, never challenged, the social order in which the attributes of family, property, rank, and intelligence were counted.

The Composition of Parliament

The elected branch of Parliament, the House of Commons, consisted of 558 members. All were men of property. Members stood for election either at the borough or county level. To be a county member required an annual income of £600 a year from land. To be a borough member required an income of £300. With national per capita income below £20, clearly all members were well-to-do.

The franchise varied considerably throughout the country. In the boroughs, represented by 432 members, historic practice and custom, not statute, determined who had the right to vote. Eligibility was widespread in a few boroughs. At the other extreme, termed "pocket" or "rotten" boroughs, the franchise was restricted to owners or occupiers of certain houses, plots of land, or property rights. "The most notorious of these places was Old Sarum, a mound of earth without a house, where a solicitor handed the seven voters title deeds to local property just before they voted and immediately took them back again after the vote had been recorded."[3]

Influence of one kind or another—government patronage, the claims of a local family, or cash bribes—governed the choice of most members. Larger electorates were more difficult to control, but only twenty boroughs had more than a thousand voters. These few became the scenes of the most active late eighteenth-century political election fights as candidates sought to demonstrate their popularity. Twenty-six boroughs had from 500 to 1,000 voters, and patrons often spent large sums to appease electors who knew their support might be critical. It was in the smallest boroughs, the vast majority of constituencies, that the pull of ownership and influence was most marked. In the tiniest of them, both vote and seat was treated as a valuable piece of real property. These tiny boroughs were bought and sold at election times through newspaper advertisements until the Act of 1809 made this practice illegal.

County seats, encompassing greater size and much larger electorates, were more expensive to win and hold, but politicians wishing to advertise their strength and electoral appeal often contested county seats. Although more independent and representative than boroughs, the aristocracy was also disproportionately strong in county seats.

In any given election, only a small fraction of constituencies was contested. Indeed, political struggles typically occurred about who would be nominated, not elected.

Since the electoral system was hardly representative, members of Parliament laid more emphasis on the deliberative rather than the representational aspect of their assembly. Most members were no more free to express their opinions than the limited electorate which had put them there. In 1783, for example, only 178 of the 558 members could be regarded as free to express their own opinion; the other 380 were readily placed into definite categories reflecting the views of their patrons. Hardly. what we envisage today as representative democracy!

Parliamentary politics witnessed factions of men struggling to assert their views and interests over those of their rivals. Party labels of "Whig" and "Tory" divided the electorate at contested elections; but, once assembled, members of Parliament were not bound together by party discipline, but by kinship, friendship, patronage, shared tactics, hopes of office, and often in response to genuine leadership. Some parliamentary seats reflected the special East India interest, the West India interest, the City of London interest, religious interests, government contractors, cotton manufacturers, and so on. These were, however, few in number compared with the landed interests.

Modern parliamentary government presupposes four conditions: an effective political party mechanism, strong ties between the political parties and public opinion to permit alternating party rule, a professional civil service free of political influence to insure administrative continuity, and a pliant monarch. Modern parliamentary government was clearly impossible in 1800. It took nearly a century to bring about these conditions.

Change occurred between 1780 and 1820. The monarch gradually lost influence. Public opinion grew in importance as larger fractions of the population expressed interest in social and political issues. Pitt gradually reduced royal patronage. As government administration grew more complex, the Prime Minister and his cabinet took responsibility for activities which the King had neither the inclination nor the ability to handle. The general public became better informed about the activities of Parliament through press reports and the publication of the proceedings of parliamentary committees of inquiry. Secret influence and royal prerogative increasingly yielded to the consequences of industrial growth, with the formation of economic associations and a variety of reform societies. Political factions increasingly reflected election results rather than coalitions among peers, although parties were still nascent.

The First Electoral Reform: 1832

Upon the conclusion of the Napoleonic War, the British economy stagnated, with the exception of Huskisson's prosperity years. During periods of economic downturn, working-class distress often spilled over into political upheaval. Members of the ruling elites knew that hard times had brought social upheaval in neighboring France, at great loss to the aristocracy. High rates of unemployment worried the government. In 1819, the worst immediate postwar year, disgruntled weavers channeled their frustrations into political agitation. Seeking complete constitutional reform, thousands of workers from hard-hit Manchester and surrounding cotton districts gathered in St. Peter's Field for a political rally. The local magistrates, scared of an uprising, called in the regular cavalry to disperse the crowds: eleven were killed and 400 wounded. The potential for revolutionary upheaval was clearly present.

Economic recovery in 1820 throttled the growth of mass meetings and political demonstrations throughout England that followed the August 1819 bloodbath at St. Peter's Field. The civil war that many respectable citizens feared withered in the boom years of the 1820s. Prosperity bred political confidence. In 1824 Parliament repealed the Combination Acts of 1800 which had banned trade unions. New unions sprang into existence throughout Britain. Intermittent violence led Parliament to amend the act in 1825, which limited the ability of trade unions to strike.

Although prosperity forestalled political agitation in the early 1820s, Parliament increasingly recognized the need for reform. Mercantile and industrial interests could no longer be dismissed. Unduly harsh criminal laws were modified. Capital punishment was abolished for a large number of crimes. With the onset of Huskisson's economic reforms, "liberality" became the watchword of the day. The middle classes talked of enlightened government and the "march of intellect." Parliamentary reform was discussed in every important town and city throughout Britain.

When the Whigs returned to power in 1830, the need for a reform bill had become inevitable. The new Whigs descended from the Rockingham tradition of anti-monarch aristocrats. Most owned splendid estates and country homes. They were supported by money interests in the City of London, manufacturing interests in the industrial provinces, religious dissidents, and utilitarian intellectuals who viewed the Tories as landed interests opposed to all change and enemies of the people.

An analysis of social-class backgrounds left little to distinguish the Whigs from the Tories. Both were exclusive and aristocratic. The difference was in attitude. Whigs believed that unless the ruling classes adapted, waves of dangerous and uncontrollable innovation would destroy the existing social order. Tories believed that parliamentary reform itself would be catastrophic. During the crucial debates of 1830 to 1832, Whigs and Tories were united in their opposition to complete representative democracy. Each insisted that landed property had a special role to play in guaranteeing social stability and preserving the Constitution. The dispute was about the choice of voting qualification that would enfranchise the middle classes without creating thoroughly popular constituencies. In creating new middle-class constituencies, some "rotten" and "pocket" boroughs would be disenfranchised. New winners and losers would emerge.

The original draft of the First Reform Bill was read in Parliament on 1 March 1831. It proposed to disenfranchise small boroughs with fewer than 2,000 inhabitants. It granted the vote in the borough constituencies to the £10 householder, a man who occupied a building of annual value of £10 either as owner or tenant. Boroughs of 2,000 to 4,000 people lost one of their two members. The bill created 168 vacancies, forty-two of which would become new borough seats, largely in industrial and commercial centers. Counties got fifty-five additional members, and nine new seats were awarded to Scotland, Ireland, and Wales. The remaining sixty-two seats disappeared.

Tories charged that eliminating small boroughs constituted uncompensated confiscation of private property and customary rights. They feared that political influence would ultimately pass from the landed to the industrial areas of the country with the largest populations. Moreover, they knew that a First Reform Bill would lead to a second and third and eventually destroy all existing political institutions, beginning with the House of Lords, the monarchy, and ultimately private property itself. One prescient critic wrote that "there would eventually be no King, no Lords, no inequalities in the social system; all will be levelled to the plane of the petty shopkeepers and small farmers; this, perhaps not without bloodshed, but certainly by confiscations and persecutions.''[4]

Whigs defended the process of orderly change in order to forestall more serious consequences. They asserted that the proposed expansion of the franchise was moderate and added commercial and industrial interests to landed property as stalwarts of the new constitutional order, thus helping to preserve the existing institutions and government of the country.

Tense exchanges in both the Commons and Lords led King William IV to dissolve Parliament and put the question of reform, almost in the fashion of a referendum, to an unreformed electorate. The election of 1830 had been concerned with many issues, but the election of 1831 was fought solely on the question of reform. The elections demonstrated an irresistible wave of excitement for reform. Pro-reform candidates were returned in virtually every large, popularly-contested constituency. Of the eighty-two county members, almost all were pledged to support reform.

In June 1831, following the election, Lord John Russell, the Prime Minister, introduced a similar reform bill. It passed its second reading by a 136-vote majority in the Commons (367 votes to 231).[5] On 22 September it received formal approval, after many delays by the opposition, and was submitted to the Lords for approval. Far more than in the Commons, the Lords symbolized Tory convictions that landed interests should remain preeminent. They duly rejected the bill on 8 October by 199 votes to 158. Their rejection of the bill led to an immediate and prolonged outburst of opposition in the country.

Lord Russell persisted and introduced a modified bill on 12 December. His adjusted bill restored the sixty-two seats previously eliminated, distributing them among a mixture of old and new boroughs. Some who would have lost their influence were assuaged by restoration of their constituencies. The bill easily passed its second reading in the Commons by a majority of 162 votes. As the Whig leadership waited for the third and final reading in the Commons, they again worried about the Lords.

The Whigs had committed themselves to reform. They staked their convictions and prestige on its success. Yet they were, at bottom, aristocrats who sought to preserve the constitutional status of Lords. Thus a severe dilemma arose in 1831—the difficult constitutional problem of creating a new group of peers, thereby packing the House of Lords to guarantee passage of the First Reform Bill. Whig leader Charles Grey obtained a promise, albeit vague, from the King to create sufficient new peers to pass the bill in the Lords. The threat proved adequate. The Lords passed the second reading of the bill by nine votes. If they succeeded, the government would have its reform bill without altering the status of the House of Lords—the best of both worlds.

The Tory Lords did not lie down and quit. In a delaying tactic, they proposed that the disenfranchising clauses of the bill should be postponed until after the new enfranchising provisions had been debated. This motion carried by 151 votes to 116 on 7 May 1832. Whig leaders confronted the King with the threat of resignation unless he immediately created 150 new peers. The King accepted the resignation of his shocked ministers.

The anti-reformers tried in vain to form a Tory government willing to sponsor a watered-down reform bill. The King, having lost all his popularity, had no choice but to ask for Grey again. Grey obtained the vital note from the King granting permission to create enough new peers to secure his Reform Bill. The King's secretary informed Tory leaders of the opposition in the Lords that approval of the bill would forestall the creation of new peers. The first Reform Bill received final approval in the Lords with a landslide vote of 106 to 22.

As an interesting aside, Sir Robert Peel opposed the bill to the last, warning that when the Corn Laws came up for consideration in the future, the government would be similarly threatened. Fate treats some men in unpredictable ways:

> By making it possible for an unreformed House of Commons to reform itself, the Whigs were successful under the leadership of a highly traditionalist peer in relieving the danger of revolution and attaching to the Constitution the middle classes who form the real and efficient mass of public opinion, and without whom the power of the gentry is nothing.[6]

The New Electoral System

Conservatism survived the 1832 reform bill. The House of Lords remained intact, and the House of Commons continued to resemble its prereform condition. The agricultural south was still overrepresented at the expense of the industrial north and London. But the changes should not be underestimated. Many of the newly created boroughs were in the industrial towns of the North and Midlands. Only five tiny boroughs with fewer than 200 electors remained. Although 115 members still sat for boroughs with fewer than 500 voters, Old Sarum and its truly "rotten" cousins disappeared. Although grossly underrepresented, manufacturing interests now took part in political decision-making. Nominees of great families were returned in the few remaining pocket boroughs until the Second Reform Bill of 1867, but the stranglehold of landed property had been cracked.

The 1832 Act expanded the franchise from one adult male in twelve to one in seven. Since it was necessary to register and pay a mandatory fee before voting, new techniques of political party organization soon followed. Parties had greater incentives to encourage registration, supervise registration, and collect information about party strength in the various constituencies.

If one in seven could now vote, six in seven could not. Over 80 percent of the adult male population lacked the franchise. The First Reform Bill of 1832 set in a motion a process of democratization by extending the franchise from the landed to the middle classes, but the working masses were still excluded. Influential families continued to dominate a large bloc of seats in the Commons. The system now accommodated the economic realities of the industrial revolution, but the growing strength of workers' organizations had not yet been recognized.

Sir Robert Peel's betrayal of his own conservative Tory followers, as he led the struggle for repeal of the Corn Laws, shows how economic conditions changed the political interests of the aristocracy. Many of the big landlords who now had urban and industrial investments had less need for agricultural protection. The most active group demanding protection was the tenant farmers who had no other economic options. The Whigs were fully converted to free trade, and even Tories accepted the new economic order a few years later. Britain's economic foundation and international political power lay in industry, not farming.

Historian G. Kitson-Clark summarized the philosophy and practice of government in mid-Victorian England:

> No doubt there was much to be said against the system of government that existed in Britain in the middle of the nineteenth century; it gave too much power to the landed gentry, it gave too much power to the aristocracy; but it was reasonably liberal, it was government by debate in which educated opinion played its part, and an intelligent man might well consider matters very seriously before he became anxious to change all this for the clumsy tyranny which seemed very likely to result from the direct rule of the people.[7]

The Second Reform Bill: 1867

As Chancellor of the Exchequer from 1859 to 1866, Gladstone completed his program of economic reform, and Britain enjoyed a period of unbroken prosperity. Indeed, economic growth so improved the conditions of working men that they held large meetings in major cities protesting the unrepresentative nature of Parliament. Gladstone, a consummate politician, turned his attention to the issue of further parliamentary reform in 1864 when he made his first famous public statement supporting a motion to reduce the franchise qualification in the boroughs from £10 to £6. Gladstone emphasized that he did not favor sudden, violent, or excessive political or constitutional change; yet, he put on the record his conviction that responsible working men had a moral right to the vote. The Commons overwhelmingly rejected the bill by

274 votes to 56. However, its debate stimulated radical agitation outside Westminster.

Gladstone firmly believed in improving the economic well-being of members of the working classes, but as individuals, not as members of a well-defined economic class. He did not favor the development of organized class pressure in the form of working-class agitation. Despite these personal convictions, the public hailed him as the new leader of a "great party of the people." Middle-class sympathizers joined forces with a variety of working men's organizations. The Reform League, established in February 1865, and the Reform Union, set up in the North of England, traced their origins to reformist activities on behalf of the working classes. Political agitation for further extension of the franchise in the 1860s paralleled that preceding the First Reform Bill. By 1865, the extension of the franchise to working men seemed inevitable, and great political figures threw their weight behind the proposal.

A break in economic prosperity in 1866 focussed attention away from economic to political issues. Gladstone was fast rising in popular esteem. He felt that he and his Liberal Party colleagues had best move quickly on reform lest the Tories gain the political credit and long-run benefits from its inevitable approval. But a small clique of Liberals led by Robert Lowe opposed reform, frustrating Gladstone's political designs.

Lowe was as gloomy about a future after reform as Gladstone was optimistic. He believed that the half-reformed Constitution, the product of the 1832 Reform Bill, provided good government. He claimed that the Houses of Commons formed since 1832 comprised the finest hour in the history of representative assemblies.

Lowe objected to extending the franchise to working men on three counts. First, it transferred power to the ignorant. He insisted that mid-Victorian prosperity already enabled most skilled workers worthy of the vote to buy it if they chose to save a fraction of their incomes, thus becoming respectable £10 householders. The way to elevate the working classes was not to change the franchise rate, but to keep it as a privilege of citizenship. From his eight-years experience in Australia where universal suffrage had been practiced, it had been ill-regarded. The evidence was that when a one shilling registration fee was introduced, the number of eligible voters fell by half. A shilling was only one two-hundredth part of the £10 requirement, scarcely beyond anyone's means.

Second, Lowe argued that a large measure of parliamentary reform destroyed the tradition of leadership by great men in Parliament. Future majorities in the Commons would solely be formed on the basis of broad electoral support. Statesmen who could not lead their party in electoral competition would not receive the opportunity to serve as had past leaders.

Third, and most important, reform led to policies that undermined national unity and prosperity. "The working classes were interested in the vote not in itself but as a means to an end, and were already looking beyond political democracy to socialism."[8] He feared that the working classes would acquire real political power and use the machinery of the state to assist strikes and foster trade union rule. Class conflict would undermine national unity. Business confidence would fall. Future prosperity would be at risk.

Lowe's warnings fell on deaf ears. Even those members of Parliament who supported his opinions and prejudices were convinced of the inevitability of reform and refused to lose public credit by opposing it.

On 12 March 1866, Gladstone introduced a mild reform bill extending the franchise to residents in counties and boroughs on a less restrictive annual rent requirement and to men with savings accounts of £50 in any bank. Many radicals felt the measure did not go far enough. Many conservatives insisted on considering changes in the subsequent distribution of seats. This coalition of disgruntled liberals and concerned conservatives defeated the measures. The cabinet resigned, Gladstone was in the opposition, and the carrying of the new reform bill fell to Benjamin Disraeli.

Historians give Disraeli the credit for granting the vote to the working classes of the towns. For Disraeli, passage of the bill was not a matter of political principle; instead, he took credit for settling the reform question and breaking the political monopoly of liberalism. The Conservatives were in a minority in Parliament, but Disraeli kept most of his party in line. Only a small minority of Conservatives complained that the results of political betrayal would be the destruction of the monarchical and aristocratic principles and the triumph of the democratic principle. Those Conservatives who held that a large-scale reform bill destroyed the influence of rank, property, and education were a minority among party leaders and in the Commons, and even their position in the Lords dwindled as the debate progressed. The Conservative Party had indeed come a long way by the second third of the nineteenth century.

Behind the scenes, a struggle took place within the cabinet between those who advocated a "comprehensive" bill and those who favored a "small" bill. Threats of resignation were hurled, but fears that the government would fall unless the Tories came forth with a comprehensive bill prevailed. A majority within the Commons was in no mood for vapid rhetoric.

On 18 March Disraeli introduced his bill. It implied no extensive redistribution of seats in favor of urban areas. Relaxing several requirements of the franchise conferred the vote on 237,000 urban ratepayers. To offset their newly-proposed political power, another provision gave about 200,000 taxpaying members of the middle class a second vote. The expanded franchise gave about one-fourth of the nation's voting power to the aristocracy, one-quarter to the working classes, and the remaining half to the middle classes. Disraeli did not go far enough in his original proposal. In the course of the debates between March and July 1867 the bill underwent a total transformation. A majority in the Commons increasingly felt that unless a truly comprehensive bill was passed, the House would be branded as an incapable, incompetent assembly. Pressures for reform were as inevitable as the new economic reality.

Disraeli adjusted to the political realities and saw the redefined reform bill as an opportunity to reestablish Toryism on a national foundation. But he was unable to control the tempo of events. Political radicals proposed, and won, amendments that went beyond his desires. They reduced the period of residential qualification for voters from two years to one year (Disraeli opposed this amendment and lost by eighty-one votes). They extended the borough franchise to all lodgers who had occupied rooms for the prior year (Disraeli accepted this amendment without a vote). A third amendment, by far the most important, established complete and unlimited household suffrage as the foundation of the borough franchise in England and Wales. No distinctions were drawn among any classes of urban residents, whether ratepayers, nonrentpaying lodgers, renters, etc. It only remained for Disraeli to drop the few remaining fancy franchises. Out went the education test, the property franchise, and the dual votes. (However, for the record, an amendment in favor of women's suffrage was defeated without any difficulty). Disraeli no longer cared what kind of bill was adopted as long as a reform bill passed while a Conservative government was in power.

There was more to come. In the past, Conservatives had always held firm on the issue of the distribution of seats and had refused to increase the representation of the cities and the populous districts in the House of Commons. An opposition member brought forward a more drastic scheme than the government proposed, and it carried over Disraeli's objections by a large majority of 127 votes. The facts of political life were fast becoming known to the Conservative party. Disraeli barely defeated by eight votes a general proposal providing a third member for large cities; this was accomplished by a backstairs compromise in which he gave third members to Liverpool, Manchester, Birmingham, and Leeds.

The Second Reform Bill that emerged from the Commons in July was far more democratic than the original proposal that Disraeli or any of his opponents had intended. The bill immediately added 1.1 million men to the franchise, severalfold the number proposed in March.[9] Workingmen gained considerably more than a one-quarter voting influence in the new Parliament.

Unlike 1832 when the House of Lords stalled the First Reform Bill and produced a constitutional crisis, the bill was successfully managed in the Lords under the able leadership of Derby. He told Conservative peers that the bill was the most conservative measure that could be passed in the Commons and that approval in the Lords would give the Tory party the opportunity to stay in power for a long time to come. It passed in August 1867. For the first time in Britain's history "numbers" counted for more in the Constitution than property or education.

Although skilled workmen, and soon all males, would have the vote, many in Parliament pondered Britain's future with apprehension. The previous seventy years of English history were dominated by the rise of the middle classes. The middle classes were the carriers of free trade and the very idea of improvement itself. Now, by granting the vote to town workers, there was little sure knowledge, but much real trepidation, about the pattern of future politics.

The most perceptive commentator of his day was Walter Bagehot, whose book, *The English Constitution*, remains a classic. In the introduction to the second edition, published in mid-1872, Bagehot displayed his personal prejudices and fears for the future constitutional government in Britain.

First, his prejudices. Bagehot firmly held that only aristocratic elements could rule wisely. He doubted the wisdom of the middle classes, the ordinary majority of educated men whom he labelled "the despotic power in England." Beneath the middle classes were found the working classes, of whom Bagehot minced no words:

> But the Reform Act of 1867 did not stop at skilled labour; it enfranchised unskilled labour too. And no one will contend that the ordinary working-man who has no special skill, and who is only rated because he has a house, can judge much of intellectual matters.[10]

And what would majority rule by working men entail?

> But in all cases it must be remembered that a political combination of the lower classes, as such and for their own objects, is an evil of the first magnitude; that a permanent combination of them (now that so many of them have the suffrage) supreme in the country; and that their supremacy, in the state they now are, means the supremacy of ignorance over instruction and of numbers over knowledge.[11]

To Bagehot, democratic politics on a broad franchise presaged the corruption of politics from the wise rule of true leaders to unprincipled full-fledged parties.

> In plain English, what I fear is that both our political parties will bid for the support of the working-man; that both of them will promise to do as he likes if he will only tell what it is; that, as he now holds the casting-vote in our affairs, both parties will beg and pray him to give that vote to them. I can conceive of nothing more corrupting or worse for a set of poor ignorant people

than that two combinations of well-taught and rich men should constantly offer
to defer to their decision, and compete for the office of executing it.[12]

Liberal leader Robert Lowe made the case against further reform during
the heat of the 1866 debate. Walter Bagehot restated his objections during
the political calm of 1872. Both warned that inalterable forces had been set
in motion which would destroy the liberal order.

The Third Reform Bill: 1884

All that remained was for Parliament to enfranchise farm laborers. In 1884,
it approved the Third Reform Bill granting universal male suffrage.[13] It also
provided for the secret ballot to prevent undue influence of landed families
and manufacturers over farm laborers and workers. Since 1870 competitive
examinations determined entry into the civil service. Professionalism totally
replaced patronage in the administration of government. The transformation
of British politics was virtually complete. Parties replaced factions. The number of middle-class and working-class voters dwarfed the landed gentry. The
House of Lords moved increasingly backstage. Gladstone became the great
popular spokesman for the Liberal Party.

As the century turned, government grew. Increased spending on social
programs accompanied higher taxes, greater staffing in the public services,
and a growing spate of social and economic regulations in industrial safety,
education, and so forth. Free trade gradually diminished as both a prevailing
doctrine and commercial policy. What brought about this transition from the
reduction of government to the growth of government?

A major cause was the rise of modern party politics, a universal male
franchise, and an emerging trade unionism which raised the demand for more
social legislation and spending. The philosophy of laissez-faire gave way to
a growing public belief that it was the duty of government to provide a better
life for all, even if it meant greater government intervention in the economy.
Accordingly, Liberal administrations between 1905 and 1915 introduced a
series of major social services: old age pensions, labor exchanges, and national
insurance. Public education and public housing programs added significantly
to the government's activities. In the twentieth century, public spending on
social programs grew from an insignificant to a very substantial share of
Britain's national income.

Accompanying the growth in social spending was an increase in taxation.
In the thirty years between 1884 and 1914, government expenditures nearly
tripled. To meet this cost, progressive taxation replaced the system of proportional taxation. Although the maximum rate of tax in 1909 had been raised
to a modest (by contemporary standards) 6.25 percent, progressivity became

a hallmark of the twentieth century British tax system. Rates rose through much of the century, with dramatic leaps in World Wars I and II, and the postwar era.

Some Thoughts on Democracy and Economic Liberty

The British Constitution of 1800 was scarcely recognizable a century later. In 1800 Continentals marvelled at Britain's intricate system of checks and balances—King, Lords and Commons—that sustained English "liberty." The franchise was not widespread; a mere 8 percent of the adult male population was eligible to vote. Parliament was a captive of the landed aristocracy. Only men of means held elective office. A few great families were disproportionately influential. Reflecting these interests, the chief preoccupation of Parliament, apart from wartime crises, was the passage of enclosure bills and the maintenance of agricultural protectionism. Disputes within the aristocratic community centered on the proper role of the monarch and the pace of social and political reform. There was no quarrel, however, about politics being the preserve of the propertied classes. Nor was there great quarrel with mercantilist policy.

By 1830 the industrial revolution had changed the economic face of Britain. The importance of agriculture waned. Manufacturing and the export trade converted Britain into a dominant world power. An unreformed electorate acknowledged the new realities in 1831, choosing candidates committed to political reform.

The Whig government of 1832 was not motivated by altruism toward the middle classes. Far better to coopt the manufacturing and commercial interests through modest constitutional reform than to drive the middle classes into a far more dangerous coalition with the working classes. In this the First Reform Bill of 1832 was wholly successful. Aristocrats retained a large measure of political influence, but they lost their monopoly over economic policy. Free trade prevailed. Protectionism died. And the new capitalist classes were as committed to the reformed constitution of 1832 as the gentry had been to its antecedent. With one-seventh of the adult male population selecting the next seven Parliaments, Britain continued to enjoy limited, stable democracy.

Under Gladstone's financial leadership, Britain continued to enjoy high rates of economic growth. Growing prosperity among skilled workers, buttressed by utilitarian intellectual currents, pushed Parliament into another round of constitutional reform. This time the Lords put up no resistance, and Parliament accommodated the working-class population in the Second Reform Bill of 1867. In turn, a greatly enlarged electorate forced political parties to develop techniques of organization. Cliques, factions, and family connections fell to well-oiled party machines. Electoral success became the prime goal of political activity.

The Third Reform Bill of 1884 completed the task of constitutional change. Monarch and Lords ceased to exercise any real influence. A Parliament chosen by the entire adult male population was now restrained largely by public opinion, custom, and limited budgetary resources. Elections to bring a new party to power became the ultimate political lever on the decisions of Parliament.

In 1800 the British economy reflected mercantilist ideas and was smothered under a yoke of wartime taxation. Peace and the growing influence of manufacturing brought free trade, low taxes, less public spending, deregulation of the economy, and the first major constitutional reform in 150 years. In the mid-nineteenth century, economic policy reflected the dominance of commercial and manufacturing interests. Repeal of the Corn Laws once and for all signalled a tolling of the bells for England's aristocracy.

But the new middle class could not sustain its monopoly position in British politics. Rapid economic growth yielded a new political class—the workers and their intellectual allies. As the Second and Third Reform Bills took hold, several million new voters, without property or the burden of income taxes, traded their support for new social programs. Modest at first, social spending grew unabated until the twentieth-century British economy looked very much like its mercantilist predecessor two centuries earlier. Economic freedom was aided and abetted by an initial limited expansion of the franchise; it was severely curtailed with complete suffrage.

Croker warned in 1832 of the perils of reform. Once set in motion, the forces of democratization would do in the traditional constitution. Lowe, too, some thirty-five years later feared that socialism would follow if workers were given the vote. It is tempting to contemplate how the British economy might have fared had Britain's Constitution froze after 1832. Tempting, yes, but irrelevant and unrealistic. It may well be that a limited constitutional democracy is inherently unstable.

Notes

1. Unless otherwise cited or referenced, the bulk of this chapter is drawn largely from Asa Briggs, *The Age of Improvement 1783-1867* (New York: McKay, 1959), pp. 75-117, 207-68, 312-25, and 489-514.
2. Sir William Blackstone, *Commentaries on the Laws of England* (1787 edition), pp. 154-55, quoted in Asa Briggs, *Age of Improvement*, p. 90.
3. Asa Briggs, *Age of Improvement*, p. 102.
4. *The Croker Papers*, vol. 2, p. 113, cited in Briggs, *Age of Improvement*, p. 242.
5. For a bill to become law in the British Parliament, it must pass through three readings. Its introduction by any member constitutes the first reading, but no

action or debate is scheduled on the bill at that time. Later, on the second reading, a vote is taken. Then the bill enters what is known as the "committee stage," where it undergoes final modification. If approved on the third reading, it is sent to the House of Lords for a similar procedure. When approved by both Commons and Lords, it receives royal assent and thus becomes the law of the land.

6. Asa Briggs, *Age of Improvement*, p. 259.
7. G. Kitson-Clark, *The Making of Victorian England* (Cambridge: Harvard University Press, 1962), p. 49.
8. Asa Briggs, *Age of Improvement*, p. 500.
9. Sydney Buxton, *Finance and Politics: An Historical Study. 1783-1885*, vol. 2 (London: John Murray, 1888), p. 11.
10. Walter Bagehot, *The English Constitution*, 2nd ed., reprint (Garden City, N. Y.: Dolphin [Doubleday]), p. 15.
11. Ibid., p. 21.
12. Ibid., pp. 20-21.
13. S.G. Checkland, *The Rise of Industrial Society in England 1815-1885* (New York: St. Martin's Press, 1964), p. 290.

7

Economic Growth and Individual Prosperity

In his book on British economic history, Professor J.D. Chambers described Britain from 1820 to 1880 as *The Workshop of the World*.[1] In 1820 Britain was changing from a primarily agricultural and commercial economy to a modern industrial state. Production shifted from supplying the domestic market to serving international buyers. Capital, entrepreneurship, and labor all came from internal sources. Britain did not depend, as do so many current poor countries, on outside aid or investment.

A few physical comparisons between 1815 and 1885 show the magnitude of the changes which had taken place.[2]

	1815	1885
Raw Cotton Imports	81 million lbs.	1,298 million lbs.
Raw Wool Imports	7.5 million lbs.	505 million lbs.
Pig Iron Output	.243 million tons	7.4 million tons
Coal Output	13 million tons	159.4 million tons
Railways	—	16,594 miles
Steamships	—	3.9 million tons
Population (England and Wales)	10 million	26.0 million

Gains in trade and output by 1885 were no simple multiple of the economy's performance in 1815. Within seven decades, output rose by multiples of tenfold to fiftyfold, depending on the commodity in question. Britain literally dominated the world's coal, steel, wool, and cotton markets, to name a few. London was the center of the world's financial markets. Britain's overseas investments played a major role in the economic development of numerous countries in the Americas, Africa, and Asia. British engineering and labor were exported all over the world. A small population living on a small island generated wealth and a standard of living that was inconceivable to earlier

111

generations of Europeans. For the first time in world history, working men and farm laborers enjoyed a wide range of goods and services that had been available only to the very rich a short time before.

During the nineteenth century, Great Britain's national income increased sevenfold. Moreover, the index of wholesale commodity prices fell by 57 percent. Expressed in terms of purchasing power, Britain's national income in 1901 was sixteen times that of 1801. Table 7.1 shows this rise in national product together with changes in the Wholesale Commodity Price Index. It also shows an especially sharp rise of 37 percent in gross national income between 1861 and 1871 (prices were virtually constant over the decade). This was the period of Gladstone's final tax and spending reforms.

Output per capita rose markedly throughout the 1800s, from £12.9 in 1801 to £52.5 in 1901 (figures expressed in constant prices). Output per capita rose almost fourfold, more than doubling in the last third of the century. These economic gains were made possible by an enormous increase in capital investment.

The economic structure underwent considerable change during the century as Britain shifted from an agricultural and trading country to the world's leading exporter of manufactured goods. During the 1850s and 1860s, for example, 80 percent of all British exports consisted of manufactured goods, of which textiles comprised the largest share.[3]

Table 7.1
Gross National Product in Great Britain, 1801–1901

Year	National Product (£ million) (current pounds)	Wholesale Commodity Price Index (1930 = 100.0)
1801	232	168.2
1811	301	157.1
1821	291	107.7
1831	340	102.9
1841	452	105.5
1851	523	77.3
1861	668	101.0
1871	917	103.1
1881	1,051	87.6
1891	1,288	74.2
1901	1,643	72.2

Sources: For national income, see Phyllis Deane and W.A. Cole, *British Economic Growth, 1688–1955* (Cambridge: Cambridge University Press, 1962); for the wholesale commodity price index, see Roy Jastram, *The Golden Constant* (New York: Wiley, 1977).

We can credit the movement to free trade with dramatic gains in foreign trade. Compound rates of growth in international trade in the eighteenth century, when royally chartered trade monopolies were prevalent, hovered just above 1 percent, reaching 2 percent per year in selected brief periods.[4] But as Huskisson, Peel, and Gladstone made free trade a reality, foreign trade grew at an annual average of 4.5 percent from 1821 through 1871—more than triple the preceding century's annual rate. This rate of annual increase over such a long period translates into dramatic results: Total gain from trade doubled from 1842 to 1858, doubled again by 1866, and yet again by 1871.[5] At this juncture, the growth rate slowed and foreign trade did not double again until 1900. In full perspective, total gain from foreign trade grew more than twentyfold between 1815 and 1900, a spectacular vindication of the free traders.

Rate of Growth of International Trade
(expressed in three-decade average)

1801–1831	2.7%
1811–1841	3.4
1821–1851	4.4
1831–1861	4.5
1841–1871	4.6
1851–1881	4.1
1861–1891	3.4
1870–1900	2.9

This robust expansion of foreign trade immediately followed sharp cuts in the customs rates and the abolition of protective tariffs. After Peel's two tariff revisions, the average customs rate (the annual net customs revenue as a percentage of net import values) fell from 35 percent in 1842 to 24 percent in 1850, to 13 percent in 1860, and, after Gladstone's final sweep of the tariff net, to about 8 percent in 1870. It hit a low average rate of 5 percent at century's end.[6]

Net revenue from customs held firm. As customs rates were reduced, the volume of imports rose quickly. Per capita tea and sugar consumption doubled between 1842 and 1857, four times the rate of population growth. Tax cuts, which led to improvements in trade and consumption, permitted more tax cuts. A broadened tax base at lower tax rates kept revenue remarkably constant.[7] Of course, the government did its part through legislating annual tax reductions rather than being tempted into higher levels of spending by higher receipts.

Year	Customs Revenues (£ millions)	Value of Imports (£ millions)
1841–1845	22.9	71.0
1846–1850	22.2	87.7
1851–1855	22.2	116.4
1856–1860	23.7	158.0
1861–1865	23.1	201.2
1866–1870	22.0	246.0
1871–1875	20.2	301.8
1876–1880	19.8	325.9
1881–1885	19.7	336.5
1886–1890	20.0	327.4
1891–1895	19.8	357.1
1896–1900	22.1	413.3

Tariff reduction encouraged import and export growth. Even more impressive was the growth in Britain's reexport trade: the island was, in effect, a great free port where British merchants could reexport on a worldwide duty-free basis. A national free port afforded much greater latitude than the previous system of bonded warehouses and drawbacks on duties paid for reshipment throughout the imperial/colonial trade routes. By 1873 the value of reexports had risen 564 percent over that of 1842, an average annual rate of growth of 18 percent, compared with 14 and 12 percent, respectively, for exports and imports.[8]

Taking all these figures together, the importance of rapidly expanding foreign trade in Britain's overall economic growth can be readily discerned. By 1881, for example, the net value of imports was equal to nearly one-third of the total national product; just four decades earlier, the corresponding figure was about one-sixth. Thus foreign trade propelled economic growth and vindicated the beliefs of both Peel and Gladstone.

Throughout this period of rapid growth in foreign trade, the balance of payments steadily improved, despite substantial deficits in the balance of visible merchandise trade, as seen in Table 7.2. An overall net surplus on the balance of payments led to an outflow of capital that took on explosive dimensions during Gladstone's stay at the Exchequer. The total balance of credit accummulated abroad rose more than 230 times from 1815 to 1900 (see figures below).[9] Thus earnings from foreign assets financed the visible deficit on merchandise trade; at the same time, invisible earnings from shipping, insurance, and commissions grew.

Table 7.2
Balance of Payments of the United Kingdom, 1816–1900
(annual averages in £ million)

Year	Balance of visible trade	Net shipping earnings	Profits, interest, dividends	Insurance brokerage, commissions	Emigrants, tourists, smugglers, government, all others	Balance of invisible trade	Net balance
1816–1820	− 11	+ 10	+ 8	+ 3	− 3	+ 18	+ 7
1821–1825	− 8	+ 9	+ 9	+ 2	− 2	+ 18	+ 10
1826–1830	− 15	+ 8	+ 9	+ 2	− 3	+ 17	+ 3
1831–1835	− 13	+ 5	+ 11	+ 3	− 4	+ 19	+ 6
1836–1840	− 23	+ 11	+ 15	+ 4	− 4	+ 26	+ 3
1841–1845	− 19	+ 12	+ 15	+ 4	− 5	+ 25	+ 6
1846–1850	− 26	+ 14	+ 18	+ 4	− 6	+ 30	+ 5
1851–1855	− 33	+ 19	+ 24	+ 6	− 8	+ 41	+ 8
1856–1860	− 34	+ 26	+ 33	+ 8	− 8	+ 60	+ 26
1861–1865	− 59	+ 34	+ 44	+ 11	− 8	+ 81	+ 22
1866–1870	− 65	+ 45	+ 57	+ 13	− 9	+ 106	+ 41
1871–1875	− 64	+ 51	+ 83	+ 16	− 12	+ 139	+ 75
1876–1880	− 124	+ 54	+ 88	+ 16	− 9	+ 149	+ 25
1881–1885	− 99	+ 60	+ 96	+ 16	− 11	+ 161	+ 61
1886–1890	− 89	+ 57	+ 115	+ 15	− 11	+ 177	+ 88
1891–1895	− 134	+ 57	+ 124	+ 15	− 10	+ 186	+ 52
1896–1900	− 159	+ 62	+ 132	+ 16	− 11	+ 199	+ 40

Source: Albert H. Imlah, *Economic Elements in the Pax Brittanica. Studies in British Foreign Trade in the Nineteenth Century* (Cambridge: Harvard University Press, 1958), pp. 70–75, summarized in Phyllis Deane and W. A. Cole, *British Economic Growth 1688–1959*, 2nd ed. (Cambridge: Cambridge University Press, 1969), p. 36.

Total British Foreign Investment
(£ million)

Year	Amount	Year	Amount
1817	25	1862	394
1822	60	1867	523
1827	100	1872	764
1832	113	1877	1,088
1837	148	1882	1,255
1842	157	1887	1,576
1847	193	1892	2,005
1852	218	1897	2,252
1857	270	1902	2,431

In the era 1842 through 1873, the British exported £787 million of new capital which was added to a large sum already placed abroad.[10] This sum alone is equal to five times the amount of total foreign investment accumulated through 1842. Thus the dramatic improvement in the balance of payments clearly starts with the advent of the liberal trade policy under Peel.

Noble deliciously revels in the performance of the British economy during Gladstone's seven years at the Exchequer.[11] From 1859 to 1866, cargoes cleared for export rose from 10 to 14 million tons, for import from 9 to 13 million. Total individual income-tax assessments jumped from £328 million to £423 million.

The general population shared in the nation's rising prosperity as seen in the consumption of basic foodstuffs. Per capita consumption of butter rose from 1.66 pounds to 4.36; cheese from 1.56 pounds to 4.32; and the number of eggs from 5 to 15. Falling duties propelled overall food imports from £48 million to £80 million.

The Standard of Living

The trends in wages and working-class standards of living in the nineteenth century have sparked controversy among economic historians. An abundance of labor kept money wages slack until 1850. But a substantial fall in retail prices from 1815 to 1850 meant that the same level of wages bought more for those who were employed.

The picture changed dramatically after 1850. Figure 7.1 reveals the relationship between money wages and retail prices from 1790 through 1910.[12]

Figure 7.1
Wages and Prices
1790–1910

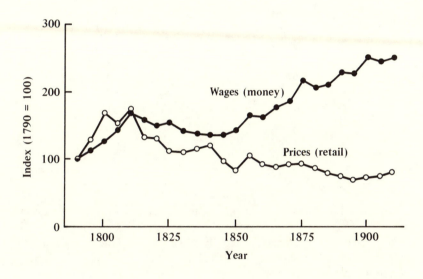

Source: C.R. Fay, *Great Britain from Adam Smith to the Present Day:*
An Economic and Social Survey (New York: Longmans, Green,
1928), p. 397.

During the second half of the nineteenth century, wages rose sharply and
prices fell gradually. Taken together, real per capita income (real purchasing
power after taking price changes into effect) nearly doubled. Note especially
the takeoff in Gladstone's era, despite the harmful impact of the American
Civil War and three successive bad harvests. To repeat, the standard of living
of the working classes doubled in the second half of the nineteenth century.

Combining the two plots in Figure 7.1 into one set of numbers provides
an index of real wages during the second half of the nineteenth century.

Real Wages, 1850–1906
(1850 = 100)

Year	Index of Wages
1850	100
1855	94
1860	105
1866	117
1871	125
1874	136
1877	132
1880	132
1883	142
1886	142
1891	166
1896	177
1900	184
1906	194

A.L. Bowley published the most extensive estimates of British wages and income. His tabulations encompass a broad range of occupations and retail price movements. For example, hourly wage rates in London rose steadily between 1860 and 1900 (see figures below) as the hours worked fell by 11 percent from fifty-six per week to fifty per week at the end of this forty-year period.[13] With prices falling 28 percent during the last four decades of the century (see Table 7.1), real purchasing power rose even more sharply than money wage increases indicate.

Hourly Rates in London (in pence)

Year	Bricklayer	Laborer
1861–64	7.0d.	4.5d.
1865	7.5	4.5
1866	8.0	4.5
1867	8.0	4.75
1872	8.5	5.25
1873–87	9.0	5.75
1888–92	9.0	6.0
1893–95	9.5	6.5
1896	10.0	6.5
1897–99	10.0	7.0

Across a whole range of trades, wages rose from no less than 25 percent to as much as 100 percent.[14] As the figures that follow show, cotton workers doubled their money wages between 1840 and 1891; other groups enjoyed somewhat less rapid increases; and for others such as wool and agricultural workers, wages peaked in the 1870s and then fell to century's end.

Average Money Wages
(Index 1891 = 100)

	1840	1850	1860	1866	1870	1874	1877	1880	1883	1886	1891
Cotton	50	54	64	74	74	90	90	85	90	93	100
Wool	74	79	87	92	97	105	114	110	105	100	100
Building	66	69	78	980	90	98	100	98	98	98	100
Mining	61	59	68	74	72	100	75	70	75	71	100
Iron	77	76	80	87	90	103	97	94	100	96	100
Sailors	61	59	70	79	72	90	86	71	82	77	100
Compositors	79	80	83	86	94	95	96	96	97	97	100
Agriculture	75	71	87	90	92	110	112	104	100	94	100

Bowley estimates that per capita income in 1880 stood at £31.5 and rose one-third to just over £40 by 1900.[15] In 1876, incomes under £150 were tax free, and incomes between £150 and £400 enjoyed a tax-free exemption of £120. The full tax fell only on incomes exceeding £400. In 1894 the bottom threshold was raised to £160. Thus, the overwhelming majority of British wage earners paid no income tax at all. All gains in wages were fully convertible into real purchasing power.

The distribution of income in Britain, largely through market forces, showed proportionately higher gains in the lower income groups. Between 1860 and 1880, for example, the weekly income of heads of households in the lowest quartile rose 38 percent, from 13s. 6d. to 21s. 4d.; by contrast, that in the upper quartile rose only 16 percent, from 27s. 6d. to 32s.[16] Thus rapid economic growth on a low tax base proportionately increased incomes more rapidly for lower income households than for upper income households, especially since lower income households paid no income taxes.

What brought about this remarkable improvement in living standards? Historian W.W. Rostow cites large capital investments, great plant expansion, cheaper sources of raw materials, a steady flow of technical innovation, and competitive forces in the marketplace, as jointly creating a regime of almost steadily falling retail prices. Since the labor supply remained stable, wage rates rose. Wealth was thus redistributed favorably to labor as the result of market forces.[17] Repeal of the Corn Laws admitted low-priced grain from abroad duty-free into the British home market. "The greatest importance [to the rise in living standards from 1873 to 1896] must, however, be attached to the importation of cheap food, if only because it represented so high a proportion of every working man's expenditure."[18]

The period encompassing the free-trade reforms of Peel and Gladstone show the beneficial effects of low duties, falling retail prices, and rising money wages on the average Englishman's consumption of basic foodstuffs. The following table shows the increased consumption per head of *imported* food.[19]

Consumption Per Head of Different Food Articles

		1840	1865	1873
Wheat & Wheat Flour	lbs.	42.47	93.08	170.79
Bacon and Hams	lbs.	0.01	2.67	9.07
Butter	lbs.	1.05	4.02	4.39
Cheese	lbs.	0.92	3.17	4.69
Cocoa	lbs.	0.08	0.13	0.26
Coffee	lbs.	1.08	1.02	0.99
Currants and Raisins	lbs.	1.45	4.12	4.29
Eggs	no.	3.63	12.23	20.56
Potatoes	lbs.	0.01	3.04	26.17
Rice	lbs.	0.90	2.05	11.37
Sugar, Raw	lbs.	15.20	37.05	43.96
Sugar, Refined	lbs.	—	2.73	7.63
Tea	lbs.	1.22	3.29	4.11

Noble can scarcely restrain his enthusiam for the benefits of fiscal reform.

From whatever point of view the subject is examined the result is the same; extensive remissions of taxation have been attended by a corresponding increase in the revenue; the foreign trade of the United Kingdom has assumed proportions truly marvellous; vast additions to our food supply, collected from all parts of the globe, testify to the increased prosperity of the great mass of the population; real property of every description has been largely augmented in value; capital has grown to such an extent that it constantly overflows the boundaries of this country and seeks channels for investment in our own colonies and foreign states; our mercantile marine equals that of all other countries combined; and our colonies have become more prosperous and more thoroughly attached to the mother country. The progress of this prosperity, traced step by step, shows that it is owing, not to the fostering care of the legislature, but to the fact, that legislative interference with trade and industry has been, to a very large extent, abandoned.[20]

It is ironic that the most glowing description of the results of Britain's economic progress in the 100 years following the conclusion of the Napoleonic War flowed from the pen of John Maynard Keynes, whose later work was to provide the intellectual justification for large-scale government programs of taxing, spending, and regulation. In his 1920 book titled *The Economic Consequences of the Peace*, Keynes provided a glowing portrait of British economic life before World War I, attributable to a century of successful economic growth.

> What an extraordinary episode in the economic progress of man that age was which came to an end in August, 1914! The greater part of the population, it is true, worked hard and lived at a low standard of comfort, yet were, to all appearances, reasonably contented with this lot. But escape was possible, for any man of capacity or character at all exceeding the average, into the middle and upper classes, for whom life offered, at a low cost and with the least trouble, conveniences, comforts, and amenities beyond the compass of the richest and most powerful monarchs of other ages. The inhabitant of London could order by telephone, sipping his morning tea in bed, the various products of the whole earth, in such quantity as he might see fit, and reasonably expect their early delivery upon his doorstep; he could at the same moment and by the same means adventure his wealth in the natural resources and new enterprises of any quarter of the world, and share, without exertion or even trouble, in their prospective fruits and advantages; or he could decide to couple the security of his fortunes with the good faith of the townspeople of any substantial municipality in any continent that fancy or information might recommend. He could secure forthwith, if he wished it, cheap and comfortable means of transit to any country or climate without passport or other formality, could despatch his servant to the neighboring office of a bank for such supply of the precious metals as might seem convenient, and could then proceed abroad to foreign quarters, without knowledge of their religion, language, or customs, bearing coined wealth upon his person, and would consider himself greatly aggrieved and much surprised at the least interference. But, most important of all, he regarded this state of affairs as normal, certain, and permanent, except in the direction of further improvement, and any deviation from it as aberrant, scandalous, and avoidable. The projects and politics of militarism and imperialism, of racial and cultural rivalries, of monopolies, restrictions, and exclusion, which were to play the serpent to this paradise, were little more than the amusements of his daily newspaper, and appeared to exercise almost no influence at all on the ordinary course of social and economic life, the internationalization of which was nearly complete in practice.[21]

Notes

1. J.D. Chambers, *The Workshop of the World* (London: Oxford University Press, 1961).
2. S.G. Checkland, *The Rise of Industrial Society in England, 1815-1885* (New York: St. Martin's Press, 1964), p. 6.

3. R.A. Church, *The Great Victorian Boom 1850-1873* (London: Macmillan, 1975), pp. 57-58.
4. Albert H. Imlah, *Economic Elements in the Pax Britannica. Studies in British Foreign Trade in the Nineteenth Century* (Cambridge: Harvard University Press, 1958), summarized in Phyllis Deane and W.A. Cole, *British Economic Growth 1688-1959*, 2nd ed. (Cambridge: Cambridge University Press, 1969), Table 8, p. 29.
5. Albert H. Imlah, *Economic Elements*, p. 113. Arthur L. Bowley also summarized these changes: "On closer inspection it is seen that the growth is naturally divided into four periods: from 1800 to 1826, when trade is almost stagnant; from 1826 to 1846, when imports increased at the continued rate of 3.5 percent per annum; from 1846 to 1872, when trade progressed at an enormous rate, imports increasing nearly fourfold in twenty-six years or at the rate of 6.1 percent per annum; . . ." See his book *A Short Account of England's Foreign Trade in the Nineteenth Century: Its Economic and Social Results* (London: Sonnenschein, 1893), p. 38.
6. Albert H. Imlah, *Economic Elements*, p. 159.
7. Ibid., p. 160.
8. Ibid., p. 169.
9. Ibid., p. 180.
10. Ibid., p. 178.
11. John Noble, *National Finance: A Review of the Policy of the Last Two Parliaments, and of the Results of Modern Fiscal Legislation* (London: Longmans, Green, 1875), pp. 29-32.
12. Figure 7.1 is sketched from a combination of four wage rates and the retail prices index series. The wages curve is from the research of G.H. Wood, published in the *Economic Journal* of 1899 (p. 591) and the *Journal of the Royal Statistical Society* of 1909 (p. 103). The curve of prices is based, up to 1850, on an index number of the cost of living constructed by N.J. Silverling and published in the Harvard Economic series in October 1923 (supplement to the *Review of Economic Statistics*) and after 1850 on the retail price index published by G.H. Wood in the *Journal of the Royal Statistical Society* of 1909 (p. 103). The halves of the curves which have been fitted together are not strictly comparable, but the differences would not greatly influence the shape of the curves. Every fifth year is recorded, with the intermediate fluctuations being ignored. See C.R. Fay, *Great Britain from Adam Smith to the Present Day: An Economic and Social Survey* (New York: Longmans, Green, 1928), p. 396.
13. Arthur L. Bowley, *Wages and Income in the United Kingdom Since 1860* (Cambridge: Cambridge University Press, 1937), p. 10.
14. Ibid., Appendix I, p. 130.
15. Ibid., p. 94.
16. Ibid., p. 46.
17. W.W. Rostow, *British Economy of the Nineteenth Century* (Oxford: Clarendon, 1948), pp. 88-89, 97.
18. Richard Tames, *Economy and Society in Nineteenth-Century Britain* (London: Allen & Unwin, 1972), p. 101.
19. John Noble, *National Finance*, p. 192.
20. Ibid., p. 224.
21. John Maynard Keynes, *The Economic Consequences of the Peace* (New York: Harcourt, Brace and Howe, 1920), pp. 10-12.

PART II

THE MIRACLE ECONOMIES
OF ASIA

8

Hong Kong: A Study in Economic Freedom

In the postwar period, many new nations, often referred to as developing countries, faced the task of transforming their poor, traditional economies into modern industrial societies. Most of these newly-independent, developing countries actively sought foreign aid. They also disproportionately followed a strategy for economic development that is state-directed and state-led. The extent of government involvement in each country's economic development has ranged from a virtual command economy to one in which government does not manage all economic activity but does assume responsibility for major capital investments and overall economic planning. This latter approach often consists of high taxation in the interests of government-directed capital formation and the prevention of inequitable distribution of wealth and income that supposedly occurs as a country develops. Governments adopting this strategy typically impose foreign exchange controls, limitations on overseas investment or ownership, high tariffs, state control of businesses, and other restrictions on the free exchange of goods and services. In the past few years, the results of this developmental strategy have disappointed both its intellectual proponents and the inhabitants of the developing countries, who are still mired in poverty with little hope for a better future.

Taking stock, we can sift through a substantial body of evidence for the successes and failures of different economies among the postwar developing countries. For example, by looking at such indicators as economic growth, real wages, productivity, per capita income, and the distribution of national income, it is becoming increasingly clear that the market economies are faring best. In Asia such economies include those of Hong Kong, Singapore, Taiwan, Korea, Malaysia, Thailand, and, recently, Sri Lanka. As a measure of the extent to which market-oriented strategies are coming into vogue, even the Peoples' Republic of China established duty-free export processing zones (copied from Taiwan and South Korea), authorized joint ownership with foreign business firms, and now offers other incentives to foreign and domestic business enterprises.

Perhaps the single best example of the market-economy model is the incredibly successful record of Hong Kong, a story of economic achievement from a starting point of almost zero.[1] Hong Kong overcame as many obstacles as any nation has ever faced and received virtually no foreign aid in the process. Its land area has almost no resources and consists largely of unproductive granitic rock formations. It suffers a population density that ranks it among the world's most overpopulated areas per square mile, and it is dependent on imports for its food, raw materials and all capital equipment. Located thousands of miles away from its most important markets, Hong Kong has been unable to control population movements across its borders; and it is ruled by a colonial government that critics regard as obsolete, antiquated, and inconsistent with the principles of independence, self-rule, and human dignity.

Thus the application of liberal economic policies in nineteenth-century Britain was not a uniquely successful historical event. The principles on which Britain flourished brought Adam Smith into the twentieth century as well. From a starting point of almost zero, several Asian countries have grown so rapidly that they are no longer considered part of the "developing" world. Low taxes, a minimum of government interference by government in private and business affairs, and responsible economic policies brought dramatic economic growth and a sharp reduction in poverty. These modern economic miracles vindicate Adam Smith more than two centuries after publication of *The Wealth of Nations*.

Despite these formidable obstacles, the rate of growth of the Hong Kong economy has been so rapid for so long that it has come to have an almost certain inevitability, despite a steady population growth of penniless refugees arriving daily by land or by sea.

The performance of the economy over the last thirty years owes much to a minimum of interference with the free play of market forces. A maximum tax rate of 15 percent on earnings and profits does not dampen the incentive to work and get ahead. The absence of tariffs and other trade restrictions, including capital movements, makes investment in Hong Kong very attractive. The result has been a rapidly improving standard of living for Hong Kong's largely Chinese population, and the continued inflow of new immigrants seeking opportunity and betterment for themselves.

The Colony and Its People

The British Crown Colony of Hong Kong lies inside the tropics on the southeast coast of China, adjoining the province of Kwangtung.[2] It consists of a small part of the Chinese mainland and a scattering of offshore islands, the most important of which is Hong Kong Island. Including reclamations through 1980, the total land area of the colony is 409.3 square miles; Hong Kong Island together with a number of small adjacent islands comprise 29.2 square miles. Kowloon and Stonecutter's Island comprise another 4.3 square miles. The New Territories, which consist of part of the mainland and more than 230 offshore islands, have a total area of 375.8 square miles.

Of the 409.3 square miles in the colony, 9.4 percent is used for farming; 74.9 percent is marginal unproductive land. Within the remaining 15.7 percent (about 38.6 square miles) of built-up urban areas, most of Hong Kong's people live and work. Hong Kong is one of the most densely populated places in the world. But the overall density figure of 4,852 per square kilometer recorded at the end of 1980 includes a wide variety of densities in individual areas. Mong Kok, situated in Kowloon, is the most densely populated district with over 150,000 per square kilometer (or 400,000 per square mile). The overall metropolitan density is 25,406 per square kilometer, and for the New Territories it is 554.

Between five and six million people live within Hong Kong's 400 square miles. Of these, over 98 percent are Chinese on the basis of language and place of origin: of these, 57 percent were born and have lived their whole lives in Hong Kong; the other 43 percent is largely refugees and immigrants from other countries, mainly China.

Throughout its history Hong Kong has coped with political refugees. Several hundred thousand entered Hong Kong in the 1930s during the Sino-Japanese War. The Japanese forcibly deported large numbers of Chinese to China during the World War II occupation of Hong Kong in order to ease the local food problems. Four years of Japanese rule reduced the population of Hong Kong to about one-third of its prewar size of 1.8 million. After Hong Kong's liberation in 1945, the deported Chinese returned at a rate approaching one hundred thousand a month; by the end of 1947 the population had regained its prewar size. Another influx took place during the Chinese civil war of 1948 and 1949 when nearly a half million people, mainly from Kwangtung province, Shanghai, and other commercial centers, entered the colony. Another flood of persons crossed the border in 1962, and nearly a quarter of a million persons from China and Southeast Asia have entered the territory since 1979. Hong Kong authorities had little control over the arrival of new immigrants, which has made it very difficult to implement such social programs as housing, schools, and health in an orderly manner.

The small colony of Hong Kong almost entirely lacks natural resources. Its mineral wealth is negligible, consisting of a modest amount of iron ore, building stone, kaolin clay, graphite, lead, and wolfram. Most of the activity in the mining and quarrying industry concentrates on the production of building stone and sand. Only one-seventh of its land is arable; the colony cannot, therefore, feed itself and throughout most of its history has encountered difficulty in maintaining an adequate water supply. Almost all industrial materials and the vast majority of foodstuffs must be imported.

Hong Kong sits on the edge of an eroded mountain chain which extends along the south coast of China, consisting mainly of sedimentary and granitic rocks. The hilly topography restricts extensive agricultural activity. The shortage of land has always been one of Hong Kong's chief concerns. The island, upon its occupation by the British in 1841, had scarcely any flat land. Reporting on this condition, *The Times* (London), candidly remarked on 17 December 1844:

> The place has nothing to recommend it, if we except the excellent harbor. The site of the new town of Victoria . . . is most objectionable, there being scarcely level ground enough for the requisite buildings, and the high hills, which overhang the locality, shut out the southerly winds and render the place exceedingly hot, close and uncomfortable.[3]

The colony's masters undertook reclamation within ten years of its first occupation in 1841. Today Hong Kong is one huge construction site and the government literally moves mountains into the sea to create land for development. Small rural villages have been transformed into modern industrial towns in a few short years, housing and providing jobs for more than a million people.

Water shortages, as mentioned, have also posed severe difficulties. There are no rivers and only a few large streams in the colony. Satisfying the colony's water needs depends upon collecting and storing rainwater by systems of catchwaters and reservoirs, the bulk of which is located in the New Territories. This problem is complicated by the fact that the rainy season is concentrated in the five summer months from May to September; within these five months sufficient water must be caught to last throughout the winter.

Between 1841 and 1863, Hong Kong Island was served by wells and hillside streams; a similar mode supplied Kowloon from 1860 until 1910. But dependence on these sources proved risky and inadequate. Accordingly, since 1864, the Hong Kong government successively built more large reservoirs and signed an agreement with China to purchase up to one-third of its fresh water consumption.

Although the water needs now seem adequately provided for, Hong Kong still has an acute lack of suitable industrial sites and premises, with no local coal, oil, or other source of power. Nor is the colony's internal market sufficiently large to offer a solid base for economic expansion. In addition, no tariff wall or other protectionist device shields the growth of its flourishing industry from overseas competition.

An Economic History: 1841 to the Present

Hong Kong became a British possession in 1841 for the simple purpose of trade with China. Hong Kong prospered as an entrepôt free port, a mart and storehouse for goods in transit to Asia and the West. This entrepôt activity diminished after World War II when the transition to an industrial economy took place.

In keeping with Hong Kong's entrepôt character, the first industrial venture was shipbuilding and repairing. A number of ancillary industries were then established to cater to the seafaring trade: a large graving dock, sugar refinery, rope factory, and other service activities. Until World War I the colony was a number of enterprises linked with the operation of the port, with few cottage industries. Hong Kong became the headquarters of the major merchant houses trading in the Far East. As a clearing house of trade between the East and the rest of the world, it soon developed specialized associated services, such as banking, insurance, accountancy, and legal services. It also developed a gold market. After World War I, the area of the entrepôt trade grew to cover much of the Far East and Southeast Asia.

Manufacturing industries are the mainstay of Hong Kong's economy. The economy is dependent upon export-oriented light manufacturing industries and a myriad of servicing industries operating within a free-port, free-enterprise environment. Highly developed banking, insurance, and shipping systems created in the entrepôt era facilitated and promoted the manufacturing industries. In its free-port tradition, Hong Kong has no tariffs and few restrictions on the import of commercial goods.

Hong Kong's post-World War II transformation from a trading to an industrial economy was so dramatic that between 1938 and 1956 it successfully absorbed a doubling of its population. In the wake of the war, many of the factors that contribute to rapid industrial development were found in Hong Kong. The Communist revolution in China produced a massive influx of refugees; but, most importantly, it resulted in the Shanghainese capital and entrepreneurial skill moving to the safe haven of Hong Kong. Hong Kong's industrial revolution is thus attributable to the three resources brought with the Chinese political refugees: labor, new industrial techniques from the North, and new capital seeking employment and security. Additional circumstances favoring industrial investment included high adaptability and diligence of this labor force, a weak trade-union organization, the lack of legislation fixing minimum wages and limiting working hours, and extremely low taxes on business profits.

Since the end of World War II, Hong Kong enjoyed a steady pattern of remarkable economic growth.[4] In 1948, per capita income in Hong Kong stood at US$180. Hong Kong's postwar transformation from a British trading post to an industrial economy was so dramatic that by 1981 per capita income reached approximately US$5,000, a more than sevenfold increase in real terms. In the early stages of its industrialization, real gross domestic product grew about 7 percent per year from 1948 to 1960. From 1961 through 1981, real GDP rose 9 percent per year. These rates of growth more than doubled national income during each of the past two decades. Hong Kong enjoyed the world's highest economic growth rate, exceeding double digit levels in real terms, during the five years from 1976 through 1981. Exports rose steadily throughout the postwar period, increasing by 9.4 percent a year in real terms during the decade of the 1970s.

During the 1970s, productivity (measured by output per work-hour) increased 8 percent per year at the same time hours worked per worker fell 2 percent per year; thus Hong Kong's labor force produced more while working fewer hours. Since the oil-induced recession of 1974, the unemployment rate has fallen beneath 3 percent and the economy has worked at a full employment level despite an inflow of several hundred thousand immigrants and refugees in the past few years. From the late 1950s, real wages more than doubled, and have risen even more rapidly in the last half of the 1970s.

Capital formation (savings as a share of the gross domestic product) exceeded 20 percent throughout the 1960s and 1970s. Hong Kong's industrial transformation occurred without foreign aid or special concessions to overseas investors.

The Political Geography of Hong Kong

A combination of circumstances in Hong Kong brought prosperity without much internal pressure for the welfare state or much outside intervention which might have closed down this haven of economic freedom. How has this come about?

Hong Kong offers more than most residents in the colony could receive elsewhere. Refugees from mainland China found physical security and an opportunity for economic improvement. They do not clamor for more state intervention in their personal lives; many of them fled from an oppressive Communist government in order to obtain the freedom found in Hong Kong's noninterventionist society. The middle class has, on the whole, enjoyed prosperity in a booming private sector. Local and overseas investors benefit from the low taxes and economic freedom not found in other Asian countries.

In turn, a prosperous free-trading and financial center, populated largely by persons of Chinese origin who constitute a ready-made export market for the Chinese mainland, has served the economic interest of the Communist government in Peking. Finally, entrepreneurs from the United Kingdom and other countries benefit from commerce in Hong Kong. Let us examine this tripod of consent to a haven of economic freedom: Britain, China, and the local people.

The Mother Country

Hong Kong became a British possession in 1841 for the purpose of trade with China; it prospered as a free-port trading post because it offered security and freedom from interference with trade. The early inhabitants, especially the Chinese, had little interest in politics; the colonial government, mainly concerned with providing a framework within which trade could flourish, did little but maintain law and order and raise taxes to pay for the cost of the civil establishment and necessary public works.

Since the end of World War II, Her Majesty's Government has willingly, but on occasion reluctantly, guided her colonial territories through a process of self-government within the Commonwealth to ultimate independence. Local pressures on the British to hand over independence, a key element in this process, has been missing throughout the postwar period in Hong Kong. The overwhelming proportion of Hong Kong residents clearly prefers British colonial rule to that of China.

Hong Kong is not a captive market for British goods; almost all British goods compete in Hong Kong's free market with those of other countries. A number of benefits flow to Britain in the form of pensions paid to retired Hong Kong civil servants in Britain, dividends paid to British shareholders in Hong Kong firms, and payments for commercial facilities arranged through the city of London; but, these benefits do not make colonial rule profitable to Britain. Still, Britain has no compelling reason to withdraw since the local population favors the stability that colonial government provides in Hong Kong.

The Chinese Connection

The history of Hong Kong is a chronicle of rising and falling trends of trade and population in response to events taking place in China. Hong Kong's rapid population increase between 1945 and 1956, for instance, was largely due to a massive exodus of Chinese refugees who wanted freedom and asylum in Hong Kong. Similarly, industrialization resulted because of the inflow of a Chinese labor force and capital during the turbulence of 1949 and 1950.

Most of Hong Kong's territory is leased from China. The New Territories were signed over to Britain in 1898 on a ninety-nine-year lease. Earlier treaties ceded Hong Kong Island, Kowloon, and Stonecutter's Island to Britain in perpetuity, but these territories are not politically or economically viable as a separate unit. Without water and industry, which are located mainly in the New Territories, the foundation of Hong Kong's economic prosperity disappears.

The post-1949 Communist government in Peking renounced the "unequal treaties" that constitute Britain's claim to sovereignty in Hong Kong, clearly stating to the United Nations Special Committee on Colonialism and Decolonization that Hong Kong's political status is an internal Chinese matter; it is not in the category of colonial territories. China thus denounced both the New Territories lease and the earlier cessions of territory as invalid while acknowledging colonial authority in Hong Kong.

In August 1982, Peking announced that China intended to reclaim sovereignty over Hong Kong by 1997 when the New Territories' lease expires. Although the Chinese authorities promised that Hong Kong's free-wheeling economy would not be integrated into China's socialistic, state-directed system, the shattering of political confidence in Hong Kong's economic future sent the stock, property, and foreign exchange markets sharply downward. These losses concern Peking because China profits from its relationship with Hong Kong and wishes to maintain the prosperity of Hong Kong in order to assist its own internal economic modernization program. Hong Kong provides major economic benefits to China. China seeks foreign exchange. Since the mid-1960s, receipts from Hong Kong are believed to account for about 40 percent of China's total earnings of foreign exchange.

China supplies Hong Kong with about 20 percent of its imports, including a wide range of inexpensive consumer goods, oil products, food, and a substantial quantity of water. It buys little in return, leaving a huge balance-of-payments surplus which underwrites China's development policies. In addition, Hong Kong is the clearing house for remittances to China. Local and overseas companies and individuals remit to their relatives and business associates in China more than US$50 million a year. Another important aspect of the Chinese-Hong Kong trade is the colony's function as a redistribution center for Chinese-made goods. Hong Kong has the largest, deepest, most modern port facilities along China's coast. Several hundred million dollars worth of goods are annually exported through the port of Hong Kong for worldwide destinations.

Apart from these quantifiable economic benefits are the indirect, but very tangible, benefits that Hong Kong provides as a convenient center for trade contacts, financial negotiations, and access to Western technology.

The Local People

The colony's government operates with two constraints. One is the need for the continued support of British public and parliamentary opinion, and the other is the continued confidence of both local and overseas businessmen and bankers. Both props might collapse in the face of a restless and discontented population.

The vast majority of the people of Hong Kong are content with the British administration. The last twenty years witnessed only three serious outbreaks of rioting. The first riot in 1956 was a faction fight between Kuomintang and Communist supporters over the flying of Nationalist flags on 10 October, the Republic of China's national day. The second riot of April 1966 erupted from the Star Ferry's proposal to raise its first-class fare by five cents (one American penny); this was the only riot specifically directed at government policy. Finally, the 1967 disturbances were a spillover of the excesses of the Great Proletarian Cultural Revolution across the border; these riots ended when the Hong Kong police force, with China's encouragement, took stern measures.

Urban workers show little inclination to protest or even organize in legally permissible ways. Unions contain fewer than 14 percent of the economically active population and strikes are infrequent. Disinterest in union activity mirrors the broader pattern of political apathy. Approximately 400,000 persons were eligible to register for the voters' list in the March 1973 Urban Council elections—Hong Kong's only broadly-elected body—but only 31,384 did. Of these, only 8,765 voted—28 percent of the registered electorate and barely 2 percent of the eligible electorate. The upper strata of the Chinese population typically channel their activism into philanthropic or community associations, or seek to be nominated for public service on the colony's appointed councils, rather than into groups with a specifically political orientation.

Why is this colonial government so readily accepted, albeit apathetically? First a large proportion of Hong Kong residents, 43 percent, are not Hong Kong born; they are mostly Chinese refugees. Most refugees, seeking comfort and security, are predisposed to political quietism; they have little interest in any form of political agitation. Living in Hong Kong makes one present-oriented: few know how long Hong Kong will survive, and all know that the wishes of the local inhabitants will not figure prominently in Peking's deliberations.

Life in Hong Kong has been materially good. During the 1960s and 1970s the index of real wages more than doubled, and this prosperity attenuates potential discontent over colonial rule.

Finally, the Hong Kong government is exceptionally efficient. Nearly half the population lives in subsidized housing at below-market rents, and great strides have been made in the development of medical and health services: the infant mortality rate fell from 99.6 per 1,000 live births in 1950 to 11.8 in 1980. The last case of smallpox was reported over twenty years ago; cholera and tuberculosis have been virtually wiped out. Roads, communications, port facilities, water supply, and public utilities have also kept pace, all financed by revenue yields from a very low tax rate.

Since most Hong Kong residents presume that Hong Kong's future will be determined by ministers in Peking and London, there is little scope or point to local political activism. Rapid economic growth is what life in Hong Kong is really all about.

An Overview of Fiscal and Economic Policy

In spending only what it can afford, the Hong Kong government is, by worldwide standards, unique. Except for a small number of tropical paradise tax havens, no other government so intently holds expenditure within means. Its standard rate of tax on earnings and profits is the lowest in the industrial world, and its official government reserves are the largest in proportion to any year's expenditure.

The colony's present-day public finances stand in sharp contrast to countries in which overspending, deficit financing, extensive use of loan finance, governmental control over the economy, and political instability are the rule. Circumstances in Hong Kong reveal a different portrait of financial and economic life:

1. Balanced budgets;
2. Fiscal reserves, which have ranged from one-half to one year's expenditure;
3. Avoidance of public debt;
4. Governmental underspending;
5. A governmental economy ethic;
6. An aversion to central planning;
7. Commercial provision of public economic services; and
8. Minimum intervention in, or regulation of, the private sector.[5]

The incentives, constraints, and ideological commitments that encourage Hong Kong's unique fiscal and economic responsibility need to be examined. These include the historical precedents of financial administration in Hong Kong, the constitutional underpinnings of its practice, and the practice and philosophy of balanced budgets and nonintervention. It also includes the personalities and competence of Hong Kong's Financial Secretaries, the men who dominate the economic dimension of public life.

Hong Kong was a barren island with no large or established community entitled to political representation. It was established as a military, diplomatic, and trading station, not as a settlement in the normal sense. For these purposes, the British Secretary of State for War and the Colonies imposed firm imperial control on the new colony; self-government was not in Hong Kong's political cards.

Administrative absolutism meant, in practice, that the colonial government did little more than maintain law and order—and raise taxes to pay for the cost of the civil establishment and necessary public works. Parliament instructed Hong Kong's Governors to take from colonial resources all public expenditures except the salaries of only three principal officers in the colonial government. In 1855 Sir John Bowring, the Governor, happily announced that Hong Kong had reached the goal of complete self-support. Although future Governors occasionally asked for assistance from the home government, the doctrine and practice of self-support was entrenched in Hong Kong financial procedure.

Hong Kong, as a Crown Colony, was administered under colonial regulations. The regulations date back to 1837 and serve as "directions to Governors for general guidance given by the Crown through the Secretary of State for the Colonies," especially in financial and administrative matters. Governors and their officials were not free agents of the Secretary of State, who was empowered to fill all important vacancies in the colonial services, maintain disciplinary control over these appointments, and impose standards for strict financial discipline. In particular, the annual estimates (the budget) of each colony required his approval well before the beginning of the financial year. It was the responsibility of the Colonial Office to see that colonies did not run into debt and impose a charge on the British Treasury.

Colonial Office policy and the colonial regulations which applied to Hong Kong reflected the prevalent economic theories of nineteenth-century Britain which stressed the passive role of government in the economy. Private individuals and companies, not the government, were responsible for the creation of wealth. Although the British Treasury ceased its oversight of colonial expenditures after 1870, Colonial Office approval was typically required until the 1930s, when convention began to replace the letter of the regulations, and the budget estimates were no longer submitted to the Secretary of State before presentation to the local legislature. Of course, the Secretary could still use his powers of disallowance if he thought that a colony's spending plans would cause recourse to the Exchequer.

Until financial autonomy was granted to the Hong Kong government in 1958, the 1951 colonial regulations provided the formal background against which the financial authorities in Hong Kong worked. The guiding principle was that all colonies should aim to be self-supporting and contribute to the cost of their own defense. This lengthy set of regulations insured financial transparency—these regulations resemble the financial and accounting regulations under which the present Hong Kong government works.

Public finance in present-day Hong Kong is a direct offshoot of colonial tradition. Hong Kong continues to follow the pattern of colonial accounting practices because they are a good set of rules for financial integrity. Where they have been refined, it has nearly always been in the direction of increased transparency. The form and scope of the budget have changed little since the granting of financial autonomy in 1958 and still resemble the traditional colonial regulations. Also nineteenth-century values of economic liberalism still influence official thinking and practice in Hong Kong.

Constitutional and Administrative Framework

Hong Kong is not a representative democracy. Administrative and executive authority lie in the hands of appointed civil servants whose personnel, at the higher levels, are recruited chiefly from the United Kingdom. Through the early 1980s, neither periodic elections nor public opinion polls guided or constrained the administrative decisions of these appointed officials. Hong Kong political activity is not party competition, the quest for votes, popularity, high standing in the polls, a share of the "pork barrel," nor the public debate of social issues. It is rather day-to-day decision making by appointed officals, sometimes within the administration, often in consultation with one of a myriad of official advisory committees, or, on occasion, by openly soliciting the public's views.

Constitutional authority for making policy is concentrated in the Governor, assisted, in practice, by his Executive Council. The Governor's powers are defined by the *Letters Patent and Royal Instructions to the Governor of Hong Kong*. He is, as the representative of the monarch, the head of government and constitutionally accepts his instructions from the Secretary of State, although, in practice, instructions are rarely given. As chief executive, the Governor has the final responsibility for the administration of the colony. He makes laws by and with the advice and consent of the Legislative Council.

Historical precedent has shaped Hong Kong's economic and budgetary policies. The incentives and constraints that dictate contemporary practice derive, in the case of budgetary policy, from the letter and spirit of the colonial regulations—the emphasis on self-support and balanced budgets. In the case of economic policy, the free-port status of early Hong Kong discouraged an interventionist government—wealth creation resided in the private sector. Nonintervention and fiscal responsibility are still the cornerstones of modern administration which, in the presence of an increasingly restrictionist world beset with deficit budgets and growing public debts, must surely seem anachronistic.

Monetary Policy

Monetary policy was the most variable element in Hong Kong's postwar economic environment.[6] When Hong Kong went off the silver standard in

1935, it adopted a sterling exchange rate, which remained intact until 1972. In July 1972, the Hong Kong dollar was pegged to the US dollar at HK$5.65 to US$1; it stayed tied to the US dollar until November 1974. Hong Kong followed gold standard rules during this fixed exchange rate period: the domestic money supply was determined by the overall balance-of-payments situation. Between 1974 and October 1983 the Hong Kong dollar floated freely as a pure fiat currency. It no longer required foreign backing for the note issue. Money could be printed at will, although the government maintained external reserves which it could use to support the currency. In October 1983 the government refixed the exchange rate at HK$7.80 to US$1 and reimposed full external backing for all newly-issued currency. Uncertainty over Hong Kong's future in light of China's stated intention to recapture sovereignty in 1997 prompted a run on the Hong Kong dollar, which reached a low of HK$9.55 to US$1. Repegging the exchange rate quelled the monetary panic. During the 1960s, inflation averaged 2.4 percent annually; it rose sharply to an annual average of 12.9 percent between 1970 and 1981.

Under the floating-rate regime, there were no effective monetary devices available to the Hong Kong government to control the domestic money supply other than prevailing on local banks to raise domestic interest rates. The liquid assets requirement introduced in 1964 was easily circumvented by accepting a deposit from a foreign bank and redepositing the funds in the same bank: the Hong Kong branch's deposit counted as a liquid asset while the deposit from abroad was not subject to the liquidity requirement. Proponents of greater monetary stability in Hong Kong forcefully advocated either that the Exchange Fund specify a monetary target or an exchange-rate target.

Central banks often create money in the process of buying government debt. Since Hong Kong has no public debt, inflationary pressure arises from private demand for money, which is often fueled during speculative binges in the property and stock markets.

Curiously, Hong Kong's period of strongest economic growth, the industrial world's highest average annual rate between 1975 and 1980, occurred during a period of monetary instability. This observation suggests that one particular monetary system is neither necessary nor sufficient for growth, so long as the economy is free to adjust its internal cost/price structure to trade profitably in world markets and enjoys business confidence! Through its floating rate regime, Hong Kong's competitive internal prices had adjusted to world prices through appreciation or devaluation of its currency, rather than through an increase or reduction in the quantity of money, which, now in the presence of a restored fixed exchange rate regime, would spur or contract economic activity.

Economic Policy

Economic affairs in Hong Kong are conducted in an environment of free enterprise. Government policy long dictated a hands-off approach toward the private sector, an approach that is well suited to Hong Kong's exposed and dependent economic and political situation. The philosophy that underlies government in Hong Kong can be summed up in a few short phrases: law and order, minimum interference in private affairs, and the creation of an environment conducive to profitable investment. Regulatory economic controls are held to a minimum, no restrictions are placed on the movement of capital, little protection and few subsidies are given to industry, and the few direct services provided by government are operated on a commercial basis.

Capital Movements

Hong Kong is a completely free money market. No barriers restrict exchange between the Hong Kong dollar and other currencies. Hong Kong is thus a genuine financial haven—financial assets are easily transferable or convertible with minimum regulation or interference. Indeed, the ever-increasing funds that have been attracted to Hong Kong banks helped finance industrial development. These capital inflows were so substantial during the postwar period that Hong Kong is today a major financial center.

Subsidies

Except for land grants in the mid-1970s to land-intensive industries that inject new technology into the economy, and the segregation of industrial land to protect it from the competition of other land users, no protection or government assistance is given to manufacturing industries, utilities, service industries, or private citizens. No attempt is made to distort factor prices to favor any particular type of development. Market forces shape the economy, and industries that lobby for protection from competitive forces in the marketplace are fiercely resisted. Postwar Financial Secretaries resolutely opposed any system of subsidy that exempted any industry from paying the full costs of the resources it consumed. Each secretary also opposed subsidies for the well-to-do.

General Business Requirements

The Hong Kong government encourages the setting up of private business enterprise.[7] Government rigorously enforces the principle of free entry into almost every line of production. Legal formalities required to set up a business, even to establish a private company, are few and inexpensive. The business registration ordinance imposes an annual fee of HK$175, but very small businesses are exempted. For approximately US$30, one can lawfully open a business in Hong Kong.

Incorporation is also inexpensive: the fee is HK$300 plus $4 per $1,000 of authorized capital. Foreign corporations with branches in Hong Kong pay neither incorporation nor annual registration fees; their obligations are simply to file with the registrar of companies a copy of the company's charter, its by-laws, its annual financial statement, and the names of persons in Hong Kong who are authorized to receive notices served on the company.

Finally, anyone who opens a factory or industrial undertaking that employs more than twenty persons must, prior to registration, comply with fire service department safety standards and labor department standards for workers' safety. Approval is, in normal circumstances, routinely quick.

Hong Kong economic and tax policies do not discriminate between residents and non-residents. Thus, overseas investors may fully own local factories. At the end of 1980, overseas interests either fully or partly owned 460 factories. Overseas capital employed a total labor force of 87,000, or 10 percent of all workers in Hong Kong's manufacturing industries. United States firms have the largest single bloc of foreign investment, which overall accounts for about 15 percent of Hong Kong's exports.

Employment and Labor Unions

Hong Kong's remarkable productivity rests, in part, on its hard-working adaptable labor force. The Chinese worker is diligent; reinforcing this diligence is the fact that the real wages available in Hong Kong markedly improved the worker's standard of living and obviated any need for trade unions. Supply and demand for labor, not trade unions, determine wage rates.

Hong Kong labor is chiefly engaged in small enterprises. At the end of 1980, for example, only forty factories employed over 1,000 workers and only 1,500 employed 100 or more; conversely, 28,000 factories had fewer than forty-nine workers, of which 20,000 engaged less than ten.

Hong Kong does not impose a statutory minimum wage. Earnings of industrial workers fluctuate with overall economic activity, although it is customary to award each worker an extra month's salary at Chinese New Year. Loyalties to firms are less important than salary and fringe benefits; thus workers respond quickly and rationally to alternative opportunities. During an economic downturn, workers generally accept a reduction in hours rather than force lay-offs and "break the next man's rice bowl."

Labor legislation consists chiefly of the Factories and Industrial Undertakings Ordinance, the Employment Ordinance, and the Workmen's Compensation Ordinance. The first of these imposes no restrictions on the working hours of men aged eighteen and over in industry. Children and women, however, are restricted. Children under fifteen years of age are excluded from all employment. Women are permitted to work a maximum of six eight-hour days per week. All women and children aged sixteen to seventeen may work no more than 200 hours of overtime per year.

The Employment Ordinance governs terms of employment for all full-time manual labor and all nonmanual workers earning less than HK$2,000 per month. It provides ten annual statutory holidays, stipulates sick leave, maternity leave, and monthly rest day conditions (although an employee may work on his four monthly rest days), states the frequency, forms, and place of wage payments, and, finally, guarantees the right of any employee to join a trade union.

Last, the Workmen's Compensation Ordinance provides personal compensation from injury or death arising from work.

The labor force is generally content; this is seen in work interruption statistics. In 1980, for example, only thirty-seven work stoppages occurred with only 21,069 man-days of work lost from an annual total exceeding 200 million man-days (a fraction of 1/10,000). Investors do not have any serious problems with strikes, work stoppages, or worker grievances. They need only pay the market price for labor to hire the requisite staff.

Manufacturing and Finance

The counterpart of employment and trade unions is manufacturing. Among the ingredients which go into manufacturing, land is perhaps the most scarce, highly prized commodity in Hong Kong. All land in Hong Kong belongs to the British Crown, and freehold tenures, except for one historical exception, are never granted. A lease is typically given for seventy-five years, renewable for a further seventy-five years, for land on Hong Kong Island and the urban areas of Kowloon, south of Boundary Street. In the New Territories and in Kowloon north of Boundary Street, leases are written to expire on 27 June 1997, three days before the termination of the original 99-year lease that granted the New Territories to the Crown in 1898.

Government makes land available to private developers and industrialists through public auctions. Again, local and foreign residents are treated equally, and each may hold title to the lease. Land goes to the highest bidder. Building covenants, attached to land-sale conditions, require a specific minimum expenditure within a reasonable period of time. The covenant prevents any individual or company from acquiring enormous banks of undeveloped land.

Trade restrictions against Hong Kong are of greatest concern to manufacturers in the garment and textile industries. The flow of Hong Kong-made merchandise is controlled largely through foreign governments' imposition of quantitative restrictions and import duties. Hong Kong is a member of the General Agreement on Tariffs and Trade (GATT) and no longer accords preferential treatment to British and Commonwealth products. Both local and overseas exporters and importers receive equal treatment.

The most comprehensive restrictions confronting Hong Kong are the quantitative limitations imposed largely on its garments and textiles, the Multi-Fibre Agreement, which was created under the auspices of GATT. The bulk of Hong Kong's garment and textile exports to EEC countries and the United States are under export quota restrictions. These work as follows. Importing countries specify quantities of each category of textiles and garments annually acceptable; permissible growth rates in these quotas are about 6 percent a year. The quotas are then administered within Hong Kong by the Department of Commerce and Industry which dispenses quota allocations on a formula basis.

Within Hong Kong itself, trade formalities are few and inexpensive. As a duty-free port, Hong Kong allows the entry and exit of most raw materials, consumer goods, and commodities with only a registration charge. To raise revenues, duties are imposed only on liquors, manufactured tobacco, and hydrocarbon oils. A handful of items require import and export licenses issued by the Department of Commerce and Industry for reasons of health, safety, or security. Certificates of origin are granted to manufacturers to qualify goods made in Hong Kong for entry under quotas, for generalized scheme of preferences tariff rates, or for Commonwealth preferences. Cars are not subject to duties, but a first registration fee of 30 percent of their Hong Kong C.I.F. (customs, insurance, freight) value must be paid to the transport department.

Finally, rent control, which is provided on some classes of residential accommodation, does not cover office accommodation.

Hong Kong is today the world's third largest gold market, and is totally free of government restrictions. Daily gold turnover on the Chinese gold and silver exchange typically exceeds 350,000 ounces on an active day—more than the average daily volume on all U.S. gold markets.

Government Economic Services

What part does government play in the operation of the Hong Kong economy? Its philosophy is noninterventionist, and its reliance on the private sector and the market mechanism for national wealth extends even to public utilities and public transport: electricity, gas, telephone services, buses, ferries, and tramways are all in private hands, although they derive monopoly franchise rights under an ordinance that requires the provision of adequate services and governmental approval of fare increases. Government, however, intervenes in such areas as the provision of water, land ownership, public housing, operation of the airport and the railway, and regulates, in part, banking, rents for domestic premises, pollution emissions, labor conditions, the rice trade, fish marketing, and so forth.

Government's management style is that of self-support except, as in the case of such specific subsidies as housing, education, and income assistance to individuals, it has overriding social reasons not to do so. These social exceptions aside, government operates its economic services on a commercial basis. Once it is determined that a service is needed to achieve social or economic objectives, either because the services cannot be found in the private market or because these are common facilities that only the public sector can provide (e.g., water supplies), it conducts its affairs with minimum cost to the general taxpayer.

"One trouble is that when Government gets into a business it tends to make it uneconomic for anyone else."[8] This comment of Sir John Cowperthwaite, Financial Secretary from 1961 to 1971, is the heart of the government's economic policy: Hands off the private sector to avoid the risk of discouraging enterprise, and provision of government economic services, when required, on a commercial basis.

> For I still believe that, in the long run, the aggregate of the decisions of individual businessmen, exercising individual judgment in a free economy, even if often mistaken, is likely to do less harm than the centralized decisions of a Government; and certainly the harm is likely to be counteracted faster. . . .
>
> It has to be recognized, and it is recognized over a large part of our daily life, that the community's scarce economic resources *can be efficiently allocated only by the price mechanism*.[9] [emphasis added]

Budgetary Policy

The principles of self-support and balanced budgets in the colonial regulations applies equally to a financially-independent Hong Kong. The government follows a fiscal policy which avoids sustained or systematic deficits and, if possible, accumulates reserves; this policy permits sustained government expenditure over a long recession without serious cutbacks, and, in the process, earns interest to meet recurrent expenses. Except for a small deficit in the immediate postwar budget, Table 8.1 shows that there was a surplus in thirty-two of the last thiry-five years through 1982. Moreover, these surpluses are computed after charging against current revenue all capital expenditures other than a comparatively small amount financed by borrowing; government traditionally financed its entire public works program and other capital investments from recurrent revenue.

The August 1982 announcement from Peking that China intended to reclaim sovereignty by 1997 destroyed economic confidence, curtailed investment and business activity, and, as a result, had a devastating effect on the public finances. In the enormous budget surplus years of 1980-81 and 1981-82, land

Table 8.1
Revenue and Expenditure of the Hong Kong Government, 1946-1984
(HK$ million)

Financial Year	Revenue	Expenditure	Surplus (+) Deficit (−)
1946-47	82.1	85.6	− 3.5
1947-48	164.3	127.7	+ 36.6
1948-49	194.9	160.0	+ 35.0
1949-50	264.3	182.1	+ 82.1
1950-51	291.7	251.7	+ 40.0
1951-52	308.6	275.9	+ 32.7
1052-53	384.6	311.7	+ 72.8
1953-54	396.9	355.4	+ 41.5
1954-55	434.5	373.3	+ 61.1
1955-56	454.7	402.5	+ 52.3
1956-57	509.7	469.5	+ 40.1
1957-58	584.2	532.7	+ 51.5
1958-59	629.3	590.0	+ 39.4
1959-60	664.6	710.0	− 45.3
1960-61	859.2	845.3	+ 13.9
1961-62	1,030.4	953.2	+ 77.2
1962-63	1,253.1	1,113.3	+ 139.8
1963-64	1,393.9	1,295.4	+ 98.5
1964-65	1,518.3	1,440.5	+ 77.8
1965-66	1,631.7	1,769.1	− 137.4
1966-67	1,817.8	1,806.1	+ 11.7
1967-68	1,899.5	1,766.0	+ 133.5
1968-69	2,081.1	1,873.0	+ 208.1
1969-70	2,480.7	2,032.2	+ 448.5
1970-71	3,070.9	2,452.2	+ 618.7
1971-72	3,541.0	2,901.0	+ 640.0
1972-73	4,936.0	4,300.0	+ 636.0
1973-74	5,240.8	5,169.2	+ 71.6
1974-75	5,875.3	6,255.2	− 379.9
1975-76	6,519.5	6,032.2	+ 487.3
1976-77	7,493.5	6,590.9	+ 902.6
1977-78	10,232.6	8,996.9	+ 1,235.7
1978-79	12,557.0	11,090.1	+ 1,466.9
1979-80	16,796.1	13,872.3	+ 2,923.8
1980-81	30,290.3	23,593.5	+ 6,696.8
1981-82	34,312.9	27,778.2	+ 6,534.7
1982-83	30,900.0	34,776.2	− 3,876.2
1983-84 (estimate)	32,269.7	35,474.9	− 3,205.2

Source: *Supporting Financial Statements and Statistical Appendices from the Estimates of Revenue and Expenditure for the Year Ending 31st March 1984*. Appendix I (Hong Kong: Government Printer, 1984), p. 135.

lease sales generated 25 percent of the public revenue; in 1982-83, this source declined to a mere 6 percent, as land values fell precipitously. Although the government scaled down some of its ambitious public works and other spending programs, it was not possible to cut so many billions of dollars from the budget so quickly. Fortunately, the government covered successive multi-billion dollar deficits by drawing on its accumulated reserves from prior budget surpluses. It has reduced these deficits over a three-to-four year period by a mixture of modest tax increases and spending reductions. After all, the purpose of maintaining fiscal reserves was to provide resources to sustain public programs in the event of an economic downturn. Thus, recent deficits do not indicate a departure from budgetary prudence, but, rather, an adjustment in sharp revenue losses due to an external political shock.

Budgetary policy in Hong Kong is unique in industrial states. Where else can one find low taxes, budget surpluses, substantial government reserves, an absence of public debt, and a vast increase in public services?

Government Reserves

The Hong Kong government is surely unique among industrial states in that it possesses very large reserves, either deposited with the local commercial banking system or held overseas; these reserves have historically ranged from one-half to one year's recurrent and capital expenditures, although this fraction declined in recent years. Existence of these reserves is, in and of itself, anomalous to a world of chronic public debt and deficit financing.

Taxation

Hong Kong does not levy an overall income tax; instead it levies four separate direct taxes on profits, salaries, property, and interest. Until 1984, when direct tax rates rose 2 percent, the maximum tax rate on corporate profits was 16.5 percent and 15 percent on unincorporated business profits, after deducting all expenses incurred in producing chargeable profits. The salaries tax, which also rose 2 percent in 1984, is more complicated: the tax is imposed on a sliding-rate scale, ranging from a minimum of 5 percent on the first assessable HK$10,000 to 25 percent on taxable income exceeding HK$50,000. (At current exchange rates, HK$7.80 = US$1.00.) The income tax permits a very generous personal allowance. Also, the total tax due cannot exceed the standard rate of 15 (now 17) percent of gross income. Thus, at some point in the income ladder, the marginal rate drops from 25 to 15 (17) percent. Personal allowances are far more generous in Hong Kong than in the United States. They are so generous that only 218,000 salaried taxpayers of a total population exceeding 5 million bore any direct income tax liability in the 1982 tax year. Exactly 13,000 salaried taxpayers, about 6 percent of the total number in the salaried tax net, contributed over half the total yield from the salaries tax. Those who can afford to pay more do so. The personal allowance is so large that the overwhelming majority of the population pay no income taxes whatsoever.

Until 1983, Hong Kong levied an interest tax of 10 percent at the source on Hong Kong dollar deposits—no tax is levied on foreign currency deposits. The payer of the interest deducted the tax and handed it directly to the Inland Revenue Department. Abolition of this tax accompanied refixing the exchange rate. Finally, property tax, set at 15 percent of ratable value after an allowance for repairs and maintenance, is levied on the owner of investment property. Owner-occupants are exempt from the charge.

Apart from these four direct taxes, the Hong Kong government collects revenue from land and property sales, stamp and excise duties, and fees and charges for publicly supplied commercial services. The relative composition of total revenue varies from year to year. However, from a low standard rate of 16.5 (18.5) percent on corporate profits and 15 (17) percent on salaries, interest, and unincorporated business profits, Hong Kong generates sufficient revenue in normal political circumstances to pay its public bills and set funds aside for a rainy day, which arrived in 1982.

Financial authorities in Hong Kong have consistently stressed one tenet of tax policy: low standard rates of direct taxation facilitate rapid economic growth. Revenue yields from rapid growth are sufficient to finance an extremely ambitious program of public expenditure on housing, education, health, welfare, and other social and community services. A succession of Financial Secretaries, the counterpart to our Secretary of the Treasury, chairman of the Council of Economic Advisers, and chairman of the Federal Reserve Board all rolled into one, have repeated the message: investment is stimulated by low rates of direct taxation.

Their words merit reproduction. Arthur Clarke, Financial Secretary during the 1950s, cautioned in his outgoing year: "We would do well to delay an increase in our direct taxation rate, the low level of which is such an incentive to our expanding economy, on which in turn we depend for increasing revenue."[10] His successor, Sir John Cowperthwaite, in 1964, asserted the same principle: "That revenue has increased in this way is in no small measure, I am convinced, due to our low tax policy which has helped to generate an economic expansion in the face of unfavorable circumstances. . . . Economic expansion remains the door to social progress and I am convinced that low taxation can in general produce a greater growth in revenue than can tax increases."[11]

To summarize, low taxes stimulate investment and rapid economic growth. Low tax rates are consonant with budget surpluses, not deficits. They permit steady growth in public spending, not sharp contractions. Between 1961 and 1981, real economic growth in Hong Kong averaged 9 percent; between 1976 and 1980, it grew at the even more incredible rate of 10.7 percent, the industrial world's highest rate. Speak to any businessman, investor, banker, government official, or scholar in Hong Kong, and he will tell you that low rates of taxation are a key to its economic growth and steadily rising prosperity.

The Hong Kong government does not adhere dogmatically to a laissez-faire style of management in all of its public economic activities. The state is the ground landlord in Hong Kong and spends between 15 and 20 percent of the national income providing roads, compulsory primary education, extensive medical and health services, subventions for numerous social welfare agencies, and public housing for about half of the population, a proportion that is scheduled to increase steadily over the next decade.

Government spending and employment are closely monitored to guarantee that the growth rate of the public sector is not out of line with the private sector. This insures that the public sector, which has a natural tendency to grow over time, does not crowd out the private sector to the detriment of Hong Kong's external competitiveness. In recent years, government spending as a share of the gross domestic product ranged from 13 to 20 percent, but the financial authorities get exceedingly nervous when the figure rises above 20 percent, as it did during the recession and political confidence-shattering years of the early 1980s.

How has the common worker fared under this system? The evidence on postwar income distribution suggests that the 70 percent of the population in the third through the ninth deciles gained the greatest share of the increase in total national income.[12] Low-paid unskilled workers benefitted most from the rapid increase in employment opportunities. The well-being of the poorest 20 percent has shown dramatic improvement: by 1976 their average household income reached US$1,300, which supasses the poverty index of all Asian countries. Since low-income households pay no income tax, rising incomes translate into more purchasing power and a higher standard of living. Thus the free-market system appears to be effective in bringing about rapid economic growth and a more even distribution of income, without any need for government-directed, tax-based redistribution schemes.

Summary

Colonial regulations and the free-port status of early Hong Kong supplied the initial constraints on budgetary and economic policies. The Colonial Office imposed the principle of balanced budgets and self-support; the absence of tariffs and other restrictive measures offered little opportunity for constructive intervention by the colonial government in Hong Kong's economy. Moreover, British economic policy in the nineteenth century strongly reflected the influence of Adam Smith's invisible hand: both wealth creation and distribution resided in the private sector.

The constitutional status of contemporary Hong Kong allows public officials to respond to internal and external economic forces, rather than to special-interest political groups. Hong Kong is a modern polity without elections and parties. Public officials in Hong Kong do not respond to the incentive of periodic popular elections, a necessary short-run view of political decision-making. Rather, career civil servants are free from popular short-run pressures to adopt a long-term view of economic efficiency. All power is concentrated in the position of the Governor, and economic and budgetary decision-making is delegated to his chief assistant, the Financial Secretary and his staff.

What incentives and constraints confront Hong Kong's financial authorities? They are, first, the reality of Hong Kong's externally-dependent economy, in which the consequences of government decisions quickly come home to roost. The lack of resources means that there is little that government can do to alter the internal cost/price structure of Hong Kong goods for the benefit of Hong Kong; the converse is not true. The government can, through intervention, alter the internal cost/price structure to the detriment of Hong Kong. Tariffs raise internal costs of production and lower external competitiveness. High taxes reduce Hong Kong's attractiveness as an investment center. Subsidies keep marginally inefficient firms in business to the detriment of total national production. Nonintervention is the cornerstone of economic policy and overlays the ideology of the free-market economy with the reality of few resources, thus encouraging a succession of Financial Secretaries to speak in the language of an eighteenth-century Adam Smith and a nineteenth-century Gladstone.

The lack of resources also means that growth in the economy must be export-led. Public sector growth comes only at the expense of reduced private investment and income. For this reason, public spending ranged from 14 to 20 percent of gross domestic product, and the financial authorities watch that public spending does not grow faster than the overall economy. Hong Kong has no plans for a central bank, and its international and domestic borrowings are restricted exclusively to self-liquidating projects at commercial interest rates.

Free trade, free markets, low taxes, nonintervention, and personal liberty combine to demonstrate that the free-market model of economic organization can be a living reality and not just an abstract textbook convention. Hong Kong can serve as a model for other developing countries that have thus far relied on a state-directed path of economic development but have failed to complete the transition to a more prosperous modern economy.

These circumstances will doubtless change in coming years as China goes ahead with its plans to recover sovereignty and administrative authority over

Hong Kong. In the transition years to 1997, the British may introduce a process of elections to select members of the Legislative and Executive Councils, thereby giving local people greater control over their government. Peking has promised that Hong Kong people can run their own internal affairs as a special region within China, but past Chinese guarantees have lacked credibility. Whether Hong Kong's free-market economy can survive these changes remains to be seen.

Notes

1. This chapter is based on ten years' research and writing about Hong Kong. It rests heavily on two of my books. The first is *Value for Money: The Hong Kong Budgetary Process* (Stanford: Hoover Institution Press, 1976). The most recent is *Hong Kong: A Study in Economic Freedom* (Chicago: University of Chicago Press, 1979).
2. Current figures on the size, population, immigration flows, and resources of the territory are found in the *Hong Kong Annual Reports*. My figures are taken from *Hong Kong 1981. Report for the Year 1980* (Hong Kong Government Press, 1980).
3. Quoted in *Hong Kong Annual Report, 1957*, pp. 2-3.
4. To accompany the financial secretary's annual budget speech, delivered on the last Tuesday in February, the government publishes a series of annual reports which contain a wealth of statistics on the performance of the economy. These include an annual *Economic Background, Economic Prospects* for the coming year, *Estimates of Gross Domestic Product 1966-1982* (through the prior year), *Supporting Financial Statements and Statistical Appendices* for the proposed budget, and a *Half-Yearly Economic Report* of the current fiscal year. The government also publishes a *Monthly Digest of Statistics*. For estimates of economic growth prior to 1966, see Edward Szczepanik, *The Economic Growth of Hong Kong* (London: Oxford University Press for the Royal Institute of International Affairs, 1958), and N. Li and M. Chang, *Economics for Hong Kong* (Hong Kong: Longman, 1970).
5. This summary is taken from the author's intensive investigation of the politics of the budgetary process in Hong Kong. See *Value for Money*.
6. For a thorough treatment of the history, analysis, and prescription of Hong Kong's monetary system, see the entire November-December 1982 issue of *Asian Monetary Monitor*, vol. 6, no. 6, pp. 1-69, published in Hong Kong.
7. For a thorough treatment of business requirements in Hong Kong, see Michel Kay, *Doing Business in Hong Kong* (Hong Kong: South China Morning Post & Amcham Publications, annual edition).
8. The Financial Secretary, *Hong Kong Hansard 1961*, p. 47.
9. Ibid., 1966, pp. 216, 218.
10. Ibid., 1960, p. 62.
11. Ibid., 1964, p. 53.
12. Steven C. Chow and Gustav F. Papanek, "Laissez-Faire, Growth and Equity-Hong Kong," *The Economic Journal*, vol. 91 (June 1981), pp. 466-85.

9

Vignettes of Growth: Singapore, Taiwan, and South Korea

Hong Kong enjoyed a remarkable record of rapid economic growth in the postwar era. But it does not stand alone among developing nations; its geographical cousins of Singapore, Taiwan, and South Korea also have enviable economic track records. These four examples demonstrate that market economies, unencumbered by massive public sectors or heavy-handed government regulation of business, can rapidly lift standards of living. Of course, political, economic, and social circumstances vary from case to case, but there is a common strategy of economic growth. In this chapter I outline that general strategy and then show its application in these three Pacific Area-Basin nations. Since Hong Kong and its Asian cousins prospered from similar market-oriented policies, the charge that Hong Kong is a unique case, and thus irrelevant for other nations, is less persuasive.

What did Singapore, Taiwan, and South Korea have in common as they entered the postwar years? Each endured major wartime disruption, each lacked abundant natural and financial resources, and each was a poor country with a low standard of living. All three initially embarked on a program of import-substitution industrial development behind a protective wall of tariffs and quotas. All sought foreign aid. Growth under this initial strategy was at best moderate.

External circumstances prompted the leaders of all three countries to switch strategies from an import-substitution policy for a limited domestic market to the development of labor-intensive, manufactured goods for export to world markets. International price competition replaced domestic subsidies and tariffs; private firms decided what to produce and where to sell. Government relaxed its grip on the economy and allowed the marketplace to determine the pattern and scope of economic development.

What ingredients go into a successful strategy of export-led economic growth?

1. The exchange rate system is reformed to make sure that a country's currency is correctly valued. An overvalued currency cheapens imports, makes exports more expensive, thus hampering the growth of exports, and invariably leads to a balance-of-payments crisis with its attendant problems.
2. Tax incentives are used to encourage foreign and domestic investment, including the establishment of special industrial estates or free-trade zones that expedite the production of goods for export.
3. Governments often raise interest rates to encourage national savings and capital formation and discourage borrowing for consumption or less efficient uses.
4. Emphasis is placed on the private sector for the creation of jobs and the distribution of income and wealth.
5. Governments hold down the size and growth of public spending, lest an expanding public sector crowd out private investment and spending. Government spending is directed at investment in an infrastructure that facilitates industrialization rather than on consumer subsidies. Public services are financed from revenue obtained from rapid economic growth, not from higher tax rates. Finally, utilities and government enterprises price their services rationally to reflect full opportunity costs.
6. Measures are taken to stabilize the labor market.

These three Pacific Basin economies coupled high growth with no adverse effects on the distribution of income. It has not been necessary to choose between growth and distribution. Because Singapore seems in many respects a twin of Hong Kong, we shall begin our economic travelogue there.

Singapore

Singapore, "the Lion City," is an island, city-state economy, located on the equator.[1] Three-fourths of its 2.4 million people are Chinese; the balance are chiefly Malays and Indians. Its land area of 600 square kilometers is largely devoid of natural resources, and its people import the bulk of their food and raw materials. Singapore's major assets are a strategic location on the trade routes connecting Europe and Japan, an excellent harbor that does not require periodic desalting, a diligent workforce, and an honest, efficient government inherited from British colonial days.[2] From relative poverty in 1946 with a per capita income in the range of several hundred dollars, Singapore is now regarded as a member of the First World, with a per capita income of about US$5,000. Sustained growth over several decades has enriched its two-plus million citizens.

Founded in 1819 by Sir Stamford Raffles, an entrepreneurial employee of the East India Company, Singapore soon became a well-known port and marketplace in Southeast Asia as well as the center of British economic interests in the region.[3] Raffles grafted a policy of economic liberalism onto a strategic location. By making Singapore a free port, he broke the Dutch trade monopoly in the region. Trade became the major economic activity, and British influence spread over the entire Malay Peninsula.

For the next century-and-a-half, the island's rulers adhered to its founder's vision of making Singapore a great emporium resting on the Victorian doctrine of free trade. Successive colonial governors zealously nurtured the port, maintained a lean and efficient administration, and allowed merchants and bankers full scope for the exercise of their talents—a nineteenth-century laissez-faire approach to government. Taxes were held to a minimum, and no harbor dues were levied as these could harm shipping and commerce. Indeed, voluntary contributions of private citizens, not government taxes, financed the construction of the island's first lighthouse. It was government policy to avoid monopolies and encourage competition in order to assure efficient business practices and low costs.

Politically, Singapore moved from a trading post under the control of the East India Company to a British Crown Colony in 1867. It was integrated into a broader political unit known as the Straits Settlements, which encompassed the British possessions of Penang and Malacca. It developed close economic ties with the nine states of peninsular Malaya that were under British influence. It adopted a financial system which pegged the Singapore dollar to the pound sterling, in which the local bank note issues enjoyed 100 percent backing in sterling. Its steady growth as a trading center and home to British regional interests was interrupted when Japan occupied the strategic port during World War II. The British returned in 1946, but Singapore had a new status as a separate Crown Colony, since Penang and Malacca were joined into a broader Federation of Malaya.

Political independence was inevitable, and elections were first held in 1947. Singapore gradually moved to internal self-government in 1959 when Lee Kuan Yew, Singapore's first Prime Minister, and his People's Action Party (PAP) took control. The PAP attained full independence through a merger with Malaysia in 1963. However, this merger was shortlived. Singapore was expelled from Malaysia in 1965, when it became an independent, sovereign nation.

Apart from having to rehabilitate a war-ravaged economy, the immediate postwar years placed three major obstacles in Singapore's path to prosperity.[4] First, a communist insurgency in neighboring Malaya between 1948 and 1960 spilled over into urban Singapore in the form of labor-union agitation. Labor unrest would complicate any plan to encourage industrialization. Political stability was a *sine qua non* of development. Second, as rising protectionism brought stagnation to entrepôt trade during the 1950s, rising unemployment threatened to become a serious domestic problem. Third, shortly after independence in 1965, Britain announced plans to withdraw its armed forces stationed in Singapore at an accelerated pace. Since British military spending accounted for almost 20 percent of the gross national product and 6 percent of employment, accelerated withdrawal threatened to create both a severe recession and a defense vacuum.

Lee Kuan Yew and the PAP proposed a political union with Malaysia, which would provide a good-sized domestic market for an industrial strategy of import substitution. Expulsion from the union with Malaysia in 1965, on political grounds by the government in Kuala Lumpur, destroyed the import-substitution strategy, since after 1965 Singapore-based goods faced a tariff wall throughout the rest of Malaysia. Producing for the smaller domestic market in Singapore alone could not generate enough new jobs. Factories which had been established with the hope of a larger market faced excess capacity. By the mid-1950s the British had largely defeated the local communist insurgency in Malaya, thus restoring overall stability to the region. The PAP set about creating jobs through a policy of industrialization and shifted from exclusive reliance on the entrepôt trade that historically had been the foundation of the economy.

Independent Singapore inherited the free port and free-trade policies of its colonial past. Until the end of the 1950s, when entrepôt trade was the mainstay of the economy, the only major import and excise taxes were on petroleum, liquor, and tobacco, levied for revenue purposes. During the import-substitution phase of industrialization from 1959 through 1967, tariffs and quotas were imposed to protect nascent industries.

To assist local entrepreneurs and to stimulate the development of import-substituting activities, the government adopted legislation in 1959 exempting approved "pioneer industries" from the 40 percent company profits tax, for five years and generous depreciation allowances.[5] It temporarily abandoned the principles of free trade in favor of modest import tariffs and quotas. The government actively directed and participated in the economy. It created an Economic Development Board in 1961 to grant loans to approved companies and to take equity positions. The Board was also responsible for planning, construction, and operation of industrial estates.

External adversity provided a golden opportunity for Lee Kuan Yew and the PAP. The withdrawal of British military forces freed-up a large piece of land that the government converted into a major industrial estate, providing choice facilities to foreign investors. Deprivation of a common economic market with Malaysia forced a change in policy away from import substitution and toward manufacture for world markets. A candid internal assessment of the poor performance of highly protected "pioneer" industries, along with recognition that import protectionism damaged the entrepôt trade and inhibited the development of new exports, reinforced the reality of a shrinking domestic market. The government also got control of the labor movement with restrictive legislation on labor activists and union activity.

Although sudden expulsion from Malaysia in 1965 prompted Singapore's shift from import-substitution to export-led development, other countries steadfastly held to an import-substitution strategy despite poor economic performance.[6] An external shock is not a sufficient condition for a radical change in developmental strategy. It also takes astute and determined political leadership.

Tax Incentives for Exports

After 1965, as a new, independent city-state with a sharply contracted domestic market, Singapore shifted quickly to the strategy of export-oriented industrialization. The government turned to already experienced foreign companies to invest and manufacture for export.[7] Adding to the "pioneer status" legislation, companies were given incentives to export. In 1965, they were permitted to deduct double the expenses of developing world markets from their taxable income. A 1967 act granted tax concessions on profits earned from exports. The consolidated Economic Incentives Act of 1967 remitted 90 percent of the profits tax if export performance was above a base level for eligible industries. Existing industries seeking to expand obtained accelerated depreciation allowances and extension of the "pioneer status," which conferred 100 percent tax exemption for an additional period of 10 years. The government treated foreigners and foreign capital equally with the local citizenry. Total foreign ownership of Singapore firms was allowed. Immigration of necessary business personnel and remittance of profits was freely allowed. No controls were imposed on capital movements. In the 1980s, new incentives encouraged research and development work in high-technology industries, and the maximum personal income-tax rate was lowered from 55 to 40 percent (similar to the company tax rate) to insure that Singaporeans did not view high tax rates as a serious disincentive to continued hard work.

To summarize, the Singapore government installed a raft of economic incentives to woo foreign investors: tax holidays, "pioneer status," accelerated depreciation allowances, export incentives, unrestricted repatriation of capital and profits, relief from double taxation, readily-available factory sites accompanied by many amenities, and subsidies for manpower training programs. Many of the tax incentives compensated exporters for the excess costs they previously endured due to the brief experiment with protectionism. The offsetting effects of these export incentives was to move the overall tax and fiscal system in the direction of greater neutrality. The response to these measures was overwhelming (see below).

Labor Regulation

A second target of economic policy was a peaceful labor movement. To secure this aim, in 1966, the PAP enacted legislation that prohibited strikes unless approved by a majority in secret ballot, required registration of all unions, and forbad noncitizens and criminals from working in union activities.[8] Further legislation in 1968 placed the promotion, transfer, recruitment, retrenchment, and assignment of tasks of workers within the sole prerogative of management—these subjects were held to be outside the scope of labor-management negotiations. The Act also encouraged collective agreements of three to five years duration. The results were spectacular. In 1961, 116 strikes cost Singapore 410,000 lost man-days of work. The communist grip on labor unions was broken in 1964. After 1968, only seven strikes erupted in the next three years. Days lost to industrial unrest fell to 1,011 in 1977 and completely disappeared in 1978. Although these measures severely curtailed the freedom of organized labor, rapidly rising wages and greater choice of jobs during the 1970s muted any desire by most workers to support labor-union agitators.

In effect the government set up a system of wage nonbargaining. With acquiescent unions, wage levels are decreed annually on the recommendation of a tripartite National Wages Council (NWC) composed of employers, unions, and government representatives. Wage awards to workers routinely exceed inflation but have not priced Singapore goods out of world markets. NWC wage-awards have not tried to repeal the laws of supply and demand. The NWC has not been concerned with holding labor costs below market rates as it has been with preventing an organized labor movement from extracting excessive wage agreements from management. Too high labor costs slow the processes of industrialization and job creation. Peace, stability, and not pricing Singapore goods out of world markets are the goals of labor policy.

Public Finance

It has been the policy of Singapore's government to concentrate on trade rather than foreign aid. Accordingly, Singapore has no foreign debt.[9] Of the government's total public debt, only one-tenth is external; this equals about four percent of the gross national product, low by international standards, and well below the government's external assets. Singapore consciously financed its own public development expenditure—infrastructure, utilities, ports, housing—from tax receipts.

The consolidated public sector consists of the government, which spends 60¢ of each public dollar, seven statutory boards, which spend the other 40¢, and the Monetary Authority of Singapore, which is the government's central bank and holds the financial reserves. Budget expenditures are divided into two categories: current spending and development spending. Approximately 60¢ of each government-spending dollar goes for such current services as defense, justice, social and community services, economic services, and debt-servicing payments, with 40¢ allocated to development projects. A portion of annual current spending consists of transfers to a development fund, which, in turn, loans funds to the seven statutory boards. The most important are the Housing Development Board and the Jurong Town Corporation. The boards develop housing which they rent or sell to the public, industrial sites, telecommunications, and port facilities. The boards conduct their affairs in accord with sound commercial criteria, relying on user charges rather than appropriations from general tax receipts.

Where does the revenue come from to finance Singapore's public spending? In 1981, for example, total government revenue, not counting the receipts of the statutory boards or the earnings from Singapore's official external reserves, came to S$9.6 billion. Of this sum, direct taxes (largely income and property taxes) supplied 32 percent, indirect taxes about 15 percent, the sale of goods and services by government about 8 percent, and investment income and miscellaneous receipts provided 12 percent. The balance consisted of loan repayments to the development fund, drawing down of development fund stocks (which exceed S$8 billion), and contributions from a special payroll tax set up to finance retirement benefits.

By 1980, Singapore had accumulated an apparent domestic public debt exceeding S$13 billion, equal to about 62 percent of GNP. Annual debt-service payments consume 23 percent of recurrent government spending. However, the debt is largely a fictional construct of the government's book-keeping structure. Indeed, Singapore's external assets exceed its public debt, which, on a consolidated basis, means the public sector is a net creditor.

Treasury securities are largely purchased through the Central Provident Fund (CPF). Established in 1955, the CPF is a compulsory savings scheme— a tax—to which most employed residents of Singapore and all employers are subject. An initial rate of 5 percent of payroll imposed both on employer and employee between 1955 and 1968 rose, by 1980, to a combined payroll tax of 37 percent. This sum is withheld and put into the national pension fund. The fund, in turn, invests its receipts in treasury securities, which are issued by, and the proceeds subsequently held by, the Monetary Authority of Singapore (MAS). Proceeds of these treasury-debt sales are then funneled into development expenditures and loans to statutory boards; most is invested overseas. Conceptually, CPF funds can be treated as public sector assets which are held by the Monetary Authority of Singapore. In effect, the CPF acts as an arm of the MAS, withdrawing liquidity (via the payroll tax) from the domestic economy. Proceeds of government securities, "borrowed" from the CPF, are initially deposited with the MAS, which converts these funds into gold, dollars, yen, deutsche mark, and other external assets which appear as assets on the MAS balance sheet. The surplus position of the MAS, its assets exceeding liabilities, include CFP contributions, past budget surpluses, and interest earnings on its currency cover, which also consists of foreign assets. The total MAS surplus exceeds the total public debt of the government. The CPF is, in effect, a mechanism for national savings that the government can direct into infrastructure, public housing, and external assets.

Individual contributions to the fund are credited with annual interest, typically exceeding the inflation rate. Payments in the 1970s averaged about 6 percent. (MAS earnings on its invested reserves usually exceed this rate.) Individuals may use CPF funds before retirement for the purpose of purchasing a flat in the new housing estates developed by the Housing Development Board. After age fifty-five, funds may be withdrawn for retirement, but, due to stable prices, it has been customary for retired persons to subsequently deposit these withdrawals into the government-run Post Office Savings Bank (which also buys some Treasury debt offerings). The CPF and the Post Office Savings Bank are the chief devices by which domestic savings are mobilized and channelled to government to finance development expenditures.

In the distant future, as the Singapore population ages, contributions to the CPF may lag behind withdrawals. At that point, residents will begin to dissave unless tax rates increase, or interest payments on CPF holdings of government securities are reduced. Singapore could then face a budgetary problem.

Economic growth has made the revenue picture so healthy that the government in the 1980s reduced marginal rates for individual income taxes and sped up depreciation for companies. High growth has meant greater tax receipts, increased public consumption and investment, and rising after-tax income. Contributing to sustained growth is the conscious determination of government to control the growth rate of public spending in order to insure that the private sector is not crowded out. Since independence, public spending has remained in a narrow range, usually below 25 percent, despite a sharp increase in defense spending following the withdrawal of British forces.

The Monetary System

Technically speaking, Singapore maintains a floating-rate exchange regime in which the value of the Singapore dollar is linked to the value of the currencies of its two main trading partners, the United States and Japan. Responsibility for the domestic Singapore dollar bank note issue resides in the Board of Commissioners of Currency, which maintains full external backing for its note issue in the form of gold, dollars, sterling, and other foreign assets. Until the Singapore dollar floated in 1973, the currency board's activities were automatic: it simply bought and sold unlimited quantities of domestic currency at the fixed-exchange rate. Since 1973, Singapore has pursued an independent monetary policy. Approximately half of the Singapore money supply consists of bank notes and half of demand deposits with local banks. The Monetary Authority of Singapore (MAS), established in January 1971, serves as the central bank, except for the note issue, and is responsible for the regulation of banking.

Over time, Singapore's money supply is largely determined by the balance of payments.[10] Exports of goods and services, earnings from other items for shipping, insurance, and services, and capital inflows (including government borrowing abroad) generate foreign-exchange accumulations by the banks. These can be converted into Singapore dollars at the currency board, thereby augmenting the currency in circulation and increasing demand deposits through multiple-credit expansion. Conversely, imports of goods and services, payments abroad for invisibles, and capital outflows (including government investing abroad) require the banks to make foreign exchange payments abroad, which tends to reduce the currency in circulation and contracts demand deposits. However, as Singapore's balance of payments has been persistently in surplus, the net effect on the money supply has been expansionary; this reflects the growth of Singapore's export-oriented economy, and its role as a financial haven for wealthy residents in less stable neighboring countries.

The government can vary the size and rate of change of the money supply by remitting the proceeds of its large foreign assets or by borrowing abroad. In so doing, it produces a net inflow of foreign exchange, and correspondingly the volume of local currency in circulation, to the extent that these funds are deposited with the commercial banks. It also pressures local banks to repatriate capital invested abroad. Conversely, to dampen an inflationary upsurge, it can contract the money supply by investing official funds abroad (removing them from the local banks), or require that a fraction of the net inflow of private funds be deposited by the banks at the MAS. The MAS can also change the cash-reserve requirement of the commercial banks and finance companies, thereby raising or lowering their capacity to lend and create demand deposits.

Overrapid monetary expansion in the United States and Great Britain in the late 1960s and early 1970s prompted Singapore to switch from an exchange-rate system pegged to the U.S. dollar to a floating-rate system in June 1973 to avoid importing inflation. Since that time, balance-of-payments surpluses caused the Singapore dollar to appreciate from a value of US$1.00 = S$3.00 to a current value of S$2.12 to one U.S. dollar. The Monetary Authority of Singapore used its assets to pursue stable prices with the result that Singapore, perhaps more than any market economy in the world, best held inflation in check throughout the 1970s. As long as Singapore maintains full external backing of its currency (in which, incidentally, its gold reserves are only officially valued at US$42 per ounce), it is likely to maintain a stable price level for the foreseeable future. Current policy allows the domestic money supply to grow in keeping with the growth of surpluses in the balance of payments. Singapore's money supply is similar to a gold-standard, balance-of-payments monetary system; the exception is that its huge control over foreign assets allows the government to manage the exchange rate in order to maintain a stable domestic price level, while remaining mindful that an appreciating local dollar does not damage the competitiveness of Singapore exports. It has done so in a consistently successful manner.

Economic Performance

The bottom-line test of any poor country is the annual rate of economic growth.[11] In Singapore, *real* growth averaged about 9.3 percent between 1960 and 1980. Throughout this period of high growth, prices remained stable: the consumer price index rose a scant 1.2 percent per year during the 1960s and, by worldwide standards, a modest 5.6 percent per year during the 1970s. As a result, real wages and purchasing power grew rapidly. A 1960 per capita income of S$1,329 became, in 1980, S$9,293 (the Singapore dollar appreciated by 27 percent against the U.S. dollar over this period).

Economic growth is ascribed to rapid increases in capital formation. Gross-domestic-fixed-capital formation grew from 10 percent of the gross national product in 1960 to an astonishing level of 40 percent by 1980, a fourfold increase in the share of national income devoted to investment. Small wonder that the index of industrial production rose 12 percent each year during the 1970s. Although the rise in capital spending has been accompanied by a corrresponding downward shift in consumption spending as a share of GNP, the absolute level of real consumption rose three- to fourfold between 1960 and 1980. The reason is that high growth rates provide the means for both greater investment and consumption. In turn, rising investment reinforces strong growth. Too, public-sector spending focussed on infrastructure, port and site development, and utilities, thus providing an attractive framework within which industrial development could occur.

Foreign investment played the major role in the export-led strategy for industrialization and growth. Foreign investment, led largely by American investors, rose at the absolutely phenomenal annual rate of 50 percent from 1967 to 1972. It grew from S$157 million in 1965 to S$3,380 million in 1975. The number of foreign-controlled manufacturing companies rose from 83 in 1959 to 383 in 1973; their paid-up capital rose from S$56 million to S$1,225 million, triple that of domestically-controlled firms. In the decade encompassing 1966 through 1975, value added in manufacturing rose from S$145 million to S$3,411 million, or by eight times. Domestically-produced goods rose from 6 percent of total exports in 1960 to exceed 50 percent by 1972. Unlike Hong Kong, the development of the manufacturing industry for export in Singapore occurred predominantly in the subsidiaries of foreign companies.

The export-growth strategy of industrialization met its jobs targets. A potentially disastrous unemployment situation in the 1950s gave way to full employment in the 1970s. This result is remarkable in that population grew from 1.6 million in 1960 to just under 2.4 million in 1980, an increase of about 50 percent. However, the number employed more than doubled, from 448,600 to more than 1,068,900. Jobs were created so fast that Singapore had a labor shortage as it entered the 1980s.

The trade statistics are staggering. Total imports and exports came to about S$7.5 billion in 1960; by 1980, the total surpassed S$92 billion. During the 1970s alone, trade rose at an annual rate of 20 percent, from about S$12 billion to S$92 billion. Total trade was four to five times the national income.

The tourist industry grew by leaps and bounds, from an annual number of 90,000 visitors in 1960 to more than two million in 1980—almost as large as the Singapore population itself.

The Future

Success confronts the Singapore government with new, but certainly pleasant, problems. Continued political stability makes Singapore's free-enterprise economic system so attractive to investors that an earlier unemployment problem has given way to a labor shortage. Also, an increasing share of the work force entered the personal income tax net. Singapore's leaders thus modified their taxation and wage policies.

First, taxes. Although tax incentives were a prime vehicle for stimulating overseas investment and manufacturing for export, the PAP adhered to a steeply-graduated rate structure for the island's personal income taxes, ranging up to 55 percent on income exceeding S$600,000. Fearing that high taxes could become a disincentive to hard work, in 1979 the government announced its policy to reduce gradually the levels of personal income tax rates in the following three years to a top marginal rate of 40 percent—the same as the company tax rate.

To facilitate business, depreciation rates of plants and machinery were accelerated. Elaborate tax incentives promoted research and development activities in an attempt to make Singapore a high- technology, highly-skilled, labor-force economy. To stimulate the growth of the financial sector, stamp duties on certain financial instruments were abolished, and a 10 percent concessionary-tax rate was granted to offshore gold transactions.

The Singapore government exercises an effective control over basic wage rates. Throughout the 1970s the National Wages Council (NWC) set annual wage increases at about 6 percent. In 1979, as part of a conscious policy to use labor more efficiently (given a labor shortage and stringent immigration controls), the government raised the average wage of a semi-skilled worker by 18 percent. However, wage increases must be related to productivity: employees whose work performance or attitude is unsatisfactory should NOT be paid the NWC wage adjustment. The government no longer wants to attract immigrants from Indonesia and Malaysia who seek low-skilled, low-wage employment. Thus, firms are told that investment should seek highly-skilled, expensive labor, as Singapore's leaders consciously try to attain a higher technology economic base.

In addition to the employer contribution to the state pension scheme, a compulsory training levy on employers now takes 2 percent of payroll. This skills development fund subsidizes the training of workers and interest payments on the purchase of new machinery and equipment.

Taiwan

Taiwan, known diplomatically as the Republic of China, is provincial home to eighteen million people of Chinese background.[12] It has a checkered history. Its most popular name, Formosa, comes from its encounter with Portuguese traders who named it "Beautiful Island." Although settled by a small number of mainland Chinese immigrants, it was not incorporated into the united Chinese empire until late in the Ming Dynasty, in the sixteenth century. It was occupied by the Japanese in 1895, but was returned to China in 1945 at the conclusion of World War II. The Civil War between Nationalist and Communist forces between 1946 and 1949 brought increased attention to Taiwan. Facing certain defeat, the Nationalist government and armies fled to Taiwan in 1948, where they set up a "temporary" provisional government. They also imposed authoritarian political rule over the native Taiwanese population. For the first decade of its island incarnation, the Nationalist government concentrated its planning on a triumphant return to the mainland.

By 1980 mainlanders diminished to a bare 15 percent of the population of Taiwan. Talk of recovering the mainland was idle rhetoric for the last two decades. In place of past military and political dreams, the leaders of Taiwan focused their energies into turning Taiwan into a rich, prosperous economy. Adopting a strategy of capitalist development with state assistance, the Taiwan economy grew so rapidly that a prosperous people of Taiwan stand in marked contrast to an economically less-well-off one billion Chinese across the straits of Formosa. With a per capita income of almost $2,500 in 1981, Taiwan is among the world's top twenty exporters, and its people enjoy a standard of living much higher than their compatriots in the neighboring People's Republic of China.

As mainland China established diplomatic ties with more nations, Taiwan became politically isolated. Still, despite diplomatic adversity, its externally oriented economy grew at about 10 percent a year throughout the 1970s. As other nations warmed up to mainland China's communist government, Taiwan demonstrated that reliance on market forces brings greater economic rewards than the listless, inefficient state-directed, state-controlled economic life of mainland China. Taiwan's economic ties with other nations thrived despite the shock of America's withdrawal of diplomatic recognition in 1979.

Political power in Taiwan is shared between the Kuomintang Party, the armed forces, and the president, Chiang Ching-kuo, son of Generalissimo Chiang Kai-shek, Nationalist China's leader for nearly four decades. Although locally-born Taiwanese have taken over an increasing share of middle-level and top positions, remnants of the mainlanders who fled China in 1948 are clearly still in charge. Taiwan maintains a formal written constitution with a division of powers among the executive, legislative, and judicial branches of government, and elections are held for members of the legislature and local government offices. This constitutional facade should not mask the reality that the Kuomintang maintains a firm grip on political life. There is no serious or effective opposition to the Kuomintang.

The government is a gerontocracy. Both the parliament and the national assembly, who choose the president, were elected in 1948 before the Nationalists left the mainland. Of the 760 members of parliament originally elected, fewer than 300 remain and all but a handful are over seventy years old. The national assembly's ranks, almost 2,700 when elected in 1947, have thinned to about 1,000. Reflecting a growing political liberalization, one quarter of the members of parliament (who now number about 400) were elected from the Taiwan provincial population; the remaining 300, shrinking each day, still "represent" all the other provinces and regions of the mainland. The key lesson drawn from this brief exposition of Taiwan's government is that persistent political stability allowed officials to take a long-run view of the economy and to adopt economic and fiscal policies conducive to rapid economic growth.

Resources

Taiwan is comprised of one large semi-tropical island and a few adjacent small islands, which have virtually no development potential; all these islands equal a total land area of about 36,000 square kilometers.[13] One-fourth of the land area is arable; the rest is mainly mountainous. Its climate consists of a long, wet summer, with a short, mild winter. Like Hong Kong, it suffers the threat of violent typhoons and torrential rains in late summer. However, its overall favorable climate permits multiple-cropping and year-round farming.

Taiwan has few mineral resources. Its main reserves are inferior-quality coal, exceptionally high-quality marble, natural gas, and few other minerals. Taiwan must, therefore, import the bulk of its industrial raw materials.

During their occupation between 1895 and 1940, the Japanese developed the power industry, built a network of railways and highways, and improved the infrastructure for their own economic goals. However, much of this was destroyed by allied bombing and the lack of maintenance during World War II. Repatriation of Japanese personnel at the end of the war reduced the number of skilled and managerial personnel on the island, and severely retarded industrial rehabilitation efforts. Taiwan's economy faced an uphill climb.

Land Reform

The first major economic policy was a comprehensive land-reform program designed to augment agricultural output and secure the Nationalists' political base in the countryside.[14] The Nationalists failed utterly on the mainland when coping with landlords in their limited efforts at land reform, thus abetting the Communist advances in rural areas. They would not fail twice.

Beginning in 1948, the government began to sell some public land to tenant farmers. The next step was the compulsory sale of land by landlords. Privately-owned land in excess of specified amounts per landowner had to be sold to the government, which would, in turn, resell that land. The purchase price was 2.5 times the annual yield of the main crops. Landlords were paid 70 percent of the purchase price in land bonds denominated in kind, and 30 percent in industrial stock of four public enterprises previously owned by the Japanese. Between May and December of 1953, tenant households acquired 244,000 hectares of farmland, 16.4 percent of the total area cultivated in Taiwan between 1951 and 1955.

The distribution of landholdings changed dramatically between 1952 and 1960. Families owning their own land rose sharply, and the proportion of land cultivated by tenants fell from 44 percent in 1948 to 17 percent in 1959. The ratio of owner-cultivators to total farm families increased from 36 percent in 1949 to 60 percent in 1957. By 1957, part-owner families and owner cultivators owned more than 83 percent of the total farm land.

Private ownership of land fostered more efficient farming practices, since families now owned the full proceeds of their production. Agricultural output rose sharply. Land was worked more intensively. Responding to market forces, farmers grew less low-valued rice, and increased their production of more profitable crops, such as vegetables, fruits, livestock, and poultry.

Industrialization

The Korean War strengthened military ties between the United States and the Taiwan government. Billions of dollars in foreign economic and military aid poured into the island. During the 1950s, U.S. aid financed approximately 40 percent of Taiwan's import bill. This huge volume of foreign aid allowed the financial authorities to grossly overvalue Taiwan's currency, which subsidized domestic consumers who purchased imports at less than half of the world prices. Each New Taiwan Dollar (NT$) bought more U.S. dollars, and thus commanded greater international purchasing power as a result of overvaluation. Behind this shield of foreign aid, Taiwan embarked on an inward-looking, import-substitution policy of industrialization. The intent was to develop industries that produce for the local market, protected behind a shield of tariffs and quotas. The overvalued exchange rate meant that domestic manufactured goods were not price-competitive in overseas markets, since production costs in NT$ translated into higher US$ trading prices.

All good things must end. In retrospect, the 1960s and 1970s demonstrated that massive foreign assistance may have hampered, not helped, Taiwan's economic growth. When the United States government in the late 1950s announced plans to phase out its massive economic assistance, the Taiwan government placed greater emphasis on export promotion. To increase exports would require massive infusions of *private* foreign capital and technology. To earn foreign exchange, trade, not aid, became the watchword of developmental policy.

From 1958 on, the government moved in a new direction.[15] It promulgated a program for improvement of foreign exchange and trade control. An initial exchange rate of NT$5 to US$1 led to a complex multiple exchange-rate system and repeated devaluations. This was replaced by an official uniform exchange rate reflecting market supply and demand, which stabilized at NT$40 to US$1 by August 1958. This simplification eliminated advance deposit requirements and other strict import and foreign exchange controls; administrative costs were also sharply reduced. As a result, the real effective exchange rate for exports remained stable during the 1960s and 1970s, which led to accelerated export expansion. The reason is that a correct exchange rate links internal prices (based on efficient, least-cost production) to world markets on a competitive basis. To compensate for distortions imposed on exporters, which had characterized the prior import-substitution regime, the government took a number of concrete steps. It gradually liberalized, and finally abolished, the commodity import-quota system. Tariffs were reduced. Import controls were liberalized. It granted three-year income-tax exemptions to certain categories of industries to stimulate investment. It revised the income tax law and the company law. It relaxed controls over the establishment of factories. It considered setting up a stock market to foster local equity participation in the economy. It instructed the Bank of Taiwan to raise interest rates to encourage private saving, and reduce excess borrowing. These steps were a modest precursor to massive new legal changes which took effect in

1960 with the promulgation of the Statute for the Encouragement of Investment.

Key elements in the 1960 financial reform package granted those export-oriented productive enterprises that met the statute's criteria were a five-year income-tax holiday and a maximum rate of profits tax (including surtax) of 18 percent compared with the ordinary 32.5 percent rate. This financial package allowed all reinvested, undistributed profits to remain free of tax, gave a tax deduction for exports equal to 2 percent of the annual export proceeds, exempted or reduced productive enterprises from stamp taxes, and permitted 7 percent of profits before taxes to be set aside as a reserve against losses due to exchange rate revisions. Annual tax refunds due to these new incentives, as a percentage of total income, stamp, customs, and commodity taxes, ranged from a low of 19 percent in 1963 to a high of 52.4 percent in 1972, with the annual average in the 30-percent range. Taiwan's remarkable economic growth is directly linked to these sharp reductions in tax rates.

The government also revised and expanded the scope of the investment statute in 1965 and authorized the creation of duty-free, export-processing zones. Developmental strategy now became wholly export oriented. Three zones grew so fast that by 1970 they provided 7 percent of all manufacturing jobs and turned out a tenth of all exports. In some years, the entire balance of merchandise trade surplus was traced wholly to the trade balance within the zones. A necessary accompaniment to an export strategy was the steady reduction in the protection rate provided by tariffs throughout the 1960s and 1970s.

A summary of Taiwan's export incentives includes reimbursement of customs duties and harbor dues imposed on imported contents of export products, refund of the commodity tax on export products, extension of foreign-exchange loans for the import of raw materials for export processing, extension of low-interest export loans, exemption of income taxes and business taxes on export transactions, cash bonuses for exports, establishment of bonded warehouses, and export-processing zones. A US$100 million trade deficit largely financed by U.S. aid was thereafter more than offset from increased export earnings.

Other Reforms

Tax concessions for exports, to neutralize the prior bias of the import-substitution period, is only one part of Taiwan's growth strategy. Other dimensions include incentives to mobilize domestic savings, control inflation, and produce domestic goods on an efficient basis. Overall, the government has adopted sound fiscal and monetary policies. It was first necessary to establish and maintain exchange rates that would not overvalue the Taiwan dollar, since an overvalued currency would discourage exports and encourage imports. Between 1954 and 1960, the government therefore carried out four successive devaluations which adjusted an exchange rate of NT$15.55 to US$1 to a more realistic rate of NT$40 to US$1. It remained in place until 1973 when the Taiwan currency was revalued upward to a rate of NT$38 to one U.S. dollar, a compromise between the revalued Japanese yen and the devalued U.S. dollar, the currencies of Taiwan's two major trading partners.

The effect of a correctly-valued Taiwan dollar meant that commodities and equipment imported into Taiwan were sold to end-users at realistic, rather than subsidized, prices, thus minimizing waste and inefficiency. Most important, a devalued Taiwan dollar enhanced the competitiveness of Taiwan goods on world markets. Exports correspondingly rose at fantastic rates.

Since 1960, Taiwan has maintained a gold-standard rule, balance of payments, fixed exchange-rate monetary system, coupled with such discretionary monetary policy measures as changes in reserve requirements, and raising deposit rates of interest. The currency enjoys 100 percent external backing in such forms as gold, foreign currencies, and other financial instruments. Taiwan's exchange rate remained virtually constant during the 1960s as the government ran substantial budget surpluses; public borrowing from the banking system declined from 45 percent of domestic credit in 1962 to 9 percent in 1970. During the 1960s, inflation averaged 3.4 percent. From time to time during the 1970s, huge balance-of-payments surpluses brought domestic monetary expansion and inflation as external balances were converted into local currency. On one occasion, Taiwan authorities lifted restrictions on luxury imports to produce a trade deficit, and a concomitant monetary deceleration. An upward revaluation from NT$40 to NT$38 in 1972 was followed by another shift to NT$36 in 1978. In 1979 a foreign exchange market was established which allowed a daily float. Domestic inflation in the late 1970s brought a devaluation to NT$38.

The government has set all institutional interest rates in Taiwan throughout the period 1960 to 1981. Taiwan's financial system is dominated by government-owned banks which often behave like a department of the ministry of finance. Only since the late 1970s have the commercial banks been allowed to vary their interest rates within a range set by the government. Thus the government could exercise a direct lever on the supply and demand of domestic credit by its interest-rate policy. To encourage savings, and to insure that credit would only be used by more efficient borrowers, the government raised the interest rate on savings deposits in the Bank of Taiwan and other banks, which is how a free market would have solved the problem of insufficent savings and excess demand for credit. This pulled more savings into the banking system, and while it meant higher charges on bank loans, it also insured that only efficient firms would have a call on the nation's scarce savings. Bank rates on secured loans rose as high as 23.4 percent in 1954 and, as the supply of savings increased, fell gradually in steps to 11.3 percent in 1972. Private and government consumption fell as an increasing share of national output was channeled into capital formation. Gross saving as a percentage of the gross national product increased from less than 10 percent during the 1950s to surpass 20 percent during the 1960s. To encourage saving, earnings from savings accounts were granted income tax exemption.

Fiscal policy has placed no strain on the island's central bankers. Overall policy is, taking one year with another, to maintain a balanced budget. The experience of the Nationalist government during its mainland rule of the late 1940s with rampant inflation, one of the five worst in world history, which also contributed to their downfall, insured that the inflationary issue of bank notes would be forsaken as a method of financing government spending on Taiwan. Despite major tax cuts in 1960, deficits in the four fiscal years through 1964 were quickly transformed into a string of steady, uninterrupted budget surpluses, which reached a high of 25 percent of annual spending in 1974.[16] Low taxes have stimulated high rates of economic growth which, in turn, have raised more than sufficient revenue to sustain sharply rising levels of government spending on both defense and social programs, sharply reducing the government's borrowing needs.

In 1974, Minister of Finance K.T. Li noted that "placing too much emphasis on increasing tax revenue is detrimental to economic development, and without economic development there can be little increase in national income. Only when national income is on the rise can the people afford to pay more taxes."[17] A conservative budgetary policy, predicated on low taxes, has eliminated inflationary pressures and promoted a regime of stable prices. With the money supply largely determined by the balance of payments and a market-determined exchange rate, Taiwan has enjoyed rapid growth and relatively stable prices.

Results

Export expansion fueled economic growth and created millions of new jobs. Even as higher productivity reduced the need for labor, sharply rising exports during the three periods 1961 to 1966, 1966 to 1971, and 1971-1976 generated net increases in employment of 377,000, 1,015,000, and 925,000. Rapid expansion of exports created jobs fast enough to allow the economy to reach full employment by 1971 and maintain that status throughout the 1970s. Export growth made it possible to maintain full employment despite steadily rising productivity and continuous migration from agricultural areas into the cities.

At the end of World War II, per capita income in Taiwan was a low, low US$70. It rose so rapidly that it reached US$2,280 in 1980.[18] Until the 1960s, population also grew at the high rate of 3.5 percent but has since levelled off at about 2 percent. Real GNP has grown at the astounding annual average rate of 9.2 percent over the past three decades: 8.2 percent in the 1950s, 9.4 percent in the 1960s, and 9.9 percent in the 1970s. Real GNP has doubled every seven years since 1963. By 1980, it was eleven times that of 1952. The whole country was literally transformed from poor to middle-income in just one generation.

The structure of the economy changed to reflect the prominent role of manufacturing for export. Employment in agriculture decreased from 51.4 percent of total employment in 1952 to less than 30 percent in 1979, while employment in the industrial sector increased from 20.4 percent to 41.8 percent during the same period.

The labor force was successfully absorbed during the 1960s. The unemployment rate fell from a worrisome 6.5 percent in 1952 to 1.2 percent in 1979. The annual growth rate of manufacturing real wages reflected this process of labor absorption, rising by 2.7 percent in the 1950s, 6.2 percent in the 1960s, and 10.7 percent in the 1970s. Increased use of unskilled labor during the 1966-1971 period seems to have caused the wage rate for unskilled labor to rise more rapidly than that for skilled labor. The poorest paid members of the work force derived the greatest benefits from the export-led industrialization of Taiwan.

The various savings reforms worked their wonders too. The average ratio of net domestic savings to national income from 1951 through 1959 was only 5 percent, and from 1960 to 1962 it was 8 percent. The savings ratio jumped to 13 percent and more after 1963. Since 1967, the savings ratio has exceeded 20 percent of national income; in the 1970s it was around 30 percent.

Almost half of all investment before 1962 was financed by U.S. aid. Almost no private foreign capital flowed into Taiwan before 1961, but this changed dramatically after 1964. Private foreign investments from 1962 to 1969 came to US$378 million. Foreign investment was about US$150 million every year in the 1970s, increased to US$330 million in 1979, and to US$466 million in 1980. Private foreign investment contributed significantly to Taiwan's prosperous transformation. In 1976 exports by private foreign and overseas Chinese firms amounted to US$2.2 billion, or 29 percent of Taiwan's total exports, reaching 82 percent of exported electronics and electrical products.

In the mid-1970s, the government of Taiwan embarked on a series of major development projects that entailed substantial government involvement in the economy. Ten basic construction projects were announced that encompassed a national freeway, railway electrification, a new railway line along the east coast, a new modern international airport, a nuclear power plant, and two harbor projects—these all fall within infrastructure development. However, the projects also included a giant shipyard, a steel mill, and a petrochemical complex; these projects were a state-directed effort to develop heavy industry to accompany Taiwan's dependence on light industry. These latter three have not been profitable ventures, and there are no current plans to embark on a new series of major projects once these are completed. While these projects are massive, they do not presage a substantially greater role for government in the future evolution of the economy.

Scholars worry a great deal about the effects of rapid economic growth on the distribution of national income. Rapid growth is all fine and well, they say, if it does not produce marked gaps between rich and poor that foster unrest and political instability. The experience of Taiwan confounds these critics, because Taiwan is now regarded, after three decades of very rapid growth, as a *low* inequality country. The poorest quintiles of the population enjoyed increases in real household income more rapidly than the richest, thus narrowing the gap between rich and poor.[19] Illiteracy has given way to near universal literacy. Life expectancy is on a par with Western societies. Ownership of cars, homes, telephones, and refrigerators, to name a few durables, is more reflective of Western standards of living than of Asian. Taiwan is prosperous *en masse*. All this in just three decades, on a relatively resourceless island that must commit a large portion of its annual budget to defense spending.

Korea

South Korea (hereafter Korea) differs from Singapore and Taiwan in several respects. It is a peninsula, not an island. It is populated by Koreans, not Chinese. Its climate is temperate, not tropical or semi-tropical.

To even the most casual observer, Korea resembles Singapore and Taiwan in many other respects. It suffered the ravages of war in the early 1950s, which literally decimated the country. It survived on foreign aid in the first few years of its postwar rehabilitation. It had to cope with the precipitous withdrawal of U.S. economic assistance in the early 1960s. It is a relatively resourceless country and must import the bulk of its raw materials for industry. It has leaped from the status of impoverished to become a middle-income nation in the short span of two decades. It has enjoyed a good measure of political stability. Export expansion was its primary engine of economic growth. Private sector enterprises have led the way in investment and job creation, although the government has played a leading part in setting interest rates and allocating credit.

Resources

Korea is a small and densely populated country of thirty-seven million people.[20] Its total land area of 99,000 square kilometers, just over triple that of Taiwan, is largely mountainous. Only 23 percent of its land is cultivated.

Sixty-seven percent is forested mountain slopes, and the cities, industrial facilities, and roads are concentrated into a small 10 percent. The rugged topography and harsh winters limit the productive potential of agriculture. Mineral resources are also limited and are largely confined to poor-quality coal. Korea's population density of 363 persons per square kilometer of land is among the world's highest. However, population pressures have abated substantially in the postwar era, falling from 3 percent annual growth in 1961 to 1.7 percent by the mid-1970s.

Political and Economic Background Before 1960

Japanese success in the Russo-Japanese War (1904-05) led to its military occupation of Korea in 1905 and outright annexation in 1910.[21] During thirty-five years of rule, the Japanese brought capital, introduced new agricultural practices, and developed the foundations of an industrial base, bringing Korea into the modern economic world.

Korea was liberated from Japanese occupation at the end of World War II, but was immediately partitioned along the 38th parallel between South Korea and North Korea. The South had a majority of the population, its most productive agricultural land, and the bulk of the light industry; most of the heavy industry and more than 90 percent of the electricity-generating capacity were in the North. What industrial facilities the South inherited were largely destroyed during the Korean War of 1950 to 1953. Thus South Korea's economic development had to overcome three obstacles in the first decade of its modern independence: withdrawal of skilled Japanese managerial personnel, partition, and wartime devastation.

Massive United States and United Nations assistance was required to rehabilitate its war-ravaged economy. Virtually the entire country had suffered extensive destruction. Three-fifths of the cultivated land had been laid to waste, property damage exceeded $3 billion, most industrial facilities had been demolished, the death toll was estimated at over three million (both sides included), and approximately one-quarter of the population roamed the countryside as refugees. Ten million people were homeless and five million survived purely on relief. Reconstruction began immediately with foreign grants. Although inflation quickly subsided, the economy registered only modest gains. During its period of dependence on aid, which totalled $2.3 billion, investment was inadequate, exports grew slowly, and output increased at much too low a rate to bring about full employment and rising real wages. Growth averaged 5.5 percent from 1954 to 1958, but fell to an annual average of 3.6 percent between 1959 and 1962.

Behind a shield of foreign aid, Korea erected barriers of tariffs and quotas in pursuit of an import-substitution industrial policy. By now, it should not be surprising that Korea initially chose an import-substitution strategy, achieved only modest gains from it, and abandoned it in the early 1960s in favor of an export-expansion policy.

The regime of Syngman Rhee held sway all through the 1950s, but its increasing autocratic rule culminated in a student revolt of 1960 which toppled the government. Rhee resigned on 26 April 1960, and elections were held the following July. Factional struggles and political turmoil after the election paved the way for a military takeover in 1961. Its leader, General Park Chung Hee, firmly ruled without interruption until his assassination in October 1979, thus providing 18 years of political stability within which Korea dashed for development on a pace that rivalled Hong Kong, Singapore, and Taiwan. When the political and economic dust had settled in 1962, Korea was a very poor country with a per capita income of US$87, total economic output of just $2.3 billion, and a high population growth rate of 2.9 percent. The prognosis for growth was not good.

Korea, too, underwent a land reform program, but it was largely completed more than a decade before rapid economic growth began and contributed little to it.[22] Japanese occupation had imposed an oppressive land tenure system on Korea, which passage of a land reform act in June 1949 began to remedy. The proportion of the rural population owning land rose from 16.5 to 71.2 percent between 1947 and 1974, reflecting greater equitability.

However, private ownership of land did not bring dramatic gains in output and rural incomes because the government sustained a policy of grain pricing and procurement that did not reflect market forces. Rhee's government and Park's first decade subsidized urban consumers at the expense of rural producers. Not until the 1971 election revealed that Park was losing support in rural areas did the government substantially increase producer prices. It had been able to suppress prices because PL 480 grain imports alleviated grain deficits, simultaneously generating local currency with which to help run the government. When the United States changed PL 480 commodities into dollar repayable loans by 1971, grain imports became a drain on foreign exchange. During the 1970s the government improved rural incentives, sharply increasing grain prices to stimulate increased yields and improve rural incomes.

In retrospect, the PL 480 foreign-aid program was a critical deterrent to reform of national grain-pricing policies, allowing the Korean government to hold down grain procurement prices. U.S. withdrawal of soft PL 480 commodity loans forced the Korean government to increase grain prices to encourage greater output, in the process raising rural incomes. Land reform, begun in 1949, did not bring full benefit to rural dwellers until pricing policies were reformed in the 1970s.

The reduction of foreign aid in the 1960s was a blessing in disguise. It prompted the new Korean leadership to adopt growth-oriented, outward-looking policies. The key to growth would be an emphasis on rapid expansion of exports. This decision brought changes in the areas of taxation, new incentives for exporters, and modifications in interest rate policy and, especially, the exchange rate. Dividends were immediate and massive: Korean exports averaged over 30 percent in annual growth from the early 1960s through the late 1970s, predominantly in the form of labor-intensive manufactured goods, in which Korea enjoyed comparative advantage in low-cost labor. In 1960, industry supplied 20 percent of national income; in 1980, the share had more than doubled to 42 percent. Agriculture's share fell from 38 to 16 percent over the same period. Thus the economy was literally transformed in two decades.

Economic, Fiscal, and Monetary Reforms

As U.S. aid was scheduled to be cut off, the government reformed the exchange rate of its currency.[23] Since imports in the 1950s had been largely financed from aid, not trade, it had not been necessary to adopt a realistic exchange rate. An overvalued Korean currency, the won, subsidized domestic consumers of imports, but retarded the growth of exports. In 1960, for example, more than half of Korea's foreign-exchange receipts were earned on government transactions, of which military procurement was the single largest item. Korean officials found they could get more dollars per soldier in uniform, whose costs were stated in Korean won, if they kept the official won exchange rate overvalued against the dollar. This method of absorbing foreign aid was devastating for the development of commercial exports. (By 1975, after exchange-rate reform, government transactions produced less than 3 percent of foreign-exchange earnings, while that of manufactured exports had grown to 74 percent.) The 1962 rate of 130 won to the U.S. dollar was sharply devalued to 256 per dollar in 1964. A unitary floating exchange rate was put in place in March 1965, and the value of the won steadily fell to 484 per dollar by 1974, where it remained during the balance of the 1970s. In effect, the successive currency devaluations produced a uniform exchange rate at a level near the free-trade exchange rate, which is the exchange rate that would exist in the absence of both export incentives and protective measures against imports.

The net real-exchange rate for exports was kept steady between 1961 and 1972. Export incentives were granted to offset the higher production costs that domestic inflation brought. Korea pegged the won to the US dollar from 1974 at W484 to US$1. The won was devalued in January 1980 by 16.6 percent and subsequently pegged to a basket of currencies and depreciated further. It is now on a managed float, falling to W745 to US$1 by late 1982. Despite the highest inflation rate among Hong Kong, Singapore, Taiwan, and Korea, export incentives were freely used to sustain a high export growth rate.

The government holds a controlling interest in all the national banks, and owns all the special banks and development institutions, which are thus subject to comprehensive government controls. Although the government has begun denationalizing state-owned banks in 1982, it dictates interest rates, lending policies, customer service, and other aspects of banking. Until 1979, when the Korean Bankers' Association began to fix deposit and loan rates within ranges established by the monetary board, the government set all institutional interest rates. The government doubled nominal deposit rates as part of the 1965 financial reform, which sustained a relatively high real rate of interest through 1971. Since 1973, however, real deposit rates have been negative.

The government has used its control over the banking system to allocate credit and has made extensive use of selective credit policies. About 60 percent of bank lending is for government-designated purposes, such as export support. Loans for exports have consistently carried rates below the deposit rate. Subsidized loans for priority sectors are usually eligible automatically for special rediscount rates at the Bank of Korea. Government guarantees have also been provided for foreign borrowing of almost any firm showing a capacity to export. The effect of selective credit allocation at below market rates has been to hold down deposit rates of interest. In turn, lower interest rates reduce the quantity of deposits (the banking system's deposit liabilities) and the total volume of funds available to lend (the banking system's loan assets). The resulting shortage of domestic saving has compelled Korean businessmen to borrow abroad, which has generated a large foreign debt.

During the post-1965 export-boom phase of Korean development, monetary policy has consisted largely of imposing reserve requirements on bank deposits, which has varied from 12 to 35 percent, often changing sharply overnight. The virtually automatic rediscount mechanism which supports priority loans for export finance tends to produce excessive monetary expansion, despite the reserve requirement provision. Institutional interest rates remain consistently below their free market levels as credit is rationed to exporters at below market prices. From time to time, credit ceilings have been used as instruments of monetary policy to control inflation. The overall effect of selective credit allocation, which has entailed negative rates of interest for savers, has been to reduce national saving and credit availability, perhaps slowing the overall rate of economic growth.

Compared with Singapore and Taiwan, foreign investment has played a relatively smaller role in Korea's industrialization, amounting to about $1.5 billion. Government guarantees of overseas borrowing by Korean businessmen encouraged foreign borrowing.

Apart from maintaining an effective free-trade exchange rate through using export incentives to offset domestic inflation, the government implemented a series of trade-liberalization and tariff-reform measures to achieve greater internal economic efficiency. In pursuit of export expansion, exporters were granted preferential credit. Other steps included indirect tax exemptions on inputs into export promotion and export sales, a 50 percent reduction on income taxes from export earnings (abolished in 1973), tariff exemption on imported raw materials and equipment for export production, and a "wastage allowance" on imported raw materials for production of exports. Following the example of the successful Kaohsiung Export Processing Zone in Taiwan, the Korean authorities passed legislation creating several tax-exempt and duty-free zones of their own in the late 1960s, which generated tens of thousands of jobs in a few short years. These measures moved the overall tax and fiscal system in the direction of greater neutrality to compensate for the bias imposed during the import-substitution phase of postwar-Korean development.

Broadly speaking, the government allowed the forces of supply and demand to prevail in labor markets. It imposed no statutory minimum wages or other labor cost-increasing measures. As a result, the economy achieved full employment by the late 1960s, after which real wages rose sharply.

The Korean public sector comprises the central government, local governments, and various public sector enterprises.[24] Most budget transactions occur at the level of the central government. Its budget, in turn, consists of a general account, an economic development special account, and a variety of small special accounts. Funds are transferred across these accounts for a variety of current and capital expenditures. What is important is to note, first, that total government spending has typically been less than 20 percent of GNP, though from time to time it has reached as high as 23 percent. In aggregate terms, the Korean public sector has not crowded out its private sector. Nor have taxes discouraged work, savings, or investment. Direct taxes only take 5 percent of the GNP, with the remaining 16 percent of the GNP collected from a value-added tax, excise taxes, customs duties, and several miscellaneous charges. The income tax takes inflation into account through regular increments in exemptions. Also, the government reduced the top marginal rates in the late 1970s from 70 percent to 55 percent on incomes exceeding $99,000; it plans still further tax-rate cuts in the 1980s. The level of company taxes has been consistently monitored, and the rate was reduced from a prior range between 33 and 38 percent to 20 percent in 1982. High rates of economic growth have enabled the government to implement periodic tax-*rate* reductions at the same time still enjoying overall increases in tax *receipts*. Korea's public finances are well managed.

Overall, the government allocates about 30 percent of the general budget to its investment and loan accounts, which largely represent investment expenditure. Thus public sector funds have not been frittered away on consumer subsidies.

In 1962, foreign transfers, largely U.S. aid, represented 8.8 percent of the GNP. It declined to 1.2 percent by 1975, reflecting both U.S.-aid reductions and increasing Korean self-reliance. In its place, the country turned to external borrowing to take up the slack. An external debt of a few billion dollars in 1971 rose tenfold, past $20 billion, by 1981 when Korea had become the world's third largest borrower on international capital markets behind Brazil and Mexico.[25] The percentage of export earnings needed for interest and repayment still remains low at about 12 to 13 percent. In borrowing so heavily abroad, Korea's pell-mell rush to industrialize parted company with its three Asian cousins, who eschewed external debt financing as a vehicle for growth. The Koreans have paid a stiff price for overheating their economy: GNP fell 6.2 percent in 1980, and real wages fell for the first time in many years. Korea's modern miracle temporarily derailed due to excessive foreign debt. By contrast, because Hong Kong, Taiwan, and Singapore followed more neutral monetary and financial policies, their economic growth was largely self-financed. Korea may face slower growth rates in the near future compared with its geographical cousins.

It is easy to criticize the Koreans for trying to move too fast into the modern technological age. However, compared with dozens of other Third World countries still struggling to surpass a poverty level of existence, the achievements of Korea's last two decades are heroic. Starting from a lower base, the country's rate of growth in exports has outpaced that of Taiwan, Singapore, and Hong Kong. But the Chinese-populated threesome, unburdened with debt, may find the path to future growth less strewn with thorns.

Results

From a per capita income of $87 in 1962, two decades of rapid growth have propelled per capita income to about $1,600 by 1982.[26] Although still lagging behind Taiwan, Singapore, and Hong Kong, the gains in Korea are nonetheless impressive. A GNP growth rate of 2.2 percent in 1962 reached 6.9 percent in 1964, 8.1 percent by 1968, and has averaged 9 percent through 1979. A trivial $41 million of exports in 1961 grew to $8 billion by 1976, rising more than 30 percent every year between 1960 and 1979. (As an aside, per capita income in North Korea, which inherited the bulk of pre-liberation heavy industry, is about 20 to 25 percent that of the South.) Predictably, rapid export growth, chiefly manufactured goods, created millions of new jobs: the open unemployment rate declined from 8.2 percent in 1963 to a low 3.9 percent in 1976. Throughout this period, the average increase in real wages exceeded 7 percent. Rising wages, in turn, fostered significant gains in nutrition, literacy, longevity, infant mortality, and the consumption of automobiles, refrigerators, and other consumer goods. Throughout this period of export-expansion, labor productivity grew 7 percent a year.

Summary

Each country, on its own, is a tale of remarkable success. Coupled with Hong Kong, the four offer convincing proof that sound economic and fiscal policies are building blocks of economic growth. They show the relevance of Adam Smith in the modern world. One is even tempted to draw the comparison with nineteenth-century Britain, whose prosperity came from an export-led industrial growth, made possible by conservative fiscal, liberal economic, and sound monetary policies.

Notes

1. I have made substantial use of several sources in preparing this brief description of Singapore's postwar development. For a comprehensive history of Singapore from its founding until the mid-1970s, see Mary Turnbull, *History of Singapore 1819-1975* (Singapore: Oxford University Press, 1975). On more concrete topics of economic development, see Lee Soo Ann, *Singapore Goes Transnational* (Singapore: Eastern Universities Press, 1977); Goh Keng Swee, *The Practice of Economic Growth* (Singapore: Federal Publications, 1977); Theodore Geiger, *Tales of Two City-States: The Development Progress of Hong Kong and Singapore* (Washington, D.C.: National Planning Association, 1973); Chow Kit Boey and Amina Tyabji, *External Linkages and Economic Development* (Singapore: Chopman, 1980); and Nicholas Harman, "The sovereign municipality," *The Economist*, 29 December 1979. A detailed analysis of the transition to and results of Singapore's export-oriented policy appears in Augustine H.H. Tan and Ow Chin Hock, "Singapore," in Bela Balassa, ed., *Development Strategies in Semi-industrial Economies* (Baltimore and London: Johns Hopkins University Press for the World Bank, 1982), pp. 280-309.
2. Goh Keng Swee, *The Practice of Economic Growth*, p. 2.
3. This political and economic history is summarized in ibid., pp. 2-3.
4. Theodore Geiger, *Tales of Two City-States*, p. 15.
5. Ibid., p. 159.
6. Ibid., p. 192. See also Lee Soo Ann, *Singapore Goes Transnational*, p. 60-63.
7. Theodore Geiger, p. 163 and Lee Soo Ann, pp. 22-23.
8. Nicholas Harman, "The sovereign municipality," *The Economist*, 29 December 1979, pp. 9-11.
9. In writing this section on Singapore's public finances I consulted the Singapore Yearbook, Singapore's annual budget documents, and the annual report of the Board of Commissioners of Currency. Thoughtful accounts of the Monetary Authority of Singapore, the currency system, the CPF, and their links to the budget are found in *The Financial Structure of Singapore* (Singapore: Monetary Authority, June 1980); Tan Chee Huat, *Financial Institutions in Singapore* (Singapore: Singapore University Press, 1978); and John R. Hewson, "Monetary Policy and the Asian Dollar Market," in *Papers on Monetary Economics* (Singapore: Singapore University Press for the Monetary Authority of Singapore, 1981), pp. 165-94.
10. Theodore Geiger, *Tale of Two City-States*, p. 189.

11. Statistics on the performance of Singapore's economy are found in Chow Kit Boey, *External Linkages*, pp. 3-5, 14, 26; Theodore Geiger, pp. 168-69, and Lee Soo Ann, *Singapore Goes Transnational*, pp. 31, 35, 60-63; and *Economic Survey of Singapore 1980* (Singapore: Ministry of Trade and Industry), entire volume.

12. This treatment of Taiwan in the postwar era depends heavily on several sources. The first is a collection of speeches delivered between 1959 and 1974 by K.T. Li, a major figure in the economic planning of the Taiwan government having long held the most important post as minister of finance. It is entitled *The Experience of Dynamic Economic Growth on Taiwan* (Taipei and New York: Mei Ya, 1976), and contains a valuable appendix of statistical tables. Another is a book-length treatment by Shirley W.Y. Kuo, Gustav Ranis, and John C.H. Fei, *The Taiwan Success Story: Rapid Growth with Improved Distribution in the Republic of China, 1952-1979* (Boulder: Westview, 1981). A third is T.H. Lee and Kuo-shu Liang, "Taiwan," in Bela Balassa, *Development Strategies*, pp. 310-50. Also useful is Hugh Sandeman, "An island on its own," *The Economist*, 31 July 1982. For a thorough review of monetary and fiscal policies, see Maxwell J. Fry, "Financial Structure, Monetary Policy and Economic Growth in Hong Kong, Singapore, Taiwan, and Korea, 1960-1981" (University of California, Irvine: March 1983, mimeo).

13. "Public Policy and Economic Development," in K.T. Li, *Experience of Dynamic Economic Growth*, pp. 35-40.

14. Shirley W.Y. Kuo, *et al.*, *Taiwan Success Story*, pp. 48-55.

15. Details of these policies appear throughout K.T. Li's public essays and speeches and are found in Shirley W.Y. Kuo, pp. 73-84.

16. See Appendix, Table 16, "Net Revenues and Expenditures—All Levels of Government," in K.T. Li, *Experience of Dynamic Economic Growth*, p. 519.

17. "The Role of Fiscal Policy in Economic Development," in K.T. Li, *Experience of Dynamic Economic Growth*, p. 470.

18. The statistics reported in this section come from Shirley W.Y. Kuo, *Taiwan Success Story*, pp. 7, 12, 23, 27-30.

19. The distribution of income is treated in ibid., pp. 34-38.

20. My exposition of Korea's postwar economic development is largely drawn from the following sources: Parvez Hasan, *Korea: Problems and Issues in a Rapidly Growing Economy* (Baltimore: Johns Hopkins University Press for the World Bank, 1976); Parvez Hasan and D.C. Rao, *Korea: Policy Issues for Long-Term Development* (Baltimore: The Johns Hopkins University Press for the World Bank, 1979); Kwang Suk Kim and Michael Roemer, *Growth and Structural Transformation* (Cambridge: Harvard University Press, 1979); Larry E. Westphal and Kwang Suk Kim, "Korea," in Bela Balassa, *Development Strategies*, pp. 212-79; Hugh Sandeman, "Asia's most ambitious nation," *The Economist*, 14 August 1982; and *Major Statistics of Korean Economy 1979* (Seoul: Economic Planning Board). This section's summary of resources is taken from D.C. Rao, "The Pattern of Economic Growth, 1961-76," in Parvez Hasan and D.C. Rao, eds., *Korea*, p. 15.

21. Further information on Korea's historical setting is found in Parvez Hasan, *Korea: Problems and Issues*, pp. 25-29.

22. For a comprehensive analysis of Korea's land-reform and grain-pricing policies see Sung Hwan Ban, Pal Yong Moon, and Dwight H. Perkins, *Rural Development* (Cambridge: Harvard University Press, 1980). See also David I. Steinberg's

review of this study in "Development Lessons from the Korean Experience—A Review Article," *Journal of Asian Studies*, 42 (November 1982): 96-97.

23. See Kwang Suk Kim and Michael Roemer, *Growth and Structural Transformation*, p. 45. For a checklist summary of the full set of economic reforms, see p. 161 of the same volume.

24. Marinus van der Mel, "Public Finance," in Parvez Hasan and D.C. Rao, *Korea*, pp. 327-64.

25. Hugh Sandeman, "Asia's most ambitious nation," *The Economist*, 14 August 1982, p. 17.

26. Rich details are contained in *Major Statistics of Korean Economy 1979*.

PART III

THE WEALTH OF AMERICA

10

What Happened to the American Dream?

Prosperity in nineteenth-century Britain and in the postwar Pacific Basin Area vindicates the doctrines of Adam Smith. These same principles were also in force during the first century and a half of our own country, transforming a small, predominantly agricultural, economy into a twentieth-century industrial giant. With the Great Depression, however, the teachings of Adam Smith fell from favor; they were replaced by new ideas that rationalized a greater role for government in the economy. The worldwide Great Depression of the 1930s led many economists and government officials to wonder if the "invisible hand" had lost control. Unemployment gripped the United States, and hyperinflation broke out in Europe. Both seemed to require immediate, massive government action. In the United States, President Roosevelt announced a "new deal," in which government became the employer of first, not last, resort. In 1933, Congress passed the Social Security Act which promised income support to older Americans. Government has since increasingly borne responsibility for full employment and a burgeoning network of human services. Although wealth creation has remained largely in the private sector, its distribution has become more and more a public matter.

By 1980 the American economy was radically different from that of 1930. A large, interventionist government had supplanted a minimalist state. "Collective responsibility," "public goods," and "government funding" assumed equal status in the American vocabulary with such traditional watchwords as "individual initiative," "individual responsibility," and the "free market economy." A lexicon of modern political economy includes "entitlements," "high marginal tax rates," "social security," "corporate responsibility," "environmentalism," "deficit spending," "managing aggregate demand," and "consumerism," to name a few. Taxation and government spending have more than tripled as a share of the gross national product (GNP). Stable prices are gone with the wind. Balanced budgets are an anomaly of yesteryear. The public debt exceeds an inconceivable one trillion dollars. As the 1970s came to a close, economists of all political persuasions decried a declining savings rate, falling productivity, punitive tax rates, and rising inflation. The historical tradeoff between unemployment and inflation evaporated into a semi-permanent condition of stagflation. These conditions restored the popularity of Adam Smith's ideas of the market and limited government and provided an intellectual foundation for Ronald Reagan's presidency.

Part Three of this book is the American dream. This chapter traces the rise of the modern welfare state, with its corresponding adverse effects on the performance of the U.S. economy. The concluding chapter offers a blueprint for renewed prosperity based on the principles of Adam Smith.

150 Years of Economic Liberty and Fiscal Prudence

Had it not been for the efforts of King George III and his ministers to tax the colonies, independence may have come much later to the American states. The notorious Stamp Act of 1765 was repealed by the English Parliament in 1766 because of colonial protest and opposition. A substitute tax on glass, paint, paper, and tea, imposed in 1767, met equally vociferous opposition and was subsequently repealed in 1770. The most famous tax of all, the 1773 Tea Act, gave rise to the Boston Tea Party, and the revolutionary war cry of "no taxation without representation."

Adam Smith's writings came alive in the new American nation. Laissez-faire was very much the order of the day. His limited functions of government were modestly funded from customs and excise duties, consuming less than 3 percent of the GNP in normal peacetime circumstances. The federal government was relatively unimportant in the production and distribution of national income.

Early colonial experience with paper money, which depreciated more than 99 percent in a few short years, put the country on a bimetallic standard in 1792 and ultimately a gold standard in 1879, which lasted in some form until 1971. The "almighty dollar" was no figment of the imagination.

Limited government, low taxes, and sound money were integral elements in the American heritage, embodied in the United States Constitution and the *Federalist Papers*. These two documents are the foundation of American political culture. The most widely discussed features of the Constitution in high school textbooks include "checks and balances" and "division of powers." Three independent branches of government were established to secure the liberties of the people from an overzealous government. Moreover, power was divided between the federal and state governments as additional guarantees of the peoples' freedom. In his book, *Economic Liberties and the Constitution*,[1] Bernard Siegan has written that the framers of the Constitution sought to perpetuate an economic system based on private property and private enterprise—economic liberties were as much a part of our Constitution as civil liberties. Other clauses of the Constitution grant Congress the power to levy and collect taxes, but not to impose a direct income tax. The Constitution also explicitly grants Congress the power to coin money, but some purists argue that this right does not encompass the *printing* of paper money without some metallic backing.

Fiscal prudence was the prevailing norm of budgetary practice. The Founding Fathers adopted two explicit constitutional provisions and assumed a third to restrain federal taxing and spending. One provision reserved powers not expressly delegated to the federal government to the states and to the people—the federalism clause. Until late in the nineteenth century, this clause worked well in restraining federal activity. A second provision provided for per capita distribution among the states of taxes on income, which made any direct income tax unconstitutional. Passage of the income-tax (sixteenth) amendment in 1913 gave the federal government easy access to a new, and seemingly limitless, source of revenue. A third provision, implicit, assumed that federal spending would not exceed federal revenue except in times of war or recession. This provision remained intact until the end of World War II, and has since been replaced by the Keynesian doctrine of deficit financing as a means of managing aggregate demand to attain full employment and stable prices.

On 26 November 1798, a decade after the U.S. Constitution was written, Thomas Jefferson wrote, "I wish it were possible to obtain a single amendment to our Constitution. I would be willing to depend on that alone for the reduction of the administration of our government to the genuine principles of its Constitution; I mean an additional article, taking from the federal government the power of borrowing."[2] The balanced budget was considered part of our unwritten constitution. The only exceptions to a balanced budget were war or economic recession. Thomas Jefferson warned that "the public debt is the greatest of dangers to be feared by a republican government." Alexander Hamilton strongly urged the repayment of national debt. Presidents John Adams, James Madison, James Monroe, John Quincy Adams, and Andrew Jackson all urged avoiding public debt. Balanced budgets were a sine qua non of sound fiscal policy.

Until the Great Depression of the 1930s, budget deficits occurred only in times of war and recession. The budget surpluses generated in good times were invariably used to reduce the national debt. Historical deficits of large proportions arose during the Revolutionary War, the War of 1812, the Mexican War of 1846, and during brief recessions in the late 1830s and 1850s. In each instance, the debts were immediately reduced at the onset of peace and prosperity, *without* any increase in taxation. Between 1795 and 1811, Congress cut the national debt nearly in half, from $84 million to just over $45 million. After the War of 1812, eighteen surpluses (of twenty-one budgets) between 1815 and 1836 virtually eliminated the national debt. A run of twenty-eight consecutive surpluses following the Civil War lowered the national debt from $2.7 billion to $960 million. Finally, throughout the 1920s, consecutive surpluses reduced the national debt from $24 billion to $16 billion, at the very time that major rate reductions were legislated in the nation's now lawful income tax. Throughout most of our history, modest revenues from customs and excises were more than sufficient to fund those activities regarded as "proper" federal functions. The consensus over the limited role for government has broken down in the past fifty years, and the greater part of the current federal budget is devoted to activities not funded fifty years ago.

From its founding until the first third of the twentieth century, Americans pursued their self-interest in a market economy, protected by the Founding Fathers' constitutional guarantees of liberty and limited government. Taxes and spending at all levels of government were a low 10 percent of our GNP. Regulatory agencies were few and modest in their actions. Gold-backed dollars made U.S. currency the envy of all nations.

By 1980, the tables were totally reversed. Taxes consumed more than one third of the GNP and more than 40 percent of our personal income. Deficit spending beyond these vast sums generated a national debt exceeding one trillion dollars. Regulatory agencies sprouted like weeds and the annual issue of *The Federal Register*, first published as two small volumes in 1936, ran to 87,000 pages. Inflation reached double-digit levels for consecutive years. The American dream was in serious jeopardy.

More and Higher Taxes

Many commentators saw California's Proposition 13, which passed on 6 June 1978, as the start of a modern-day tax revolt, the biggest since the original Boston Tea Party.[3] It is not too difficult to understand the sentiment behind tax-cutting state-ballot initiatives, growing tax avoidance, tax evasion, and a booming cash or barter underground economy. What is surprising is that it took so long to burst forth.

Our early government made ends meet on today's small change. In 1800 the federal government collected $10.8 million in taxes. This figure rose fourfold to $43.6 million by 1850, reflecting overall growth in the economy. Another thirteenfold increase raised total federal taxes to $567.2 million by 1900. During the nineteenth century, the prices of consumer goods actually fell by 50 percent, which means the dollars received by the federal government in 1900 could buy more of the country's goods and services than in 1800. In real terms, federal taxes were seventy-five times higher in 1900 than in 1800, reflecting a growing population and greater public responsibilities. Still, all levels of government taxed away less than one-tenth of the GNP.[4]

The growth of government receipts in the twentieth century has dwarfed what was itself a phenomenal growth during the nineteenth. Table 10.1 traces this expansion. In 1929, the first year for which national income and product accounts information is available, federal taxes amounted to $3.8 billion, state and local totaled $7.6 billion; and total taxes equalled 10.9 percent of the GNP. By 1980 the federal government collected $540.8 billion; state and local governments had $384 billion; this total take of $836.8 billion equalled 31.9 percent of the GNP. Every decade saw a higher and higher share of the national income going to government. It was fed by a steeply-graduated income tax and an ever-increasing burden of social security taxes.

Prices have increased about fivefold since 1929, with the sharpest increases occurring since 1965. Taking inflation into account, federal taxes have increased twenty-sevenfold in real terms, and state and local receipts tenfold.

The federal tax dollar comes from four main sources: individual income taxes, corporation taxes, social insurance taxes and contributions, and excise taxes. In 1980, individual income taxes contributed 47.6 percent of federal receipts; corporate taxes gave 13 percent (down sharply from 22.2 percent in 1960, reflecting the declining profitability of corporations); excise taxes and customs duties were 7.5 percent; and social insurance taxes and contributions totalled 31.8 percent (up sharply from 18.3 percent in 1960). Social security taxes have risen so rapidly that more than half of all American households pay more in social insurance taxes than they do in personal income taxes.

Table 10.1
U.S. Government Receipts, 1929–1980
(in billions of current dollars)

Calendar Year	Federal Government ($)	State and Local Government ($)	Total Government ($)	Total Govt. as Percent of GNP (%)
1929	3.8	7.6	11.3	10.9
1940	8.6	10.0	17.7	17.7
1950	50.0	21.3	69.0	24.1
1960	96.1	49.9	139.5	27.5
1970	191.9	135.4	302.8	30.5
1980	540.8	384.0	836.8	31.9

Source: Economic Report of the President 1982, Table B-75, p. 320. Figures are from the national income and product accounts.

Individual Income Taxes

The income tax took effect in 1913 after three-fourths of the American states ratified the sixteenth amendment to the Constitution of the United States.[5] In that first year, the personal income tax return, Form 1040, was two pages long and the accompanying instructions only filled two pages. Moreover, only 0.4 percent of the American population earned enough money to file a return.

The income tax of 1913 granted a personal exemption of $3,000 for a single person and $4,000 for married persons. The basic tax rate started at 1 percent. In addition to the normal rate of 1 percent, a surtax was levied on the net income of individuals exceeding $20,000 at a rate of 1 percent. The rate of this surtax rose in stages to 6 percent on incomes over $500,000.

Things looked rather different in 1980. A complete Form 1040 booklet included seventeen pages of the most frequently used schedules, and forty-four pages of instructions to assist taxpayers in preparing their returns. Eighty-three million returns, encompassing virtually the entire population, were filed in 1979. Over half of all taxpayers feel compelled to use commercial tax-preparation services to file their returns. In 1980, taxpayers faced a federal income-tax system in which marginal tax rates rose from a low of 14 percent to a high of 70 percent. The marginal rate is the amount by which the tax goes up for each additional dollar of income.

This transformation is remarkable!

During congressional debate on the sixteenth amendment, proponents of the income tax promised that the top rate could never pass 10 percent. World War I quickly gave the lie to these promises. Wartime needs for revenue reduced the personal allowance, imposed a normal rate beginning at 4 percent, and raised the surtax to 50 percent for those with incomes over $1 million. Still, only about one-fifth of the adult population filed income-tax returns.

Secretary of the Treasury Andrew Mellon reduced the structure sharply during the 1920s, bringing the top marginal rate down to 25 percent. But the depression and war years of the 1930s and 1940s pushed the top rates back above 50 percent. Indeed the top marginal rate stood at the incredible level of 91 percent when President John F. Kennedy proposed in 1963 to reduce it to 70 percent.

The sharp rise in the income-tax burden appears in Table 10.2. The individual income tax barely surpassed 1 percent of personal income after the Mellon reforms in the 1920s, remaining at that low level through the 1930s. Since the end of World War II, the share has typically exceeded 10 percent, contributing between 42 and 46 percent of total federal receipts.

Table 10.2
Growth of U.S. Individual Income Tax, 1930–1981

Year	Individual Income Tax As a Percentage of:	
	Total Personal Income	Federal Receipts
1930	1.4	33.3
1935	0.9	15.0
1940	1.3	11.6
1945	10.9	43.5
1950	7.7	34.8
1955	9.8	41.9
1960	10.4	43.5
1965	9.4	41.1
1969	12.1	46.5
1970	11.0	46.3
1972	10.8	45.2
1974	10.8	43.9
1976	10.2	42.7
1978	10.9	43.9
1980	11.6	46.4
1981	12.0	46.3

Source: Bureau of Economic Analysis, *Survey of Current Business,* "The National Income and Product Accounts of the United States" (September 1981), pp. 73–75, 122–23; (July 1981), pp. 14, 23; (April 1982), pp. 12, 13; (July 1982), pp. 12, 47.

Changes in Marginal Tax Rates

Marginal tax rates apply only to the last dollar earned. As increases in income push people into higher tax brackets, a greater proportion of each additional dollar of income is paid in taxes. Someone paying a marginal rate of 20 percent gets to keep 80¢ of each additional dollar. At 30 percent, he keeps 70¢. And at a 50 percent marginal rate, he divides the last dollar equally between himself and the government. Many American families have incomes of $50,000, pay an average tax between $5,000-$10,000 (between 10 and 20 percent), yet face marginal tax rates from 30 to 50 percent. It is this top marginal rate, not the average rate, that sets incentives. The marginal rate determines whether the taxpayer decides to work harder or spend more time fishing.

Twenty years ago few Americans paid high marginal tax rates on their income. Today, millions of middle-class Americans face the high marginal rates that were intended only for the very rich just a short while ago. "Bracket creep," caused by the inflation of the 1970s, pushed taxpayers into higher marginal tax brackets even with no change in their real disposable (after-tax, after-inflation) income. In 1961, although statutory rates were steeply graduated from 20 to 91 percent, the income tax was essentially a flat-rate tax for all but the highest-income taxpayers. Table 10.3 shows that 88 percent of all taxpayers paid a marginal tax rate of 20 to 22 percent in 1961. By 1969, 64 percent faced marginal tax rates above 22 percent; by 1979, actual marginal tax rates resembled the graduated statutory rates.

According to Treasury Department figures, a family of four earning the median income in 1965 faced a marginal tax rate of 17 percent. In 1980, its marginal rate was 24 percent. For families with twice the median income, the marginal rate increased from 22 to 43 percent. If a family's income only kept pace with inflation during this period, the purchasing power of its take-home pay would have declined as the family paid taxes at increasingly higher rates, leaving it with a smaller, after-tax share. As this process accelerated during the high inflation years of the late 1970s, taxpayers faced a growing squeeze on real take-home pay.

Figure 10.1 plots the sharp rise in marginal tax rates faced by taxpayers in the 70th and 95th percentiles of taxable returns. The 70th percentile watched its marginal tax rate increase by two-fifths, from 20 to 28 percent, between 1966 and 1981; the 95th percentile experienced a four-fifths increase, from a marginal rate of 25 to 46 percent.

Table 10.3
Distribution of U.S. Tax Returns by Marginal Tax Rate[1]
1961, 1969, 1979 (in percents)

Marginal Tax Rate	1961	1969	1979
1–14	0.00	9.59	10.06
15–19	0.00	16.97	24.70
20–22	87.80	9.38	19.94
23–31	10.04	57.48	27.36
32–72	2.15	6.57	17.93
73–91	0.01	0.02	0.00
Total	100.00	100.00	100.00

1. Includes only tax returns with positive tax liability.
Source: Eugene Steuerle and Michael Hartzmark, "Individual Income Taxation 1947–1979," *National Tax Journal* (June 1981): 164.

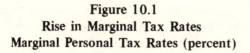

Figure 10.1
Rise in Marginal Tax Rates
Marginal Personal Tax Rates (percent)

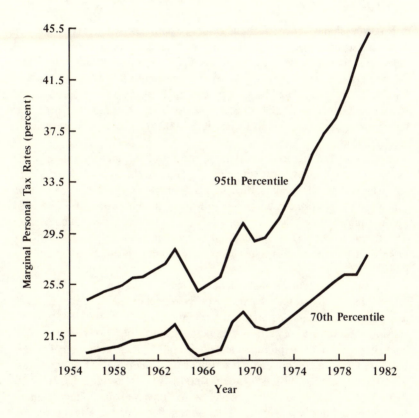

Source: Robert J. Genetski, "The Impact of the Reagan Administration's Economic Proposals," Shadow Open Market Committee, Policy Statement and Position Papers, March 15–16, 1981, p. 25 (Graduate School of Management, University of Rochester).

The complexity, costs, and disincentives embodied in our graduated income tax are three reasons for growing tax evasion, the proliferation of fancy tax shelters, some questionable, and an expanding underground economy that cost the government an estimated $87.2 billion in lost revenue in 1981, a figure that tripled from $29.3 billion in 1973. Table 10.4 shows that the underground economy has mushroomed from a modest 2 to 3 percent of the GNP in 1950 to 12 percent by 1978. The trend line is especially worrisome.

Social Security Taxes

No discussion of federal receipts would be complete without some mention of social security taxes. Signed into law by President Roosevelt in 1933, individual contributions did not surpass $100 until 1950. Table 10.5 shows that the tax rate (shared equally between employer and employee) rose from a low 2.0 percent in 1937 to 13.3 percent in 1981. The tax base has simultaneously risen from $3,000 to $29,700. As a result, the maximum contribution has jumped from $60 to nearly $4,000 by 1981. It is estimated to reach $6,000 by 1986.

In the past few decades, taxes have risen more rapidly than other major expenses facing Americans, suppressing gains in real take-home pay. Table 10.6 shows how the median U.S. family (married couple with two children supported by one worker, employed full-time) fared between 1971 and 1981. Median family income more than doubled. However, federal income taxes tripled, social security taxes quadrupled, and inflation cut purchasing power more than half. Real disposable income fell, with an especially sharp drop in 1980.

One final comment on the federal income-tax system. It was originally proposed and adopted for the purpose of raising additional revenue. By 1980, it had also become a major tool of social policy. Tax preferences or tax subsidies are used to reward or encourage specific types of behavior (e.g., home buying, energy exploration and conservation, local government bonds). In 1982, the joint committee on taxation of the United States Congress classified 109 separate provisions of the tax code as tax-subsidy items. If all 109 items in the fiscal year 1983 budget were converted into direct spending outlays, their value would exceed $292 billion. Seen another way, the revenue lost to the treasury from granting these 109 functions preferential tax treatment was about $243 billion.[6] Tax subsidies have become an end run around the outlay side of the budget, where it is more appropriate to consider questions of social policy.

Lost revenue from tax subsidies points up a general problem with the federal income tax, namely, the erosion of the tax base. In 1979, for example, total receipts from the personal and corporate income taxes were $280 billion, amounting to 11.6 percent of the GNP. Thus a straight tax of 11.6 percent

Table 10.4
Rise of the U.S. Underground Economy, 1948–1978
Gross National Product

	Billions of Dollars		Percent Change	
	Official	Underground[1]	Official	Underground
1948	259.1	17.8	11.3	6.5
1949	258.0	15.9	−0.4	−10.6
1950	286.2	13.4	10.9	−15.7
1951	330.2	14.5	15.4	8.2
1952	347.2	15.9	5.1	9.7
1953	366.1	17.1	5.5	7.5
1954	366.3	13.3	0.0	−22.2
1955	399.3	13.7	9.0	3.0
1956	420.7	14.7	5.4	7.3
1957	442.8	16.7	5.2	13.6
1958	448.9	13.6	1.4	−18.5
1959	486.5	14.2	8.4	4.4
1960	506.0	14.4	4.0	1.4
1961	523.3	13.6	3.4	−5.6
1962	563.8	17.3	7.7	27.2
1963	594.7	21.9	5.5	26.6
1964	635.7	25.0	6.9	14.2
1965	688.1	29.2	8.2	16.8
1966	753.0	38.1	9.4	30.5
1967	796.3	37.8	5.8	−0.1
1968	868.5	39.9	9.1	5.6
1969	935.5	50.7	7.7	27.1
1970	982.4	56.5	5.0	11.4
1971	1,063.4	63.1	8.2	11.7
1972	1,171.1	67.2	10.1	6.5
1973	1,306.6	83.5	11.6	24.3
1974	1,412.9	113.7	8.1	36.2
1975	1,528.8	145.6	8.2	28.1
1976	1,700.1	181.3	11.2	24.5
1977	1,887.2	212.8	11.0	17.4
1978	2,107.6	264.5	11.7	24.3

1. Computed by the Congressional Research Service using methodology developed by Peter Gutmann.

Source: Reported GNP is from the U.S. Department of Commerce, Bureau of Economic Analysis. Underground GNP is calculated from data published by the U.S. Department of Commerce, Bureau of Economic Analysis and Board of Governors of the Federal Reserve System. Reproduced in Bruce Bartlett, *Reaganomics: Supply-Side Economics in Action* (Westport, Conn.: Arlington House, 1981), p. 20.

Table 10.5
History of U.S. Social Security Tax Rates

Period	Combined Employee-Employer Tax Rate	Tax Base	Maximum Contribution
1937–49	2.0%	$ 3,000	$ 60
1950	3.0	3,000	90
1951–53	3.0	3,600	108
1954	4.0	3,600	144
1955–56	4.0	4,200	168
1957–58	4.5	4,200	189
1959	5.0	4,800	240
1960–61	6.0	4,800	288
1962	6.25	4,800	300
1963–65	7.25	4,800	348
1966	8.4	6,600	554
1967	8.8	6,600	581
1968	8.8	7,800	686
1969–70	9.6	7,800	749
1971	10.4	7,800	811
1972	10.4	9,000	936
1973	11.7	10,800	1,264
1974	11.7	13,200	1,544
1975	11.7	14,100	1,650
1976	11.7	15,300	1,790
1977	11.7	16,500	1,930
1978	12.1	17,700	2,142
1979	12.26	22,900	2,808
1980	12.26	25,900	3,175
1981	13.3	29,700	3,950
1982*	13.4	32,400	4,340
1983*	13.4	35,400	4,644
1984*	13.4	39,000	5,226
1985*	14.1	42,900	6,049

* Estimated

Source: Senate Finance Committee. Office of Management and Budget. Reproduced in Bruce Bartlett, *Reaganomics: Supply-Side Economics in Action* (Westport, Conn.: Arlington House, 1981), p. 172.

on all gross income would yield the same revenue as the 1979 system, which taxed corporate profits at 46 percent and an individual's "taxable income" at rates from 14 to 70 percent. The reason for the huge disparity between the hypothetical 11.6 percent flat rate and the higher corporate and individual rates is the erosion of the GNP into a smaller taxable base of income. Sub-

Table 10.6
Median U.S. Family Income Before and
After Direct Federal Taxes and Inflation,
1971–1981 ($ U.S.)

Year	Median family income[1]	Direct Federal Taxes			After-tax Income	
		Income tax[2]	Social Security	Total	Current dollars	1971 dollars[3]
1971	10,314	933	406	1,339	8,975	8,975
1972	11,152	982	468	1,450	9,702	9,392
1973	11,895	1,098	632	1,730	10,165	9,264
1974	13,004	1,267	761	2,028	10,976	9,014
1975	14,156	1,172	825	1,997	12,159	9,149
1976	15,016	1,388	878	2,266	12,750	9,071
1977	15,949	1,466	933	2,399	13,550	9,056
1978	17,318	1,717	1,048	2,765	14,553	9,034
1979	19,097	1,876	1,171	3,047	16,050	8,955
1980	20,900[4]	2,197	1,281	3,478	17,422	8,563
1981	23,700[4]	2,801[5]	1,576	4,377	19,323	8,548

1. Median income for all families with one earner employed full-time, year-round.
2. Married couple filing joint return, two children.
3. Adjusted by Consumer Price Index, Bureau of Labor Statistics.
4. 1980 and 1981 estimated by Tax Foundation.
5. Assumes no change in current law.
Source: The Tax Foundation.

tracting from GNP such items as fringe benefits, indirect business taxes, unreported income, itemized and standard deductions, and personal allowances, shrinks that tax base by half. To raise the same 11.6 percent of GNP in revenue from this smaller base requires much higher rates.

New and Higher Spending

Accompanying the rise in taxation is even more rapid growth in spending. Table 10.7 shows that total government spending as a share of GNP has risen from 10 percent in 1929 to an even 33.3 percent by 1980. A comparison of the 1929 and 1980 federal budgets shows that the bulk of current federal budget activities did not exist fifty years ago. Consensus on limited government has been replaced by a welfare-state mentality.

The way in which the public dollar is spent has changed markedly.[7] Defense consumed 49¢ of the public dollar in 1952, falling to a modest 16¢ by 1978. Income support programs, commonly called transfer payments (including

Table 10.7
U.S. Government Expenditures, 1929–1980
(in billions of $ U.S.)

Calendar Year	Federal Govt.	State and Local Govt.	Total Govt.	Total Govt. as Percent of GNP (%)
1929	2.6	7.8	10.3	10.0
1940	10.0	9.3	18.4	18.4
1950	40.8	22.5	61.0	21.3
1960	93.1	49.8	136.4	26.9
1970	204.3	133.4	313.4	31.5
1980	602.0	355.0	869.0	33.2

Source: Economic Report of the President 1982, Table B-75, p. 320. Figures are from the national income and product accounts.

social security), rose from 7¢ to 23¢. Education doubled from 9¢ to 18¢; health tripled from 3¢ to 9¢. Defense lost two-thirds of its share of the public dollar, while the share of domestic functions doubled. Expressed in constant (inflation-adjusted) dollars, defense spending fell 4 percent between 1952 and 1978 while domestic spending increased 498 percent. The latter was fueled by a sharp growth in state and local government spending.

All governments shifted their primary spending from the purchase of goods and services to transfer payments. In 1952, for example, transfer payments at all levels of government amounted to $44.4 billion. By 1978 they reached $218.7 billion, a real increase of 527 percent. Roger Freeman, in *The Wayward Welfare State*, documented this shift away from the service state. In the three areas of income support, health, and education, total government expenditures in constant dollars multiplied eight times between 1952 and 1978, in a quarter century in which population increased only 39 percent and personal consumption 153 percent.

By itself, federal spending on domestic purposes increased twenty-twofold between 1952 and 1978, from 18 to 62 percent of all federal spending by 1978, or from 3.6 to 13.5 percent of the GNP. Both the size and scope of the government in 1980 bear little resemblance to its 1930 predecessor.

Deficits, Deficits, Deficits

In sharp contrast with historical experience, the federal budget process has failed to show restraint in the post-World War II era. For the better part of 200 years, Americans held to a limited role for the federal government. Except for periods of war or recession, revenues from customs and excises were sufficient to fund those activities widely regarded as proper federal functions. This consensus has broken down in the last fifty years.

Since 1960, deficits have become the accepted practice of federal budgeting.[8] Apart from one modest surplus of $3 billion in 1969, Congress has imposed a regime of persistent deficits. A national debt of $300 billion in fiscal year 1962, a legacy of World War II, rose to $437 billion in fiscal 1972, surpassing $1 trillion in October 1981. Eight deficits in the 1970s were $40 billion or greater. Interest payments, which absorbed approximately 6 percent of the national budget twenty years ago, consumed about 12 percent in 1981. It is a figure half as large as spending for national defense and one-third as large as spending for income security programs. Even these sums pale against the nearly $200 billion deficits of the early 1980s. Deficit financing is the reason that federal spending has been able to outstrip federal receipts, which on their own rose more than eightfold as a share of the GNP.

Due to the unwritten norm of budget balance, the federal government was rarely troubled by budget deficits through 175 years of our history. The breakdown of the balanced-budget norm, replaced by a Keynesian rationale that government could use deficits and surpluses[9] to smooth out the business cycle, thereby sustaining full employment and stable prices, enabled spending to outpace revenue by an increasingly wider margin. "Bracket creep" and "deficit gallop" have joined hands in the waltz toward bigger government.

The Heavy Hand of Government Regulation

Laissez-faire, the watchword of government's relationship to the economy during the nineteenth century, has yielded to regulation since the mid-twenties. Regulation is somewhat more invisible than taxes, but it is no less a direct cost imposed on business activity. Government can achieve its policy objectives through spending on specific programs, granting tax subsidies, or ordering business to bear costs in the form of regulations. Murray Weidenbaum's textbook, *Business, Government, and the Public*,[10] describes government regulation of automobile production, consumer products, job safety, the environment, energy, personnel practices, and paperwork, to name a few areas, most of which has occurred since 1960.

In 1930, only twelve federal regulatory agencies existed. By 1980, the number stood at fifty-three. Table 10.8 shows that twenty-six new agencies were christened during the 1960s and 1970s. This fact bears repeating: half of all the federal regulatory agencies were born in the past two decades, most during the Nixon administrations.

The growth in the page count of the *Federal Register*, which records all rules, regulations, and notices issued daily by federal agencies, quantifies

Table 10.8
Chronology of U.S. Federal Regulatory Agencies

Field	Prior to 1939	1930s	1940s	1950s	1960s	1970s	Total
Consumer safety and health	1	2	1	0	1	6	11
Job safety and other labor conditions	0	2	0	0	2	5	9
Environment and energy	2	0	0	0	1	2	5
Finance	2	2	0	0	0	3	7
Industry	3	5	1	1	2	2	14
General business	4	0	0	1	0	2	7
Total	12	11	2	2	6	20	53

Source: Compiled from data contained in Marsha Wallace and Ronald Penoyer, *Directory of Federal Regulatory Agencies* (St. Louis: Center for the Study of American Business, Washington University, 1978). Cited in Murray L. Weidenbaum, ''Government Power and Business Performance,'' in Peter Duignan and Alvin Rabushka, eds., *The United States in the 1980s* (Stanford: Hoover Institution Press, 1980), p. 215.

rising federal regulatory activity. As seen in Figure 10.2, the *Federal Register* had only 2,411 pages in 1936, a mere two volumes. In 1960, it was still a modest 14,479 pages. Then the government went into the business of regulation full throttle. The page count grew 50 percent between 1960 and 1970, and then quadrupled, from 20,036 to 87,011, between 1970 and 1980—an annual compound rate of nearly 16 percent.

Members of Congress embarked on an unprecedented regulatory binge. Between 1970 and 1978, Congress enacted twenty-seven major new pieces of regulation (see Table 10.9). Protecting safety in the workplace, maintaining air and water quality, and encouraging automobile safety are all worthy goals, but they must be weighed against the additional costs that are entailed. The costs of government regulation are pervasive: 1) to the taxpayer for supporting a galaxy of government regulators, 2) to the consumer through higher prices to cover the added expense of producing goods and services under government regulations, 3) to the worker in the form of the jobs eliminated by government regulation, 4) to the economy as a result of the loss of smaller enterprises that cannot afford the onerous burdens of government regulations, and 5) to society through a reduced flow of better products and a slower rise in the standard of living.

Figure 10.2
Growth in the Federal Register

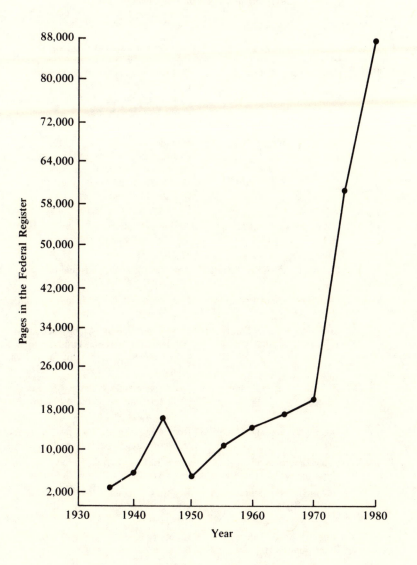

Source: Richard B. McKenzie, *Bound to Be Free* (Stanford: Hoover Press, 1982), p. 27

Table 10.9
New U.S. Government Regulation of Business, 1970–1978

Years of Enactment	Name of Law	Purpose and Function
1970	Amendments to Federal Deposit Insurance Act	Prohibits issuance of unsolicited credit cards. Limits customer's liability in case of loss of theft to $50. Regulates credit bureaus and provides consumer access to files
1970	Securities Investor Protection Act	Provides greater protection for customers of brokers and dealers and members of national securities exchanges. Establishes a Securities Investor Protection Corporation, financed by fees on brokerage houses
1970	Poison Prevention Packaging Act	Authorizes standards for child-resistant packaging of hazardous substances
1970	Clean Air Act Amendments	Provides for setting air-quality standards
1970	Occupational Safety and Health Act	Establishes safety and health standards that must be met by employers
1972	Consumer Product Safety Act	Establishes a commission to set safety standards for consumer products and bans products presenting undue risk of injury
1972	Federal Water Pollution Control Act	Declares an end to the discharge of pollutants into navigable waters by 1985 as a national goal
1972	Noise Pollution and Control Act	Regulates noise limits of products and transportation vehicles
1972	Equal Employment Opportunity Act	Gives EEOC the right to sue employers
1973	Vocational Rehabilitation Act	Requires federal contractors to take affirmative action on hiring the handicapped
1973	Highway Speed Limit Reduction	Limits vehicles to speeds of 55 miles an hour
1973	Safe Drinking Water Act	Requires EPA to set national drinking water regulations
1974	Campaign Finance Amendments	Restricts amounts of political contributions
1974	Employee Retirement Income Security Act	Sets new federal standards for employee pension programs

Table 10.9 (Continued)
New U.S. Government Regulation of Business, 1970–1978

Years of Enactment	Name of Law	Purpose and Function
1974	Hazardous Materials Transportation Act	Requires standards for the transportation of hazardous materials
1974	Magnuson-Moss Warranty Improvement Act	Establishes federal standards for written consumer product warranties
1975	Energy Policy and Conservation Act	Authorizes greater controls over domestic energy supplies and demands
1976	Hart-Scott-Rodino Antitrust Amendments	Provides for class-action suits by state attorneys general; requires large companies to notify the Department of Justice of planned mergers and acquisitions
1976	Toxic Substances Control Act	Requires advance testing and restrictions on use of chemical substances
1977	Department of Energy Organization Act	Establishes a permanent department to regulate energy on a continuing basis
1977	Surface Mining Control and Reclamation Act	Regulates strip mining and the reclamation of abandoned mines
1977	Fair Labor Standards Amendments	Increases the minimum wage in three steps
1977	Export Administration Act	Imposes restrictions on complying with the Arab boycott
1977	Business Payments Abroad Act	Provides for up to $1 million penalties for bribes of foreign officials
1977	Saccharin Study and Labelling Act	Requires warning labels on products containing saccharin
1978	Fair Debt Collection Practices Act	Provides for the first nationwide control of collection agencies
1978	Age Discrimination in Employment Act Amendments	Raises the permissible mandatory retirement age from 65 to 70 for most employees

Source: Murray L. Weidenbaum, *Business, Government, and the Public,* 2nd ed. (Englewood Cliffs, N.J.: Prentice-Hall, 1981), pp. 8–10.

Murray Weidenbaum and his colleagues at Washington University's Center for the Study of American Business have tried to measure the direct and indirect costs of federal regulatory activity.[11] The first layer of costs is the

direct budgetary expenditures of federal regulatory agencies. These have grown
from under $3 billion in 1974 to over $6 billion in 1980. Much of this
expenditure is the salary and fringe benefits awarded to more than 80,000
employees of all federal regulatory agencies. Second-order effects, the costs
of compliance with 87,011 pages of new federal regulations in 1980 alone,
are much greater, perhaps twenty times as high as the direct costs to taxpayers.
Robert DeFina estimated that such compliance costs came to $63 billion in
1976. The corresponding 1980 sum is a round $100 billion, representing a
substantial hidden tax of $500 imposed on every American.

Federal paperwork requirements is one concrete example of compliance
costs. Professors James Bennett and Manuel Johnson estimated that in 1977
the federal government had a total of 5,473 repetitive forms for businesses
to complete, which required 427 million responses and consumed 210 million
man-hours (a 36 percent increase over 1973).[12] These figures do not include
the 600 million man-hours spent filling out tax forms and non-repetitive
business forms. The 1980 paperwork burden for individuals and businesses
exceeded a billion man-hours, which is equivalent to the work load of 500,000
full-time employees.

Third-order effects imposed by regulation on business are harder to quan-
tify. These are actions taken by a firm to respond to the direct and indirect
effects of regulation. Examples include cutting back on research and development and on new capital formation because of the diversion of funds to
meet government-mandated social requirements. Regulation slows the pace
of innovation and rising productivity.

Regulation has spawned a growing number of vested interests—people,
firms, and organizations—that have a major stake in maintaining, or even
expanding, the regulatory activities of government. Regulatory agencies, set
up ostensibly to protect the interests of consumers, are often used by the
industry to reduce competition, divide the market, and set prices, benefitting
producers and penalizing consumers. Regulation politicizes American life
because individuals and groups vie with each other for the regulatory favors
governmental agencies can grant. Washington's K-Street corridor is home to
hundreds of lobbying organizations. The annual *Directory of Washington
Representatives* lists thousands of groups and individuals registered to lobby
the United States government. Every candidate for high office feels obligated
to rail against the "special interests" that influence politics.

From Sound Money to Fiat Currency

The United States has run the gamut from paper money to a specie currency
throughout its history.[13] At the very beginning of colonial times, the English

Kings forbade the minting of coins in the colonies, regarding it as an infringement on royal prerogative. However, foreign silver and gold coins obtained in commerce with the West Indies, especially the Spanish silver dollar, circulated as currency within the colonies.

Beginning in the late seventeenth and through much of the eighteenth century, every colony issued paper money, which was not backed by a precious metal. Silver coins disappeared from circulation during this period as people were not prepared to exchange a silver dollar coin for a one dollar note which lacked convertibility into gold or silver. Cycles of inflation, deflation, boom, and bust characterized the colonial economy. To finance the Revolutionary War, the Continental Congress issued fiat paper money. The total money supply in the United States rose from $12 million to $225 million in five years, with a marked erosion in the value of the paper notes. Continentals, as the notes were called, fell to a value of $1.25 to $1 in specie in 1777. By December 1778 the value was 6.8 to 1; by December 1779 it was 42 to 1; and by spring of 1781 it was a worthless 168 paper dollars to one dollar in specie.

When President Washingon took office, he appointed Alexander Hamilton as secretary of the treasury. Hamilton produced the famous *Report on the Establishment of a Mint*, which culminated in The Coinage Act of 1792, creating a bimetallic monetary system. The dollar was defined as both a weight of 371.25 grains of pure silver and/or a weight of 24.75 grains of pure gold— a fixed ratio of 15 grains of silver to 1 grain of gold. Anyone could bring gold and silver bullion to the Mint to be coined, and silver and gold coins were both to be legal tender at this fixed ratio of 15:1. Whenever this 15:1 ratio changed, as it often did, one of the two metals would disappear from circulation, as it became profitable to exchange the coins of one for the other at the Mint, melt them down into bullion, and export the bullion for profit at the higher price. From 1810 to 1834, for example, undervalued gold disappeared from circulation. However, so long as one of the two metals remained in circulation, prices remained relatively stable.

During the Civil War, all banks suspended specie payments from 30 December 1861, and the U.S. Treasury soon followed. The government printed legal-tender note issues, called greenbacks, and the country went on a paper-money standard until 1 January 1879. In terms of specie, greenbacks depreciated rapidly. Within six months only copper/nickel pennies remained in circulation—gold and silver coins had disappeared. When the United States returned to a specie basis on 1 January 1879, it was de facto on a gold standard, since a revision of the coinage laws in 1873 discontinued the privilege of free coinage of silver. Twenty-one years later Congress legally recognized the gold standard by the Gold Standard Act of 1900. Thereafter, silver served only as small change.

Until 10 March 1933, the United States was on a classic gold standard. On that day, President Roosevelt prohibited by executive order the export of gold and gold certificates as well as payments in gold by banks, thus bringing the classic gold standard era to an end.

What happened to the price of gold and the purchasing power between 1792 and 1933? Setting 1930 as the index year equal to 100.00, the price of gold, expressed in dollars, remained at an index of 93.8 every year between 1800 and 1833; it moved up to an index price of 100.0 in 1835 where it remained almost every year until 1933.[14] Only during the Civil War and post-war years of 1862 to 1876 did the price of gold rise in terms of dollars. It peaked at 203.3 in 1864, which reflected a more than 50 percent depreciation in the value of paper notes. The steadily rising value of paper money after the war permitted resumption of specie at par in 1879. With the exception of the wartime greenback years, the Treasury sustained an almost perfectly stable gold-dollar price.

Recall that in nineteenth-century Britain, a stable price of gold neither guaranteed short-run stability in commodity prices, nor prevented commercial and banking crises. The American experience was similar. Between 1808 and 1933, Jastram designated four periods as inflationary and three as deflationary. Table 10.10 shows that in each of the four inflationary periods, gold lost purchasing power in terms of what it could buy in commodities; in all three deflationary periods, gold appreciated handsomely in value.

Table 10.10
Purchasing Power of Gold, 1808 to 1976

Years	Inflation		Deflation	
	Prices (%)	Purchasing Power of Gold (%)	Prices (%)	Purchasing Power of Gold (%)
1808–14	+ 58	− 37		
1814–30			− 50	+ 100
1843–57	+ 48	− 33		
1861–64	+ 117	− 6		
1864–97			− 65	+ 40
1897–1920	+ 232	− 70		
1929–33			− 31	+ 44
1933–51	+ 168	− 37		
1951–76	+ 101	+ 80		

Source: Roy Jastram, *The Golden Constant* (New York: Wiley, 1977), p. 172.

From a long-run perspective, gold held its purchasing power very well. The purchasing power of gold, exchangeable into dollars at a fixed price throughout this period, was roughly similar in such disparate years as 1802, 1820, 1836, 1855, 1865, 1874, 1882, 1916, and 1927.[15] The gold standard went hand-in-hand with long-run price stability.

The key element in the system was convertibility. Overrapid expansion of credit or currency by banks, made possible by a fractional reserve banking system, often led to cycles of boom and bust. Whenever holders lost confidence in notes due to their overissue, the process of conversion into specie contracted credit and business activity. So long as convertibility was sustained, hyperinflation was impossible.

Money Since 1933

During the worldwide depression of the 1920s, most European nations abandoned the gold standard. Despite official statements that America would maintain the gold standard, the public grew increasingly anxious about the safety of their money. Runs on banks by depositors in early 1933 anxious to get cash, and runs on the Federal Reserve Banks by holders of cash anxious to get gold, accelerated rapidly. On 3 March the big New York banks agreed to close. Roosevelt was inaugurated on 4 March, but he kept all banks closed until 13 March. During these nine days, Congress granted the president emergency powers, which he used to take the United States off the classic gold standard.

On 5 April it became illegal to own or hold any form of monetary gold, either coins, bullion, or certificates. Convertibility disappeared! By 1936 all gold countries ceased redeeming their paper currencies for gold. In the absence of a regulating gold standard, currencies all over the world depreciated. An international monetary conference was held in mid-1944 at Bretton Woods, New Hampshire, to establish a new postwar monetary order so as to restore the currency stability of the gold standard.

Under the Bretton Woods arrangement, the dollar would be convertible into gold at $35 an ounce; it would be so only to foreigners, and, after 1962, only to foreign governments. All other currencies were defined in terms of the dollar. No currency was allowed to either rise or fall more than 1 percent against the dollar. The dollar remained literally "good as gold" so long as foreign holders of dollars could present American currency to the U.S. Treasury at any time and receive one ounce of gold for thirty-five paper dollars.

The Great Society programs and the Vietnam War in the late 1960s brought a massive dollar inflation which made the U.S. dollar overvalued in terms of gold. A recession in 1969-70 moderated inflation and encouraged foreigners to hold dollars. But renewed inflation presaged the imminent collapse of the dollar. Money flowed across the Atlantic into the European money markets, which forced European currencies against their upper ceiling in terms of the fixed-exchange regime of Bretton Woods. Rumors of an upward German revaluation saw dollars pour into Germany, forcing the Bundesbank to buy them in billions. On 5 May 1971, the German central bank let the mark float. Fears that the U.S. government would suspend its pledge to redeem gold for currency became a self-fulfilling prophecy. In August, $5 billion in gold or other reserve assets were drained from the Treasury in one week. During the next week, the U.S. Treasury borrowed $3 billion in foreign currency in a futile attempt to halt the dollar's decline. On 15 August 1971, President Nixon announced that we would no longer exchange gold for dollars.

The drain of U.S. gold supplies stopped instantly. Shutting the "gold window" also removed all restraints on the ability of the U.S. government to inflate the currency, since floating exchange rates, not convertibility, now determined the value of the dollar in world commerce and finance.

What has happened to the stock of money and the price level since 1971? The money supply has grown at an unprecedented rate. Defined in terms of the monetary base, which is the sum of bank reserves and currency held by the public, the money supply has risen from $86.6 billion in December 1971 to $169.8 billion ten years later. Other popular indicators of the money supply show a similar doubling, or more. Depending on the choice of indicator, the increase in the money supply ranged from a low of 58 to a high of 184 percent in the short span of one decade.

The effect on prices is clearly visible. The consumer price index (CPI), using the base year of 1967 = 100, showed a corresponding ten-year rise from 123.1 to 281.5. Rising prices imposed an inflation premium on interest rates, the price of credit, as lenders tried to preserve the real value of their assets. Between 1971 and 1981, conventional home mortgage rates more than doubled, the prime lending rate tripled, and Treasury bill rates went up two and one-half times.

The Emergence of Stagflation

Since 1965, the U.S. economy has experienced progressively higher rates of inflation and unemployment, a combination of conditions commonly called "stagflation." It accompanied growing federal involvement in the economy. The concurrent rise in inflation and unemployment during the 1970s signalled that something was radically amiss in the American economy.

Until the Great Depression of the 1930s, the American economy and its government reflected the visions of the Founding Fathers. A combination of liberal economic policy, conservative budgetary policy, and sound money brought the American dream to millions. The last fifty years have brought political and economic changes that the Founding Fathers would scarcely recognize or tolerate.

Americans prospered from the end of World War II until the first oil shock hit in 1973. However, the oil shock is not the cause of our economic difficulties. What it did was to crystallize several adverse trends that have intensified since 1965. The analogy with smoking makes this point. One can smoke for decades and yet damage to the human body is reversible if the habit is kicked in time. If not, sustained persistent smoking brings irreversible, life-threatening damage. Up to a point, the U.S. economy could withstand the costs imposed by a growing government. By the 1970s these costs drove the economy onto a path of slow to no growth.

Productivity

Let's start with changes in productivity. Rising productivity allows the economy to produce more goods and services at lower cost, thus increasing our ability to consume more. It is the foundation for economic growth and a rising standard of living.

Between 1950 and 1967, the average annual percentage change in productivity was 2.4. It fell by more than half to 1.1 from 1967 to 1972. It fell yet again by about half to an annual average of 0.6 from 1972 to 1977. During the three years from 1978 to 1980, output per hour of all persons in both the private business and nonfarm business sector fell every year. Declining productivity has put the U.S. economy at a disadvantage against our major industrial competitors, who have enjoyed higher productivity growth.

Personal Savings

Paralleling the downward trend in productivity, personal saving as a percentage of disposable personal income has steadily declined since 1965. Table 10.11 shows that an annual savings rate of 7 to 8 percent settled into the 5 percent range in the late 1970s. This savings rate is lower than in all of our major industrial competitors. Without true savings, capital formation is impossible. A declining savings rate means a reduction in the supply of new funds available for business to borrow. It has occurred at the very time the U.S. Treasury upped its borrowing to finance runaway deficits.

People have saved less in recent years for a variety of reasons. Many have invested their funds in real estate, precious metals, jewelry, art, and other collectibles, seeking a hedge against inflation. Another reason is that the return to savings, after taxes are taken into account, has been negative throughout the 1970s. Table 10.6 reveals a third reason: real, after-tax family income has declined, forcing Americans to dip into their savings to sustain living standards.

Table 10.11
Personal Savings as a Percentage of U.S. Disposable Personal Income,
1965–1980

Year	Savings
1965	7.1
1966	7.0
1967	8.1
1968	7.1
1969	6.4
1970	8.0
1971	8.1
1972	6.5
1973	8.6
1974	8.5
1975	8.6
1976	6.9
1977	5.6
1978	5.2
1979	5.2
1980	5.6

Source: Economic Report of the President 1982, Table B-23, p. 260.

Prices

Recall that prices fell by about half from 1800 to 1900. Thus increases in wages in the nineteenth century translated into even greater increases in purchasing power. Since 1929, however, the price level approximately doubled in the forty years ending in 1967. During the Eisenhower and Kennedy years, the annual rate of inflation averaged below 2 percent. The story changed in 1965. Between 1965 and 1970, the annual rate of inflation averaged 4.2 percent; it was 6.7 percent from 1971 to 1978; and then attained back-to-back double-digit levels in 1979-80. Using 1967 = 100 as a base year, the consumer price index reached 272 in 1981, an increase of 272 percent. Put another way, a 1967 dollar was worth 37¢ in 1981. Inflation was literally eating away Americans' purchasing power and eroding the value of their savings.

The average daily closing prices of the thirty stocks that comprise the Dow Jones Industrial Average reached a postwar high of 910.88 in 1965. Sixteen years later it stood at 932.92, for a gain of 22 points. During the same period, the CPI rose from 94.5 to 272.4 or roughly threefold. In a nutshell, the market value of the bellweather stocks which comprise the Dow Jones Industrial Average fell about two-thirds.

Bond prices fared no better. Between 1950 and 1978, the annual average of monthly prices of a $100 long-term U.S. government bond fell by half from $102.53 to $51.26. Corporate bonds fell by an even sharper 53 percent.

Per Capita Income

The major task of any economic system is to make each of its participants better off. Annual increases in per capita, disposable income are a good measure of economic success or failure. Disposable personal income is what remains after personal tax and nontax payments are subtracted from personal income.

Table 10.12 shows the changes in per capita disposable income in *constant* 1972 dollars from 1929 through 1980. Note that per capita income fell sharply in the depression years, but began a sustained upward rise in the late 1930s.

Table 10.12
U.S. per Capita Disposable Income, 1929 to 1980
(in constant 1972 dollars)

Year	$
1929	1,883
1933	1,349
1939	1,754
1940	1,847
1945	2,416
1950	2,392
1955	2,582
1960	2,709
1965	3,171
1970	3,665
1971	3,752
1972	3,860
1973	4,083
1974	4,013
1975	4,055
1976	4,161
1977	4,266
1978	4,409
1979	4,493
1980	4,473

Source: Economic Reort of the President 1981, Table B-24, p. 261.

It rose from $1,847 in 1940, to $2,392 in 1950, to $2,709 in 1960, and to $3,665 by 1970. It hit the $4,000 mark in 1973, remaining at that level during the first oil-shock recession. It increased again between 1976 and 1980, from about $4,200 to $4,500.

Several observations are in order. First, the annual increase in per capita income (PCI) has slowed since 1973. PCI increased 22 percent during the 1940s, 13 percent during the 1950s, a whopping 30 percent during the 1960s, 11 percent in the first three years of the 1970s, and a very modest 10 percent during the next seven years. Overall, the seventies witnessed a 22 percent gain in PCI, which is higher than the 1950s. These statistics do not reveal a nation in deep economic trouble, and clash with the plight of the median family income reported in Table 10.6, which has suffered a fall of more than 5 percent in real disposable income since 1976.

The answer to this apparent contradiction is found in the changing composition of the labor force. Examine Table 10.13. From the end of World War II to 1981, the civilian labor-force participation rate increased from 57 to 64 percent, a rise of about one-eighth. The reverse side is that the fraction of the labor force which stayed home fell from 43 to 36 percent. Growth in labor force participation outpaced the overall increase in population by a considerable margin in the postwar era.

The most dramatic change occurred in female participation, which rose from about 34 to 52 percent in the last three decades, a proportional increase of half. The number of women at work went from about seventeen million to over forty million during this period, a nearly two-and-a-half-fold increase.

Table 10.13
U.S. Labor Force Participation Rates, 1940–1980
(in percentages)

Year	Total	Male	Female
1940	55.7	83.7	28.2
1945	57.2	84.8	35.9
1950	59.2	86.4	33.9
1955	59.3	85.3	35.7
1960	59.4	83.3	37.7
1965	58.9	80.7	39.3
1970	60.4	79.7	43.3
1975	61.2	77.9	46.3
1980	63.8	77.4	51.5

Source: Economic Report of the President 1982, Table B-29, p. 266.

Note from the table that the great bulk of the rise has occurred since 1965, suggesting that women entered the work force in increasingly greater numbers partly to cope with inflation.

The continued rise in PCI throughout the 1970s can be explained by the growth in the share of women at work. More and more families had two earners, whereas the median family in Table 10.6 presumes only one full-time employed worker. Although PCI has continued to rise since 1973, the same is not true for income computed on a per-worker basis, which fits with the prior fact that output per man hour has been negative between 1978 and 1980. A rise in the female labor force participation rate has been accompanied by a corresponding decline in productivity. Each additional worker who has joined the labor force has been less productive than her predecessor. Furthermore, the time will come when men will run out of spare girl friends and wives to put to work. Unless productivity rebounds, there is a risk that per capita income will decline in tandem with the current erosion in per worker income.

Since 1975 analysts have sought explanations for America's dismal economic performance and suggested a variety of remedies. Some have become rich telling us to follow Japanese work and management practices. Others advocate a partnership between government, business, and labor to rebuild our antiquated industrial base. Calls for protection from foreign imports are increasingly tendered. Lester Thurow's *Zero Sum Society* said that gains for one could only come at the expense of another since the era of growth had come to an end. But this search for elixirs and magic formulas is misdirected. Parts I and II of this book provide all the insights we need to map out a blueprint for a return to economic growth.

Notes

1. (Chicago and London: University of Chicago Press, 1980).
2. Paul L. Ford, ed., *The Writings of Thomas Jefferson*, vol. 7 (New York, G.P. Putman's, 1896), p. 310 (Jefferson to John Taylor, November 26, 1798). The next few pages are taken from Alvin Rabushka, "A Compelling Case for a Constitutional Amendment to Balance the Budget and Limit Taxes" (Washington, D.C.: Taxpayers' Foundation, May 1982), pp. 7-8.
3. Alvin Rabushka and Pauline Ryan, *The Tax Revolt* (Stanford: Hoover Institution Press, 1982).
4. These numbers and ratios appear in Richard B. McKenzie, *Bound to Be Free* (Stanford: Hoover Institution Press, 1982), p. 16.
5. This treatment of individual income taxes is drawn from Robert E. Hall and Alvin Rabushka, *Low Tax, Simple Tax, Flat Tax* (New York: McGraw-Hill, 1983), pp. 2-16.
6. Ibid., p. 111.
7. See Roger A. Freeman, *The Wayward Welfare State* (Stanford: Hoover Institution Press, 1981), pp. 124-32.

8. Alvin Rabushka, "A Compelling Case," p. 13.
9. The last few American presidents might have cried out, "A surplus, a surplus— my presidency for a surplus."
10. (Englewood Cliffs, N.J.: Prentice-Hall, 1981).
11. Murray L. Weidenbaum, "Government Power and Business Performance," in Peter Duignan and Alvin Rabushka, eds., *The United States in the 1980s* (Stanford: Hoover Institution Press, 1980), pp. 205-10.
12. Cited in Richard B. McKenzie, *Bound to Be Free*, p. 28.
13. For a history of money and banking in the United States, see Ron Paul and Lewis Lehrman, *The Case for Gold* (Washington, D.C.: Cato Institute, 1982).
14. Roy W. Jastram, *The Golden Constant* (New York: Wiley, 1977), pp. 143-44.
15. Ibid., p. 173.

11

Recipe for Prosperity

In 1776 two glorious documents appeared—Adam Smith's *The Wealth of Nations* and the American Declaration of Independence. Each called forth fundamental principles of economic and political liberty which have survived to this day. The Declaration of Independence asserted the inalienable rights to life, liberty, and the pursuit of happiness. Adam Smith asserted, on his side of the Atlantic, the benefits of economic freedom. English historian Henry Thomas Buckle has called *The Wealth of Nations* "probably the most important book that has ever been written." Most economists regard Smith as the father of modern-day economics, no small achievement! Perhaps more important, his exposition of the principles of sound political economy remain as vital in the 1980s as when they were set forth more than 200 years ago. Like the Declaration of Independence, Smith's truths are timeless. Whenever and wherever they have been applied, people have enjoyed prosperity and freedom. Just exactly what are these principles?

> Political economy, considered as a branch of the science of a statesman or legislator, proposes two distinct objects: first, to provide a plentiful revenue or subsistence for the people, or more properly to enable them to provide such a revenue or subsistence for themselves; and secondly, to supply the state or commonwealth with a revenue sufficient for the public services. It proposes to enrich both the people and the sovereign.[1]

These are profound words of purpose. Sound practice of political economy does not pit citizen against government. A prosperous people can better afford to support their government than an impoverished people. It only takes a modest level of taxation to pay for the primary tasks of government: national security, maintaining a system of law and order, and providing the essential public works that private individuals will not or cannot maintain. But the activities of most governments go well beyond these few essential tasks. It takes a high level of taxation to pay for a much bigger government. This insatiable demand for revenue soon pits citizen against government. As government grows, the economy often contracts. In the long run, neither the people nor the sovereign are enriched.

My recipe for American prosperity calls for three major sets of ingredients. First we add the staples, which consist of the four principles of sound political economy on which to judge the pros and cons of public policies. Then we blend in the practice of sound fiscal, economic, and monetary policies. Finally, we throw in the remaining ingredients of historical evidence. Properly assembled, we have a truly valuable product: economic and political principles which bring about prosperity and individual freedom.

Four Principles of Political Economy

Smith's definition of the science of political economy identified the first two principles. The overriding purpose of any economic system is to make its people better off. The primary goal of the government is to provide the stability within which productive economic activity can take place. To the extent that the government maintains an environment conducive to profitable investment and hard work, more goods and services will be produced. A steadily rising standard of living brings with it better education, housing, health, and human development in all its social, cultural, and spiritual aspects. On this one test alone—the prosperity of its people—any government can be judged a success or failure.

The second principle, a corollary, is that the people should supply the government with sufficient funds to carry out its basic tasks. Two norms are embedded in this principle: that the tasks of government are limited, and that government's demand for revenue should not violate the first principle of allowing the people to make themselves better off. The exception would be a serious threat to national survival and the very freedom of the people. I accept Smith's brief list of primary public tasks, with the slight dissent that he, too, might have attached less importance to the Navigation Acts had he written one hundred years later.

As government grows, the first two principles of political economy increasingly come into conflict with each other. The need for more public revenue prompts higher taxation, which often has the counterproductive effect of slowing economic growth. In turn, the public revenue will wane. At some exhorbitant level of taxation, the productive capability of the economy will weaken and tax receipts may actually decline. To the extent that a low rate of taxation fosters sustained economic growth, public revenue will rise in tandem. This is the story of Hong Kong.

The key to political economy is to limit the size and scope of government activities to the revenue generated by a low level of taxation. As economic growth continues, new or expanded public programs should remain within the level of these additional resources. Excessive growth in public spending invariably brings higher taxes, inflation, reduced output, and, ultimately, the loss of prosperity.

The third principle of political economy is human freedom. Each person should be free to pursue his or her own economic, social, cultural, or spiritual objectives, subject, of course, to respecting similar rights of others. This concept of freedom does not repeal the economic reality of scarcity. The freedom to pursue one's desires is limited by one's resources. Freedom does not mean the right to steal or take from others against their wishes.

Free societies have typically flourished within a constitutional framework, written, or, as in the case of nineteenth-century Britain, unwritten. The United States Constitution is the best example of a written constitution that has secured the liberties of its people for nearly two centuries. Democracy is a highly desirable form of government, one in which the people freely elect their leaders, but it does not guarantee economic liberty. Sweden, for example, takes more than 60 percent of its people's income in taxes. Governments in Singapore, Hong Kong, and Taiwan offer their citizens an enormous amount of individual freedom, yet none of these displays the form of Western democracy. Remember that the full flowering of freedom in nineteenth-century Britain took place alongside a limited franchise in which politics was dominated by aristocratic elements.

One can add a fourth principle to political economy: that of social welfare. Social welfare must not be equated with the practices of modern-day welfare states. No one would quarrel with the desire to help others who, through no fault of their own, cannot take care of themselves. Compassion is indeed a virtue. Helping the disabled, the handicapped, the blind, the frail, or abandoned children has a place in public life. But these needy people differ from able-bodied men and women who choose the dole over work. They are not the same as widows whose husbands chose not to buy insurance. They are not in the same class with alcoholics, drug addicts, or criminals.

Where private charity fails to help these "truly needy" people in our society, few would totally oppose that we give them any public help. Once again, the key is to limit the size and scope of government help to the few who really need it, without imposing damaging taxation or counterproductive regulations. The most successful welfare-oriented policy is one that brings strong economic growth, full employment, and a rising standard of living—these enable people to look after themselves and their families. Policies that retard economic growth in the name of compassion for the poor only assure that the poor will multiply.

Against these four principles of political economy, we can write a prescription for sensible economic policy. But first it is necessary to identify those aspects of our political process that have been so conducive to the growth in government.

A Bias towards Big Government

During the past half century, public spending, taxes, and federal budget deficits have grown wildly out of control.[2] The facts suggest that the American political process is biased toward higher levels of public activity that does not reflect the genuine will of the people on the overall size of the government. Government activity is skewed toward these artifically higher levels because members of Congress and the executive bureaucracies have powerful incentives to spend the taxpayers' money and regulate their affairs; yet they face few offsetting incentives to watch out for the taxpayers' interests or to keep their hands off private business activity.

The objectives of economic policy and the political process are in direct conflict. The Congress, as a whole, is concerned with stable prices, low interest rates, and full employment, which require some check on the scope of government spending, taxes, and regulation. As individuals, however, each congressman confronts pressures to increase spending, grant a tax preference, or proffer a regulatory favor. The reality of our system has shown convincingly that the collective need to control spending, taxes, and regulatory costs is no match for the pressure each individual member in the Congress, or officials in the agencies of the executive branch, face to increase them.

This bias towards more spending, taxing, and regulation is due, first, to what analysts of government call the phenomenon of "concentrated benefits versus dispersed costs." This describes the fact that the benefits of any given spending program, tax preference, or regulatory privilege normally are concentrated among a small number of persons, while the costs of such a program are dispersed throughout a much larger class, either the general taxpayer or consumer.

The competition between taxspenders and taxpayers, or between the highly concentrated trade or industry organization and the general consumer, is highly unequal: it is simply not as worthwhile for an individual taxpayer to spend much time and effort to save a few dollars in taxes as it is for the spending interests to secure millions or billions of dollars for themselves. Thus, whenever government programs are considered individually, as they are in our budgetary system, there is a bias toward government growth. Similarly, hundreds of special interests with a stake in the current tax code will fight radical reform that could benefit the country at large, but perhaps at the expense of their unique tax preference.

The explosion in spending, tax breaks, and ever-higher deficits is not due to the failure to elect the "right" people; it is an institutional defect. The federal budget process is inherently biased toward deficits, higher taxes, and greater government spending. The trends toward bigger government and economic instability reflect the decisions of reasonable men and women in Congress who, as individuals, cannot successfully resist the pressures they face to increase spending.

A second source of bias is the separation of benefits, which are short-run, from costs, which are typically more long-run. The benefits of government programs are immediate, both to the recipients and the congressmen who supported them. The costs of government programs—in the form of potentially higher future taxes, higher future unemployment, or higher future interest rates—will be evident only at some future time, to be borne, perhaps, by future congressmen. Since the electoral time horizon of all house members and one-third of the senators is never more than a year or two away, short-term benefits invariably take precedence over potentially long-run adverse economic effects due to higher levels of government activity.

A third bias arises within the structure of Congress itself. The committee system, whatever its original intentions, finds members of Congress gravitating to those committees that allow them to serve geographic constituencies by bringing home their "fair share." Reelection rewards those congressmen who successfully serve their constituencies; at the same time, the actions of Congress as a whole damage the growth rate of the economy. The driving elements in each congressman's calculation is protecting his turf, getting his share of the pork barrel, not transgressing his colleague's committee jurisdiction; in short, concerns about self come first. The same situation fits all 535 members of Congress. Unless the entire membership can agree to limit the overall budget, or put a halt to granting special tax or regulatory favors, no one member or group of members dare risk their constituents' wrath by surrendering benefits that have no appreciate effect on the total scope of government activities, while their colleagues, who conduct business as usual, continue to earn the support of their respective constituents. Asking the Congress to restrain overall spending and control deficits is tantamount to giving the same American Express card number to 535 people, with a polite request that they consider the impact of their individual purchase on the total bill as each person embarks on his or her shopping spree. You can guess the result. It will not be in the interest of any one person to curtail spending since his/her purchases will have an imperceptible effect on the total bill. Also, any one cardholder's prudence can be offset by any other cardholder's improvidence. Spending under this system will stop only when the company imposes an overall credit limit on these 535 "good" men and women. It is a pity the government has no such credit limit!

Under our present tax system, members of Congress have an incentive to encourage inflationary policies and programs. The reason is that our progressive tax code works to transfer more and more of our personal income to the government through "bracket creep." During the 1970s, for example, government income-tax collections rose by about 16 percent for each 10 percent increase in personal income, largely as a result of inflation pushing taxpayers into higher brackets. This system of steeply graduated tax rates allowed Congress to raise taxes without having to vote an explicit increase either in tax rates or the size of the tax base. Federal income-tax yields have grown about 75 percent faster than the GNP, which has allowed the Congress to go through the charade of cutting taxes some eight times in the postwar era, while overall tax burdens and average marginal tax rates on real incomes have increased. To deliver the goodies to their constituents, congressmen face incentives to support inflationary policies which net them greater command over resources. In 1981 Congress voted to correct inflation-generated "bracket creep" by indexing tax rates to inflation, to take effect in 1985, but this measure must perpetually fend off attempts at repeal if it is to halt the progressive transfer of resources from private to public hands.

Thus in sharp contrast with historical experience, the federal budget process has failed to show restraint in the post-World War II era. For the better part of 200 years, Americans held to a limited role for the federal government. Except for periods of war or recession, revenues from customs and excises were sufficient to fund those activities widely regarded as proper federal functions. This consensus has broken down in the last fifty years. The lack of direct constitutional restraints on taxing, spending, and deficits has fostered ever-larger government intervention in the economy. By 1971, these pressures forced us to shut the "gold window" to foreign holders of dollars, thus severing our final monetary link to gold. Inflation soon became the most important economic problem of the 1970s.

Many politicians, scholars, and taxpayers believe that we can change the way our government conducts business by statutory reform, without resorting to the extreme of amending the Constitution. Statutory reform is a less time-consuming and cumbersome process. However, the belief that Congress can draft legislation to put its fiscal house back in order has been repeatedly proven false.

A recent attempt—the Budget and Impoundment Control Act of 1974—established budget committees within each house, the creation of the Congressional Budget Office to supply timely information and analysis, and the development of a budgetary timetable. These measures were deemed necessary to enable Congress to consider individual spending measures in light of overall budget objectives. In the Humphrey-Hawkins Full Employment Act, a balanced budget was declared to be a national priority. An amendment offered by Representative (now Senator) Charles Grassley and Senator Harry Byrd, Jr., to an International Monetary Fund loan program measure was enacted into law and requires that, beginning with fiscal year 1981, total budget outlays of the federal government "shall not" exceed its receipts (P.L. 95-435). In 1979, a provision in a measure to increase the public debt limit stated that "Congress shall balance the federal budget" (P.L. 96-5), which required the congressional budget committees to propose balanced budgets for FY 1981 and subsequent years.

None of these measures has effectively constrained deficits. None has reduced the share of national income taxed or spent by government. The most obvious reason is that no Congress can bind a succeeding Congress by a simple statute. A balanced budget or tax limitation statute can itself be repealed by the simple expedient of adopting a new statute or new budget which is in conflict with the earlier measure. The Byrd-Grassley amendment, which required a balanced budget for fiscal year 1981, provided no deterrent whatsoever to the adoption of a budget with a $50 billion deficit for that year.

Indeed, a convincing case can be made that control over the budget has steadily declined since the 1974 act. Despite congressional adherence to the budget timetable, deficits have assumed record proportions.

The source of this failure lies in the fact that there is a structural bias within our political system that causes higher levels of spending, taxing, and deficits than are desired by the people, even though most members of Congress believe that large deficits and excessive government spending damage the eonomy. This spending bias has yet to be corrected by internal reform, because none of these reforms allow members to cope with spending pressures. The removal of prior constitutional constraints calls for the imposition of a new constraint. A constitutional amendment that would reimpose those constraints which the framers of the Constitution originally imposed or assumed would go a long way toward correcting the serious defects in the institutional setting within which our government now operates.

In recent years, a growing number of scholars, members of Congress, and taxpayers' organizations have favored amending the Constitution to eliminate the spending bias inherent in our present political system. By 1980, a "consensus" view had emerged, which took the form of a proposal that was developed by members of the Senate Judiciary Committee in consultation with scholars and leaders of such organizations as the National Taxpayers Union and the National Tax Limitation Committee. This "consensus" amendment banned deficit budgets, subject to a three-fifths majority vote of the whole membership of both houses of Congress, and restricted tax increases to the annual rate of growth in the private economy (see the Appendix for the text of Senate Joint Resolution 5, the Balanced Budget/Tax Limitation Amendment proposed at the start of the ninety-eighth session of Congress). The purpose of this amendment is to overcome the spending bias of Congress by restoring the linkage between spending and taxing decisions. It would accomplish this by constraining overall spending to available revenues. In turn, revenues could rise no more rapidly than the growth of the economy, thus halting the transfer of steadily higher proportions of national output from private to public hands.

It is important to recognize the difference between an ordinary statute and a constitutional amendment. The reason that our civil rights have survived for 200 years is because they are expressly set forth in our Constitution. Without constitutional protection, it is quite likely that Congress would have eroded many of our individual freedoms in the name of some political or economic crisis. A constitutional requirement of budget balance and tax limitation—granting constitutional protection to economic liberties—is more likely to succeed where ordinary statutes have failed.

On 20 January 1981, Ronald Reagan was inaugurated as president. He promised to cut federal spending, reduce tax rates, deregulate the economy, and arrest inflation. By restoring economic incentives, these policies would stimulate economic growth, raise productivity, increase savings, create jobs, raise living standards, and stabilize the purchasing power of the dollar. Shrinking the size and scope of government would also enhance individual liberty.

Ronald Reagan brought impeccable conservative credentials to the presidency. Upon taking office, he articulated the means and goals of economic policy in *A Program for Economic Recovery* (18 February 1981) and in his many subsequent speeches. In these, he blamed the expansion of government for unemployment, declining productivity, and slow economic growth. Government spending more money than it receives in taxes was the culprit of inflation. To restore economic growth, he proposed a four-point program.[3]

1. Immediate passage of a 30 percent, across-the-board reduction in personal income-tax rates and a system of accelerated business depreciation.
2. A reduction in government spending as a share of GNP from 23 percent in 1981 to 19 percent by 1986.
3. A reduction in costly and unnecessary government regulations.
4. A steady reduction in monetary growth to a rate consistent with the economy's real output of goods and services.

Reagan's election mandate was overwhelming, but the implementation of his program has been disappointing. His tax cut, adopted in August 1981, was scaled back from the original plan to 5 percent beginning 1 October 1981, with subsequent 10 percent cuts on 1 July 1982, and 1 July 1983. The accelerated depreciation system for business was stretched out, and then partly repealed in the August 1982 tax increase measure (supported by the president). In the end, his original tax reduction package was distorted almost beyond recognition. The reasons for this will doubtless be the subject of numerous books throughout the 1980s as friends and foes wonder what went wrong!

What about spending? Exactly the opposite of what was planned. Government spending is expected to take almost 25 percent of the GNP in fiscal year 1984, which runs from 1 October 1983 through 30 September 1984. If this estimate turns out to be correct, it will mean that President Reagan, committed to reducing the share of national income consumed by the federal government, will have presided over the most rapid peacetime increase in the size of the federal government in history. It is apparent that the Reagan administration failed to recognize the overriding importance of indexed entitlement programs, such as social security, medicare and medicaid, and food stamps in the growth of the budget. A few reductions in spending were attained on some discretionary programs, which produced small, one-time savings. Instead, it is clear that the only way to reduce the size of government is to attack entitlement formulae in order to get continuing savings.

Measured by the pages in *The Federal Register*, the Reagan Administration has scored some gains against excessive federal regulation: it has fallen by more than 10,000 pages. However, real reform requires that Congress rewrite the statutes that underpin business, consumerism, safety, and other regulations. True deregulation has eluded the Reagan administration.

In one area, controlling inflation, great success has been enjoyed. A 12.4 percent increase in the consumer price index in 1980 has fallen to a much more palatable 3.9 percent increase in 1982. This fall can be attributed to a slowdown in money-supply growth on the part of the Federal Reserve Board. However, critics claim that the fall in money supply growth was erratic, not steady, thus producing wild swings in interest rates. Interest rates remained far above their historic levels, throwing the economy into a sharp recession. Reagan devotees were disappointed that he failed to give clear direction to the Federal Reserve Board, or to appoint a new member who could have effectively represented his monetary policy.

The president's four-point plan has been undermined by his own decisions. Chief among these is his successful support for a $99 billion tax increase package, the Tax Equity and Fiscal Responsibility Act which won approval in Congress in August 1982. This measure repeals some tax-cutting provisions in the 1981 bill and imposes several new taxes. Since August 1982, the president supported a new gasoline tax, higher social security taxes, and once proposed a contingent surcharge to take effect in 1986 depending on economic and budgetary conditions. He appears to have abandoned his own tax-cutting philosophy.

It is not my purpose in reviewing President Reagan's program and its implementation to either praise or condemn his efforts to reverse the course of government. Rather, my intent is to show how difficult that task really is, even when the "right" people have been elected to office in the White House and the Congress. Ronald Reagan has been emphasizing the importance of a constitutional limitation on government spending since he first proposed such a measure in California in 1973; yet he too failed to throw his full support to the federal campaign for such an amendment until it was too late. It is not enough to replace big spenders with officials committed to smaller government. It is just as important, if not more so, to alter the rules under which our government conducts its business.

Free marketeers, gold bugs, libertarians, and traditional Republican conservatives may have been guilty of expecting too much too soon. The complete transformation from mercantilism to the market economy took some fifty years in Britain. Overnight changes in economic policy were possible in Singapore, Taiwan, and Korea only because strong leaders, facing immediate cutoffs in foreign assistance, did not have to overcome determined political opposition within their own countries. Democracies are not conducive to radical swings in economic policies, except in very rare circumstances.

Just to whet our imagination, let's transport Huskisson, Peel, and Gladstone to contemporary Washington and replace our Congress with the Parliament of the mid-nineteenth century. Peel, of course, becomes president, Gladstone assumes the mantles of secretary of the Treasury and chairman of the Council of Economic Advisers, with Huskisson taking charge of the Federal Reserve Board. As leaders of their party, they naturally deserve and receive the support of a majority in Congress. What might the course of public policy look like under this leadership?

Blueprint for Economic Policy

America adhered to the principles of Adam Smith from the Founding Fathers until one-third of the way into the twentieth century. Thereafter its leaders embarked on a path of more spending, higher taxes, increasing regulation, and ultimate abandonment of the gold standard. The main goals of economic policy are simply to reverse direction: reduce government spending, cut high tax rates, free up the economy, and restore sound money, preferably on a gold standard. What specific measures will our historical heroes propose?

Reducing Government Spending

The composition of federal spending has shifted dramatically in the past few decades. Nearly half of the budget went to defense in 1960; by 1982, that share had fallen to 22 percent. Conversely, payments to individuals (e.g., retirement, unemployment, medical care, food, nutrition, and public assistance) increased from 26 to 50 percent during the same period. Interest payments consumed about 13 percent of the budget in 1982, compared with 9 percent in 1960. All other programs take approximately the same 15 to 16 percent in both years. This last category includes justice, energy, natural resources, the environment, agriculture, commerce, community development, transportation, education, and training.

The mathematics of federal spending are sobering. When defense, income transfers, and interest payments on the national debt are added together, 85 percent of public spending is accounted for. Outright cancellation of the entire "other" category of nondefense discretionary programs would not, by itself, balance the budget. Since interest payments must be met lest the federal government be wholly unable to sell future debt, it is simply impossible to reduce government spending without substantial modification of the "entitlement" programs. Bluntly put, this means that legal residents of the United States must not automatically be entitled to levels of cash, housing, food stamps, medical care, and other social services which the country cannot afford. Harsh words! The failure to grasp this point is the failure of the Reagan administration to curtail federal spending. Each year the Congress must establish who is eligible for federal benefits and must tailor the size of those benefits to the available public resources, not to the putative "need" of the intended recipients.

Given the political pressures that members of Congress and the executive branch face to be compassionate, it is imperative that some broader principle than compassion govern the nation's public finances. It is essential that every time Congress proposes an additional dollar of spending it also propose a dollar less for some other program, or a dollar to be raised in taxes. A constitutional amendment may be the only device which reconciles compassion with rationality, humanity with scarcity. Surely the leaders of Bangladesh are as compassionate as members of Congress; they simply have no resources to feed, house, clothe, or treat their impoverished millions. An amendment that restrains the size of government and in the process stimulates economic growth holds more hope for the needy than the proliferation of government income transfer programs.

Cut Tax Rates

The structure of taxation plays a major role in shaping peoples' incentives to work, save, and invest. Throughout the postwar period, Americans have suffered steadily higher marginal tax rates. Many have chosen borrowing over saving, spending over investing, and leisure over work. To reverse these trends, tax reform is essential.

The evidence of nineteenth-century Britain and postwar Hong Kong suggests one solution: replace the present steeply graduated income tax code with a low, flat-rate tax levied on a broad base of income. The plan that Robert Hall and I proposed in *Low Tax, Simple Tax, Flat Tax* demonstrates that a standard charge of 19 percent would raise the same amount of revenue we now collect from the current corporate and personal income taxes.[4] Scholars have estimated that a simple flat tax would bring sharply higher economic growth, thereby increasing real after-tax personal income. In the long run, it would also raise more revenue than the present high tax-rate system. The real losers would be the tens of thousands of tax lawyers, accountants, sellers of tax shelters, and Internal Revenue Service employees, who would have to find honest work.

It makes good sense to combine a flat-rate tax with a constitutional amendment limiting the total size of federal receipts. Neither inflation nor real economic growth would then transfer a greater share of private resources to government. Indeed, a provision that all taxable income be assessed at the same rate could be incorporated into an amendment.

Regulatory Reform

The Founding Fathers would not recognize the regulatory apparatus of the federal government. Over fifty agencies issue tens of thousands of pages of new regulations each year, imposing costs on business that run to the hundred-billion dollar range.

But regulations do more than increase the costs of production. The federal government currently grants billions of dollars in subsidies to inefficient and unproductive enterprises.[5] It also protects many industries from foreign or domestic competition. Improving the efficiency of the American economy requires ending all subsidies to American business, eliminating all regulatory restrictions on free entry, and paring down unnecessary and costly regulations. Only those essential to the preservation of public health and safety should be preserved.

A brief lecture on the workings of the free-market economy may be in order here. In a free, competitive economy, consumers determine which products and businesses will succeed and which will fail. Companies that satisfy the demands of consumers will prosper. Those that do not will fail, in the process releasing resources to other firms that are more efficient in satisfying consumer demand. The free flow of resources in the market economy insures that capital and labor will move to where they will be employed most efficiently, making products people want. Think of the market economy as a democratic economic system. Consumers vote for or against goods and services with their dollars. For political reasons, the government may decide that a particular firm or industry that has failed to satisfy consumers should not be allowed to go out of business, and thus grants it a subsidy. Subsidies distort the pattern of the efficient allocation of resources. They reward companies that fail to meet the test of fair competition. They penalize successful firms by helping less efficient competitors. Subsidies thus lead to lower output and a lower standard of living than if the free play of market forces is allowed.

The federal budget is replete with business subsidies, loan guarantees, and other favors granted to specific companies or industries. The American automobile industry is protected from foreign competition by quotas on the importation of Japanese cars. The steel industry is protected from low prices by a mechanism that limits the quantity of foreign steel which may be imported. The federal government directly subsidizes the American merchant marine industry with thousands of dollars for every employed worker. In 1983 farmers received price supports worth some $10 billion. Federal loan guarantees kept Chrysler Corporation and Lockheed afloat. Preferential loan rates have caused a massive overinvestment in residential construction. It would be easy to write a whole book documenting the extent and effects of government subsidies on American business.

In addition to subsidies, government regulations often prevent free entry into many sectors of the economy.[6] It is necessary to get a license from some unit of government to operate all kinds of business activities: trucking, airlines, shipping, radio, television, banking, and so forth. When government restricts free entry and competition, consumers pay higher prices. There is simply no reason, apart from considerations of national security, or public health and safety, for the government to restrict anyone's right to buy or sell as he pleases.

Restore Sound Money

There is less agreement among economists, bankers, financial analysts, politicians, and civil servants on the subject of monetary policy than on virtually any other aspect of political economy. Areas of controversy include the definition of money itself, which changes from month to month in the current era of financial deregulation and innovation, the velocity of money, the inherent workability of any system of fiat currency that requires the discretionary jurisdiction of a central bank, the pros and cons of a return to some form of gold or specie standard, and even the desirability of completely free banking in which the government does not have a monopoly on the issue of legal tender bank notes.

Since 1971 the United States has been on a pure fiat monetary system, in which Federal Reserve notes are issued without backing of any form. Since 1971 the United States has also experienced its most destructive peacetime inflation. It may well be that proper administration of a purely fiat monetary system would result in stable prices, but the experience of this system so far is not encouraging.

Despite the alleged drawbacks of a gold-based monetary system—the difficulty of insuring a steady increase in new gold supplies to support expanding economic activity, the importance of South Africa and the Soviet Union in new annual output of gold, the inability of the government to quickly increase or decrease liquidity—the long-run success of a gold standard in controlling inflation in Great Britain and the United States make it a preferred candidate to the present fiat system. An automatic monetary mechanism, in which government stands ready to buy and sell gold within a fixed price range, is clearly superior to a central bank which must decide some appropriate quantity of money at all times and under all circumstances to an ever-changing level of economic activity. A gold standard would prevent potential mistakes of human misjudgment, a point that concerned the Committee which released the 1810 bullion report:

> The most detailed knowledge of the actual trade of the Country, combined with the profound science in all the principles of Money and Circulation, would not enable any man or set of men to adjust, and keep always adjusted, the right proportion of circulating medium in a country to the wants of trade.

The 1810 report concluded that the suspension of cash payments, when notes could not be converted into bullion, had fostered an overissue of paper currency by the Bank of England, causing the pound to fall in value on the European exchanges.

> For upon a general view of the subject, Your Committee are of opinion, that no safe, certain, and constantly adequate provision against an excess of paper currency, either occasional or permanent, can be found, except in the convertibility of all such paper into specie.

We would do well to heed the wisdom in these two passages!

The correct approach to monetary policy is to bring the same freedom to this area that fits a free-market economy. All federal legal tender laws should be repealed, allowing freedom of contract to apply in all financial transactions. Second, the dollar should be defined as a fixed weight of gold. Third, all taxes on gold transactions should be eliminated: capital gains, excise, and sales taxes. Free of tax, gold coinage would constitute an alternative monetary system to the present paper monopoly. Fourth, private mints should be allowed to issue coins under their own trademarks. Fifth, private citizens should enjoy the right of free coinage at the Treasury (except for a nominal minting fee). Finally, all restrictions and regulations on the export, import, minting, and hoarding of gold coins and bullion should be repealed. In short, the government should restore a free market in money to go along with a free market in all other goods and services.

These recommendations in taxing, spending, regulation, and money are not derived from the idle chatter of college classrooms or the mathematical expositions in learned journals. They are based on nearly two centuries of practical application, encompassing different eras, geographical locations, resource endowments, and cultures. Wherever and whenever the economic principles of Adam Smith have been applied, prosperity has followed.

How do we get from here to there? The political pressures that brought the welfare state will work for its retention. The demise of laissez-faire in Britain is traceable, partly, to the extension of the franchise and the emergence of mass parties. In the United States, and Western Europe for that matter, it is hard to see how the old principles of limited government and economic freedom can be restored against the backdrop of universal suffrage, mass parties, and the millions who benefit from the welfare state. Perhaps the most challenging task is to find rays of hope upon which to argue that individual freedom and the market economy are compatible with democratic practices, that the general interest can transcend hundreds and thousands of special interests. Somewhere, the sound application of political economy must overcome the political incentives of short-run electoral time horizons, entrenched bureaucratic interests, and millions who receive checks from the government.

Advocates of limited government and the market economy fear that a golden opportunity to transform the American economy and its government was lost in the early months of Ronald Reagan's presidency, in his failure to accomplish wholesale reductions in taxing, spending, and regulation. They see in liberal and Democratic gains in the 1982 Congressional elections a return to business as usual in government: tax, tax, tax, spend, spend, spend, elect, elect, elect. Can they hope for another opportunity in the near future?

A Concluding Note of Optimism

Liberal reform does not come easily. We began this book with a review of the British economy of 1820. Deep in recession, Britain was strangled by agricultural protectionism. Unemployed workers threatened political unrest. Manufacturing and trade were stagnant. Half of all public spending went just to pay interest on a colossal national debt. The complexity of the tax system literally defied description. William Huskisson courageously set in motion the first round of liberal reform. Between 1823 and 1825, he began the arduous task of rolling back the regulatory and tax structures that suffocated the spirit of enterprise among the British people. His reforms were modest, to be sure: yet, in his day they constituted a monumental step away from the command and control economy to the free market. He proposed and accomplished these reforms despite opposition from within his own party and the vested interests that sought to retain their existing privileges.

Seventeen years passed before Sir Robert Peel maneuvered the next major round of tax and regulatory reform. Free trade in grain became a reality in 1846, an event even Adam Smith dared not contemplate.

William Gladstone brought Britain to a pinnacle of economic liberty during his years as Chancellor of the Exchequer from 1859 to 1866. He reduced public spending, sharply cut tax rates, cleaned up the tariff, and finished the task of economic deregulation.

Altogether, it took nearly fifty years to transform a highly-regulated, heavily-taxed nation into a lightly-regulated, lowly-taxed, free-trading, gold-standard nation which brought unparalleled prosperity to the British people. Nor did reform come easily. Huskisson, Peel, and Gladstone all had to overcome formidable obstacles. Peel was abandoned by his own party for supporting free trade. Gladstone prevailed by the sheer strength of intellect.

Adam Smith published *The Wealth of Nations* in 1776. Seventy years later Britain enjoyed free trade in grain. On the first centenary of *The Wealth of Nations* Britain epitomized the spirit and reality of laissez-faire. A coherent system of economic liberty slowly materialized, fulfilling Smith's visions of freedom and prosperity.

On this pattern, Ronald Reagan has taken a modest first step, perhaps no more than that of William Huskisson. But a first step has been taken. And some modest reforms have been achieved. It will take sustained effort by determined leaders, perhaps stretching well into the twenty-first century, to liberate the full productive potential of the American people. But the determination and success of three giants in nineteenth-century Britain gives cause for optimism in our country. As the intellectual currents increasingly demonstrate the flaws in big government and the benefits of the market economy, politicians of all stripes will find the attractions of more economic freedom irresistible. On this view, the future is not so bleak.

Notes

1. Adam Smith, *An Inquiry Into the Nature and Causes of the Wealth of Nations*, ed. with an introduction by Edwin Cannan (New York: The Modern Library, 1937), p. 297.
2. This section draws from my essay, "A Compelling Case for a Constitutional Amendment to Balance the Budget and Limit Taxes," a paper prepared for the Taxpayers' Foundation (Washington, D.C., May 1982), pp. 8-13.
3. For an interesting account of Reagan's economic principles, see Bruce Bartlett, "Coordinating Economic Policy," in Richard N. Holwill, ed., *Agenda '83: A Mandate for Leadership Report* (Washingon, D.C.: The Heritage Foundation, 1983), pp. 11-16.
4. Robert E. Hall and Alvin Rabushka, *Low Tax, Simple Tax, Flat Tax* (New York: McGraw-Hill, 1983).

5. Three examples of business subsidies, the Economic Development Administration (EDA), the Minority Business Development Agency (MBDA), and the U.S. Travel and Tourism Administration (USTTA), that should be terminated are persuasively discussed in David Boaz, ''Ending Business Subsidies,'' in Richard N. Hollwill, ed., *Agenda '83*, pp. 57-64.
6. Walter Williams, *The State Against Blacks* (New York: McGraw-Hill, 1982).

Appendix

The following is the text of Senate Joint Resolution 5: Balanced Budget/ Tax Limitation Amendment (Introduced 26 January 1983):

ARTICLE—

SECTION 1. Prior to each fiscal year, the Congress shall adopt a statement of receipts and outlays for that year in which total outlays are not greater than total receipts. The Congress may amend such statement provided revised outlays are no greater than revised receipts. Whenever three-fifths of the whole number of both Houses shall deem it necessary, Congress in such statement may provide for a specific excess of outlays over receipts by a vote directed solely to that subject. The Congress and the President shall, pursuant to legislation or through exercise of their powers under the first and second articles, ensure that actual outlays do not exceed the outlays set forth in such statement.

SECTION 2. Total receipts for any fiscal year set forth in the statement adopted pursuant to this article shall not increase by a rate greater than the rate of increase in national income in the year or years ending not less than six months nor more than twelve months before such fiscal year, unless a majority of the whole number of both Houses of Congress shall have passed a bill directed solely to approving specific additional receipts and such bill has become law.

SECTION 3. The Congress may waive the provisions of this article for any fiscal year in which a declaration of war is in effect.

SECTION 4. Total receipts shall include all receipts of the United States except those derived from borrowing and total outlays shall include all outlays of the United States except those for repayment of debt principal.

SECTION 5. This article shall take effect for the second fiscal year beginning after its ratification.

SECTION 6. The Congress shall enforce and implement this article by appropriate legislation.

Index

Aberdeen, Lord, 56,57
Abyssinia, 62
Act of Union (1707), 4
Agricultural protectionism, 5, 93, 102, 108.
 See also Corn Laws
Aix-la-Chapelle, Peace of (1749), 11
Alexander's (brokers firm), 90
Althorp, Lord, 48
American Revolution, 10, 12, 38, 74, 94
Amiens, Peace of (1802), 13
Anti–Corn Law League, 55
Aristocracy. *See* Agricultural protectionism;
 Electoral reform; Parliament
Artificers and Apprentices, Statute of (1563),
 7, 8, 72
Australia, 75, 103

Bagehot, Walter, 106–7
Balance of payments, 114, 137, 157, 165.
 See also Gold standard
Balanced Budget/Tax Limitation Amend-
 ment, 217–18, 229
Bank Act (1844), 89
Bank notes. *See* Bank of England
Bank of England, 15–19, 75–76, 82–92, 224
Bank of Korea, 172
Bank of Taiwan, 163
Bank Restriction Act (1797), 17
Banking and fiscal policies: American, 203;
 British, 15–19, 56–66, 75–76, 82–92,
 224; Hong Kong and, 134–36, 137, 140–
 41, 147; Korean, 171–74; Singapore and,
 157; Taiwan and, 163, 165–66. *See also*
 Monetary policies
Baring, Alexander, 40–41
Bennett, James, 200
Birmingham, England, 90, 105
Blackstone, William, 95
Bowley, A.L., 118, 119, 122n5
Bowring, Sir John, 4, 135
Bracket creep. *See* Marginal tax rates

Bretton Woods, New Hampshire: monetary
 conference at, 203, 204
Briggs, Asa, 24, 27
Bright, John 55, 79
Britain: agrarian protectionism in , 5, 93,
 102, 108; banking in, 15–19, 56–66, 75–
 76, 82–92, 224; Constitution of, 94–96,
 99, 103, 106, 108, 109; ecomomic and
 fiscal policies of, 38–81, 111–21; 220,
 225–26; government spending in, 24–36;
 governmental regulation in, 72–81; income taxes in, 13, 21, 38, 39–40, 49–
 50, 55, 56, 58, 60–61, 62–63, 66–67,
 93–94, 107–8, 114, 119; industrial development in, 4, 5, 75–76, 93, 102, 108;
 mercantile system of, 4–22, 24–36; population of, 4–5. *See also* Hong Kong;
 Singapore
British Constitution. *See* Constitution, British
Brougham, Lord, 40
Bubble Act (1720), 76
Buckle, Henry Thomas, 211
Budget and Impoundment Control Act (1974),
 216
Budgets: British, 12–13 (1792–93), 13–14
 (1815), 46–57 (1825), 57–60 (1860), 60–
 62 (1861–66); Hong Kong, 142–44; Korean, 173; Taiwan's, 166; U.S., 183–84
Bullion Report (1810), 18–19, 82–83, 84,
 224
Buxton, Sydney, 29, 31, 35–36, 49, 60, 63,
 80n3
Byrd, Jr., Harry, 216–17

Canada, 74
Canning, George, 41
Central Provident Fund (CPF), 155–56
Chambers, J.D., 111
Chartered and joint stock trading companies,
 9, 75–76